LIBERTY
UNDER SIEGE

LIBERTY UNDER SIEGE

American Politics
1976-1988

Walter Karp

FRANKLIN
SQUARE
PRESS

NEW YORK

Published by Franklin Square Press, a division of Harper's Magazine,
666 Broadway, New York, NY 10012

First Franklin Square Press edition 1993

Library of Congress Cataloging-in-Publication Data

Karp, Walter.
Liberty under siege: American politics, 1976-1988 /
Walter Karp.
—1st Franklin Square Press ed.
p.   cm.
Originally published: New York : Holt, 1988.
ISBN 1-879957-11-6 : $14.95
1. United States—Politics and government—1981-1989.
2. United States—Politics and government—1977-1981.
3. United States—Politics and government—1974-1977. I. Title.
(E876.K38 1993)
973.92—dc20
93-21851
CIP

This edition edited by Ellen Rosenbush

Book design by Deborah Thomas

Manufactured in the United States of America

CONTENTS

BOOK FIVE:
OLIGARCHY RESTORED

ACKNOWLEDGMENTS

This acknowledgment appeared in the first edition.

I would like to express my gratitude to David Hunter of the Benchmark Fund and to the J. Roderick MacArthur Foundation for their generous help in supporting this book; to David Anker and Alan Burdick for helping me prepare this manuscript; to my beloved wife Regina; for her unfailing support and affection; to my good friend Marvin Gelfand and my dear brother Richard Karp for the many hundreds of hours we spent together discussing the work-in-progress.

1.
GLORIOUS FOURTH

On the Fourth of July 1976, the American people celebrated the two hundredth anniversary of the American Republic and, sub rosa, unofficially, the sixteenth year of a vast, chaotic upheaval that was mainly democratic in spirit, purely democratic in its outcome and deeply threatening to the nation's political establishment, which watched with increasing anxiety as its power and authority steadily eroded. Not since the Progressive movement had died in the trenches of France in 1918 had Americans demanded a greater voice in their own government, or felt so keenly the ancient republican hostility to arbitrary power and secret procedures, to the rule of the self-serving few. For the first time in half a century men of power found themselves pressed, and pressed hard, by a free people's immense vitality. For a half-dozen years they had been retreating before an awakened democracy, but by the summer of 1976 events had reached a crisis point and political leaders began to think about preparing a counteroffensive. Few who celebrated the joyful bicentennial Fourth could have had the slightest inkling that the sixteenth year of the democratic awakening was destined to be its last.

The democratic spirit seemed to be triumphing everywhere. For the first time in many decades the Congress of the United States ceased to be in the paralyzing grip of a handful of committee chairmen, aged obstructionists who were answerable to nobody, not even the electors of their one-party districts—those rotten boroughs and pocket boroughs of America's two-party system. For the first time in decades the illicit surveillance of the law-abiding had ceased to be practiced by the federal government. Revelations in the press in late 1974 that the Central Intelligence Agency and the Federal Bureau of Investigation had been secretly spying on American citizens had so outraged the awakened democracy that President Ford in fright abandoned the system without a fight. The awakened democracy had grown disgusted, too, with the corrupting influence of money in the nation's elections. Legislation providing for federal funding of presidential elections, enacted in 1974, ensured that the election of 1976 would be free of bought financial interest for the first time in our history. The awakened democracy had grown deeply distrustful of official secrecy and so light now shone where darkness had hitherto prevailed. For the first time, committee meetings of Congress and House-Senate conferences had to be kept open to the public. The executive agencies of the government were required, too, to open their meetings to the public light. By the Freedom of Information Act, enacted in 1966 and greatly strengthened in 1974—that *annus mirabilis*—virtually all the unclassified documents of the Executive Branch could be obtained on demand by the public. Under this law, a sovereign people could judge for themselves how well or badly the vast federal bureaucracy was carrying out its duties, how honestly officials were exercising their power, how disinterestedly they were formulating their regulations and guidelines. The awakened democracy distrusted unchecked power, and so for the first time since its creation in 1947 the CIA ceased to be the personal instrument of the White House and had now to withstand the steady scrutiny of a number of congressional committees. Even the ancient republican hostility to private economic power had begun to surface in the democratic awakening. Armed by legislation enacted in 1975, the Federal Trade Commission for the first time in living memory was preparing to challenge price-fixing, mergers and monopoly practices.

All these concessions to the awakened democracy (many of them secretly riddled with loopholes) paled before the one democratic reform which threatened the very survival of the existing political establishment. This was the great change which the Democratic Party had been compelled to make in the way it chose its candidates for the presidency. The change had been made in the aftermath of the tumultuous Democratic National Convention of 1968, when millions of Americans, watching the proceedings on television, discovered that regardless of public opinion, regardless of the outcome of primary elections, regardless even of winning the presidency, the leaders of the Democratic Party had the power to choose whomever they wished to carry the banner of the party. That power, the power of an oligarchy answerable to no one, could be measured with arithmetic precision. It consisted of the 1,760 delegates who nominated Vice President Hubert Humphrey, who had not even dared to present himself that year to the suffrage of his fellow Democrats. That power was nothing abstract. It was visible, vivid and intensely personal. It could be seen in the iron jaw and tyrant's will of the convention's leader himself—the famed boss of Cook County, Mayor Richard Daley of Chicago, seething with televised rage and hatred against all those Democrats who dared to challenge the party magnates, and whose thugs could be seen on the convention floor, bullying, harassing and silencing them.

Party power at its most ruthlessly self-serving had been laid bare with the utmost vividness before scores of millions of astonished Americans. The leaders of the Democratic Party had four years to consider how to deal with the crisis which that revelation had created. At stake was a complicated system of party rules, procedures and state laws, evolved over 140 years, which put into the hands of a few hundred party officials—themselves controlled by a still smaller number of party magnates—the legal and formal authority to name the majority of delegates to a presidential nominating convention. To preserve this system or scrap it was the grand question weighed by the party. Few Presidents in our history have faced decisions more weighty than this.

Vehemently opposed to reform stood the trade union chiefs, national ward heelers of the Democratic syndicate. Stand fast by the oligarchic system, they insisted, and ride out the democratic storm, which in due course was bound to abate. Union leaders tolerated no elections in their own unions—only voting—and saw no reason why the Democratic Party should be subjected to ordinary Democrats. Vehemently opposed to reform, too, were Democratic Party intellectuals—the future "neoconservatives"—trembling with fear of an American people unchecked by a powerful oligarchy, professing fear of "totalitarian democracy," which many saw taking shape already in new laws protecting air and water from industrial pollution.

A preponderance of party leaders thought otherwise. Open defiance, they believed, might prove fatal to the whole party enterprise. Timely concessions to the democratic spirit could always be taken back once that spirit abated. This had happened before in our history. In the years prior to World War I, the progressive reformers, too, had laid siege to party power, had introduced twenty-six presidential primaries into the nominating system. In the bitter aftermath of the war, an exhausted and disillusioned people ceased to care about having a voice in the choosing of presidential candidates. The primaries quickly fell into desuetude. Since they ceased to matter to the people—until the shock of 1968—they ceased to matter at all. Without a democratic spirit to drive them, democratic institutions are as lifeless as sailing ships on a windless sea.

Present fears and future hopes decided the issue, and by 1972 the die had been cast. Henceforth in the Democratic Party, delegates to the national convention were to be chosen by the millions who voted in presidential primaries or participated in party caucuses, which had to be conducted in accordance with rules that prevented a few party leaders from controlling them.

In a decision of extraordinary sweep and magnitude, the Democratic Party leadership had boldly scrapped the old oligarchic system. The change was truly momentous. For the first time in 140 years the Democratic gateway to the White House had ceased to be guarded by a few party potentates. For the first time in American history the banner of the "party of the people" was actually in the people's hands. It was now possible for someone to win the Democratic nomination for President without the support of a single party leader and even, in theory, against the wishes of party leaders. Thanks to the power of the democratic awakening it was possible in 1976 for a man to become

President of the United States with the approval of nobody save the American people. No such political freedom, no such democratic prospect, had existed in the American Republic since the rise of Andrew Jackson.

In every aspect of public life, Americans in the year of the bicentennial were falling back on ancient republican principles. Nowhere was this more apparent than in the conduct of foreign affairs. For nearly thirty years U.S. foreign policy had been conducted in an atmosphere of almost continuous crisis by Presidents who claimed unprecedented power to safeguard the "national security," which was deemed to be threatened by the most trivial events in the most remote and backward places.

That entire system of global intervention had almost completely collapsed. In 1961 the nation had thrilled with pride when President Kennedy promised that America would "pay any price, bear any burden" to defend liberty on foreign shores. Had a President made the same declaration in 1976, the country would have shaken with fury and fear. In April 1975, one week before Saigon fell to the onrushing North Vietnamese armies, President Ford had won tumultuous applause for a speech in which he assured his still-anxious compatriots that Vietnam was "a war that is finished as far as America is concerned." In January 1976, Congress, in the same spirit, had voted overwhelmingly to prohibit U.S. military involvement in a civil war raging in Angola, although the ban assured the swift victory of the faction favored by the Soviet Union. The vote, however, faithfully reflected the new public conviction about the scope and requirements of national security. In this bicentennial year the great majority of Americans had ceased to regard as just grounds for armed intervention a trifling accession of Soviet influence that posed no demonstrable harm to the vital interests of the country. "America goes not abroad in search of monsters to destroy," John Quincy Adams had advised his countrymen one Fourth of July long ago. "She is the well-wisher to the freedom and independence of all. She is the champion and vindicator only of her own." By the time of the bicentennial Americans had returned to that long-forgotten wisdom—to the profound dismay of the enemies of popular government.

They had the best of reasons for dismay. The interventionist system had been the political establishment's single most powerful prop. It had imposed upon the country an iron discipline. With the "national security" of the country perpetually at hazard, "loyalty" to the national leadership had become the citizens' chief virtue, servility the new patriotism. Dissent was deemed guilty until it proved itself innocent of weakening the country. "Perhaps it is a universal truth," James Madison had written to Jefferson in 1798, "that the loss of liberty at home is to be charged to provisions against danger, real or pretended, from abroad." The interventionist system had amply attested to that truth, for it was used for three decades to justify repression, to justify official secrecy, to justify tapped telephones, police spies and agent-provocateurs. The system justified unchecked and overwhelming executive power; it inspired American Presidents to claim the power to wage war at will under their inherent authority as Commander-in-Chief, a claim without the slightest constitutional foundation. In a word, the interventionist system had buried the Republic—but the Republic was buried alive, and well before the bicentennial it had burst free of its imperial sepulcher.

In 1961, Senator William Fulbright had remarked, with no show of regret, that "in a world of aggressive totalitarianism," the United States had to "give up some of the democratic luxuries of the past." By 1969 he was frantically warning the Senate that "our government will soon become what it is already a long way toward becoming, an elective dictatorship." The senator's odyssey was a voyage the entire country had taken. This was the cause of President Nixon's undoing. Struggling to justify his lawless abuse of his office, he invoked the requirements of "national security," claimed he was obeying an "unwritten constitution" forged by Presidents in times of crisis, warned that impeachment would fatally "weaken the presidency." But the American people would no longer allow loss of liberty at home to be charged against pretended dangers from abroad. The people listened calmly and judiciously and then said a firm nay to all of Nixon's pretexts. "We are a government of laws, not of men" was the ancient maxim, and to that maxim the country repaired.

The grip of the political establishment had weakened and the American people had become not a mob, but a citizenry.

Yet the democratic awakening goes virtually unsung. "The common wisdom of the day," notes *Newsweek* in its special 1976 Fourth of July issue, "pictures Americans sunk in malaise—the legacy of Vietnam and Watergate, inflation and recession, the decline of civility at home and authority in the world." The *New York Times* prepares a front-page bicentennial essay filled with the gloomiest forebodings. Americans are suffering from "self-doubts uncharacteristic of the nation." They are "moving toward an uncertain future, waiting for a day when a clear national cause develops to quicken their energies and national pride." Is the American Republic not a matter of national pride? Is its defense, its reform and its regeneration not the one true national cause? Apparently not. The *Times* detects "a wild disorientation about the state of American life, as though the national compass had been lost." Had it not pointed with unerring accuracy to a despot's departure from office a mere twenty-four months before? Professor Eric Goldman, author of an apologia for Lyndon Johnson, informs the *Times* that "the word that best describes the mood today is malaise," which he ascribes to America's "defeat" in Vietnam. The polltaker Louis Harris provides the *Times* with the information that in 1966 only one American in three felt that his voice did not count in the country, whereas today two of three Americans are discontented with the state of democracy in America. This desire to count, to matter, to be heard is referred to as the people's "alienation," and it has plainly grown worse in the last decade.

The democratic awakening, in short, is a *spiritual disease*. The reversion to a more modestly republican foreign policy, the refusal to "go abroad in search of monsters to destroy," is widely known in 1976 as "post-Vietnam trauma" and the "Vietnam syndrome," medical terms for the republican revival. Secretary of State Henry Kissinger is widely reported to be sunk in "Spenglerian" gloom by the American people's "loss of will and resolve" to defend the values of Western civilization in Angola. President Ford is deeply distressed, he tells us in his memoirs, by "the precipitous decline in the faith that Americans traditionally placed in their nation, their institutions and their leaders." Loss of "confidence" in everything except the republican institutions of the country is deemed the most dangerous spiritual ailment of all. It is nothing less than a "crisis of authority," say pundits and political scientists. We are living in "the twilight of authority," says the eminent historian Robert Nisbet, although it is the authority of the Constitution which has triumphed so magnificently over the pretensions of lawless power. To challenge lawless power and secret power and usurped power, as Americans are doing, raises grave questions about "the governability of democracy," reports an eminent organization called the Trilateral Commission. The press have grown "increasingly critical," says the report, and "significant measures are required to restore the appropriate balance between the press, the government and other institutions of society." And they will be taken, soon enough.

The eminent historian Barbara Tuchman, writing for *Newsweek*'s July 12 issue, believes that the American "idea of democracy" is now, at this very moment, on the verge of disappearing entirely. It "survives in the disenchantment of today, battered and crippled." An awakened democracy is pronounced near-dead! Mrs. Tuchman, sounding bleak, thinks it may just be barely "possible to reconcile democracy with social order and individual liberty." What reconciliation is needed? Was it not public outrage that put a stop to illicit domestic spying, that set in motion against official criminality the ponderous engine of impeachment? It is the awakened democracy which has upheld law and protected liberty and democracy's enemies who have been subverting both.

This popular lawfulness is yet another spiritual illness of the people. It is widely condemned as "post-Watergate morality" and the "post-Watergate appetite for scandalous implication." What republicans of old had praised as a "virtuous jealousy of public men" is now cried down as a vice. The eminent social scientist Daniel Bell fears that popular participation in public affairs is a menace to "constitutional democracy." Now that it has proven quite otherwise—the people defending, their leaders subverting, constitutional government—Professor Bell complains in this manifestly calm bicentennial season that "we are becoming moralistic and extreme in our politics."

Walt Whitman spoke of the "Union, always surrounded by blatherers and always calm and impregnable." So it is with the American people this bicentennial season: We are surrounded by blatherers and quacks bent upon twisting every revived republican virtue into a vice and every resurgent republican principle into an ailment.

How is it that the democratic awakening can be so readily distorted and reviled? This is an important question for the history of the Reaction which is about to unfold—which, in truth, is already unfolding in these very misrepresentations.

One reason, not the main one, is that the democratic awakening has no eminent high-hearted champions. No political party speaks for it; no organized movement rallies around it. No eminent savants retort to the blatherers who revile and distort it. "Confidence is everywhere the parent of despotism—free government is founded in jealousy and not in confidence." So said Jefferson, but who pits Jefferson's republican understanding against the swarms of "confidence" mongers? Who pits John Quincy Adams against the blatherers of "will and resolve"? And who will remind the Trilateral Commission that a free press is, in Victor Hugo's words, "a light thrown from all points at once upon all questions, the perpetual warning of the nation"? Certainly not America's "conservatives." They are preparing at this very moment to lead the Reaction.

The only articulate, intellectual opposition active in America is the Marxist Left, and the Left, intellectually speaking, has been worse than useless. Its younger adherents have become hysterical Maoists, while their elders belabor their "infantile" doctrinal errors. A lingering loyalty to trade unionism has lured some of the Left, unwittingly, into the anti-democratic camp. The republican cause is mere "bourgeois formalism" to much of the Left, and what use is that to the democratic awakening? The failures of the Left are gently alluded to by the Marxist historian Eugene Genovese in *Newsweek*'s Fourth of July issue. "What I think the Left will have to understand," says Genovese, a scholar with rare gifts of heart and mind, "is that the American people's commitment to the Constitution is a healthy thing, and the battle, as far as possible, has to be fought out on that terrain."

The democratic awakening has been heartfelt and intuitive, but it has no intellectual strength whatever, so moribund is republican thought, a politically perilous defect, truly, for, says Hazlitt, "Power never slumbers and fear and self-interest wait upon it as its shadow."

The shaken political establishment has no wish to praise the awakened democracy; it expects to bury it at the first opportunity. This is the main reason why the democratic awakening goes unsung. A party oligarchy, unchallenged for half a century, has its allies and apologists everywhere, ready to wait upon it as its shadow. The conduct of the Democratic leadership and its shadows is so extraordinary that it may have no parallel in history. The Democratic Party has promulgated a truly noble reform of an ancient abuse, but it does not laud its handiwork: It wages a relentless war to discredit it. The first Democratic presidential nominee under the reformed system is George McGovern, a senator from South Dakota. He has gained his popular support chiefly because he was chairman of the party's reform commission, made chairman by the party leaders themselves, who, in effect, secured his nomination. Within hours of McGovern's victory, however, the party chiefs and their AFL-CIO ward bosses begin vigorously sabotaging his candidacy, thereby providing Richard Nixon with perhaps the most factitious landslide victory in the history of the presidency. Strange things happen in democratic eras.

Party leaders then offer McGovern's disastrous showing as proof incontrovertible that the new nominating system, so far from being democratic, completely misrepresents the true sentiments of ordinary Americans. Taking its cue from unsleeping Power, Political Science springs into action, led by Jeane Kirkpatrick. Close examination of statistical and demographic charts bears out the intuitions of the Democratic leadership: When millions of Americans have a voice in the choice of a Democratic candidate the result is elitist. When a handful of party potentates do the choosing, further scientific study suggests, democracy thrives in America!

A Democratic "front" group is quickly organized to spread this impudent lie as widely as possible. It is chiefly a combination of trade union officials and party intellectuals under the informal leadership of one of the most powerful Democratic oligarchs: Senator Henry Jackson of Washington, a skilled and rancorous enemy of communism abroad and democracy at home. The trade union chiefs are coarse, crafty operators such as Albert Shanker, president of the United Federation of Teachers, who in 1969 had fought with savage zeal to prevent an outburst of local democracy in the public-school system of New York City. The party intellectuals are mainly "liberals" who tremble at the idea of liberty. Professors Bell and Kirkpatrick are among the founding leaders. So, too, is Norman Podhoretz, editor of *Commentary*, who increasingly fits Hazlitt's description of the editor of the reactionary *Quarterly Review:* "the fine link which connects literature with the police." This vehicle for the Democratic oligarchy calls itself the Coalition for a Democratic Majority. It has an important role to play in the coming Reaction; it already forms a vanguard of sorts.

In the three and a half years since its founding, the Coalition and its members have been issuing a steady stream of articles, studies and polemics purporting to show that the Democratic Party has been "taken over," not by millions of rank-and-file Democrats, but by feminists and homosexuals, by New Left extremists, by upper-class elitists and "countercultural gurus," by a sinister "new politics" which despises "as morally unworthy," says a full-page Coalition advertisement, "the long-range values and daily concerns of tens of millions of ordinary people," whom the Democratic oligarchy is bent upon silencing.

The restoration of oligarchy at home requires the revival of danger from abroad. Since the summer of 1974 the Coalition has been waging a rancorous campaign against the new republican foreign policy, although with few signs of success. To strengthen their hand when the 1976 elections are out of the way, Coalition leaders have been quietly organizing a separate Committee on the Present Danger to revive dormant fear of the Soviet Union. Members of the committee are already at work in the bowels of the Central Intelligence Agency construing new evidence of the "present danger." They form part of a group of outside experts—Team B, so-called—appointed by President Ford to compel the CIA to produce a more ominous estimate of Soviet power and ambition than the agency would make on its own, the CIA being "soft on Russia," as one of the group says. Through "crisis, mortal danger, shock, massive understandable challenge," America's "will" can be restored, says one of Team B's White House promoters—and the Republic buried once again in the imperial tomb.

Thus the awakened democracy goes unsung and unrecognized while its enemies are gathering to destroy it.

The democratic awakening enjoys one day of glory, nonetheless. The celebration of the Fourth of July reveals with wonderful force and clarity that the American people, supposedly sunk in malaise, wildly disoriented and cankered by mistrust of our leaders, are actually bursting with pride in ourselves and in our ancient rejuvenated republic. We are *secretly* happy and the secret is out on the bicentennial day. "Nations and Millions in City Joyously Hail Bicentennial," exclaims the *New York Times* in broad headlines. The newspaper's spirited account of the people's joy runs side by side with its portentous essay on the people's gloom. The newsweeklies duly chronicle the success of the "lovely party," as *Time* magazine calls the bicentennial day. In Los Angeles, a 10.8-mile parade snakes through streets not known for pedestrians. In Boston, 400,000 people, the largest crowd in the city's history, gather along the Charles River to hear the Boston Pops orchestra and hail one another. In Philadelphia, one million people gather to witness the official bicentennial ceremonies at Independence Hall. At Valley Forge, there is a great rendezvous of horse-drawn wagons, which had set out from every part of the country days, weeks and possibly months before. It is New York, ordinarily the least civic of cities, which holds the national spotlight. There, seven million people crowd the city's great harbor to watch a slow parade of square-riggers, barks and barkentines glide up the Hudson River. "In parks, and on piers, on fences, balconies, ramps, rooftops, chimneys, ledges, abutments and the ladders of water storage towers, they sat, stooped, stood and clung," the *New York Times* reports, "chiefly to watch the great ships come sailing out of the distant past and go up the hazy Hudson like a vision."

Through sheer force of bad habit the city fathers mark the bicentennial of the Republic with a "salute to ethnic diversity" and twenty-three separate "ethnic festivities." But *divide et empera* cannot work on this day, not even in America's Babel. "I've never seen the city like this," a visitor exclaims to a *Times* reporter. "Everyone feels so united." Gathered together as citizens, we recognize the citizen in one another.

The police had feared an outbreak of crime and violence, but there is none; the crime rate actually plummets for the day. Ten years later, New Yorkers can still recall an almost miraculous feeling of safety as they strolled home in the darkness through streets that had perhaps not seen in decades a respectable pedestrian at night. The civic happiness of the day has restored for a brief hour the criminality of crime and the majesty of law. What is true of New York is true across the country. "Despite the immense crowds and huge traffic jams, people almost everywhere were remarkably good-natured and mutually helpful," reports *Time* magazine. "There was evidence of good will everywhere."

The public happiness of the people is completely unexpected, so well have the quacks and blatherers done their work. "The feeling of the day sort of crept up on many of us, took us by surprise. There was a spirit to it that could not have been anticipated." So Elizabeth Drew reports to readers of the *New Yorker.* "The celebrating seemed genuine. There was a kind of inventiveness about what people were doing. Wagon trains and bicycle trips and improvised local festivities. . . . It was a people's day. The Tall Ships—the great sailing ships from around the world—captured the national imagination and they seemed to do so simply because they did, not because we were told that they should."

It is perhaps closer to the truth to say that the national imagination has captured the Tall Ships, which have appeared in New York before without stirring more than a ripple of interest. Something glows in the public mind which makes the barks and barkentines so moving a bicentennial spectacle. They are "a remarkably appropriate tribute to a nation that was settled from the sea," according to one explanation offered in the press. Something far deeper seems to be at work, however. Americans are celebrating the two hundredth anniversary of the American Republic. We feel it to be a relic, but a relic still quick with life. What is the democratic awakening if not just this happy and heart-felt realization? And the living antiques calmly gliding upriver seem, to glowing minds, like palpable counterparts of the Republic itself.

This year, says a polltaker, 68 percent of the American people believe that during the past ten years "America's leaders have consistently lied" to them. Yet Americans are intensely proud of their country. How do public men navigate these strange new currents of popular feeling?

One public man understands how. He goes before Democratic audiences all over the country delivering the same message over and over, month after weary month. The message is simple, clear and bold. The great follies and betrayals of the recent past are not the fruits of our system of government; that is as sound as a bell. It is not the fault of the people; you and I have never been consulted. "We didn't decide as a people to start a war in Vietnam." We had voted overwhelmingly for no wider war there in 1964. "Our government" started the war anyway. "We didn't decide to plot assassinations and murder against leaders of nations with whom we are not at war—but our government did it. We didn't make the decision, but it happened, in my and your government." These crimes and follies are the bitter fruit of secret government and unaccountable power. They happened "because the American people have basically been excluded from participation" in the nation's decisions. He himself is an "outsider," a former governor of Georgia, one Jimmy Carter, by name, a peanut farmer. "It's time for someone like myself to make a drastic change in Washington. The insiders have had their chance and they have not delivered." He is running down the new wide-open road to the White House with bottomless stamina and iron determination. What he wants, what we all want, he says in the peroration of his standard speech, is "a government as good and decent and compassionate and filled with love as are the American people."

Such speeches are not often heard in America. Political parties do not take kindly to party members who try to curry the people's favor by abusing the party leadership. George McGovern, quietly groomed by party leaders to represent "reform," said, "Come home, America," as if we, the people, had been responsible for the war in Vietnam. Governor Ronald Reagan is engaged this bicentennial summer in a furious struggle with President Ford for the Republican presidential nomination, but he cautiously blames our ills on "government," which accuses everybody and nobody for everything and anything. Jimmy Carter, however, boldly blames the governors, not the government, the leaders and not the led, the powerful few, not "the system." He is the candidate of the democratic awakening, the tribune of the people against the oligarchs. That is his strength with the voters. In a matter of months the strength of that tribune's role has carried an utterly obscure figure into the very center of the struggle for power. The strength of this would-be tribune gives him, moreover, a shield of immunity against his enemies. The party oligarchy dares not put out its full strength to stop this declared enemy of Oligarchy. The awakened democracy would not tolerate it. Carter understands this clearly and exploits it adroitly. "A lot of insiders are saying that Jimmy Carter has to be stopped, but I want to tell you there's no way to stop me."

In Pennsylvania this shield of immunity saves him just when his campaign is dangerously faltering. It has been weakened by the gnawing suspicion that Carter is not the popular tribune of so many people's hopes, but merely an ambitious interloper, playing a daring game in a democratic age. His main adversary in the state is Senator Henry Jackson, the well-organized candidate of most of the party regulars, most of the unions and most of the party's intellectuals. In highly industrialized, highly unionized Pennsylvania, Jackson hopes to retrieve his own sagging fortunes. On April 13, a Philadelphia newspaper carries the front-page story "Stop-Carter Alliance Is Formed"— truly a gift from the gods for a would-be tribune of the people. At once Carter calls a press conference in Philadelphia, brandishes the front-page headlines and vows defiantly: "I'm not going to yield anything to the political bosses. Jackson is being used"—and dearly will Jackson make him pay for that condescending slur! "I am letting the voters know that I belong to them and not to the political bosses."

Publicly accused by the people's tribune, most party officials in Pennsylvania flee from Jackson as from a leper. Carter's candidacy triumphs in the state and Jackson's is ruined. "Stop Carter" efforts continue; fresh aspirants enter the contest; Jackson even urges George Wallace, the party's former *bête noire*, to enter primary contests in the South to undermine Carter's chief bastions. But the national party leadership dares not direct an organized campaign against the tribune. On June 8, Mayor Daley, the grand sachem of the Democratic Party, announces that no further efforts should be made to deny the nomination to Carter, who has amassed far more delegate support than any of his rivals. Surrender to the tribune will be safer in the long run than a suicidal victory over him today. Such is Daley's advice to his party. The "boss" has no doubt weighed Carter's character in his calculations and has perhaps concluded that Carter will prove much more manageable in the White House than he appears to be on the hustings.

These are not the confident calculations of a powerful governing party but the desperate dodges of a party establishment on the brink of extinction. Carter's victory lays bare once and for all just how deadly the 1972 reforms really are. It sweeps away false hopes and delusions. When the 1976 campaign began, Democratic leaders thought it likely that a large field of candidates competing in twenty-eight primaries in every region of the country would produce a deadlock. The nomination would be decided at the convention and the ultimate disposal of the great prize would stay firmly in the oligarchy's hands. Instead, the new nominating system has produced a clear-cut victor. The banner of the party of the people is truly in the hands of the people. And worse, far worse is this revelation: The candidate chosen by the people is the avowed enemy of the party establishment. Unless something drastic is done the Democratic road to the White House not only lies open to a tribune of the people, it will remain open *only* to popular tribunes, only to avowed enemies of the powerful few. The winning candidate in the *next* struggle for the Democratic nomination will almost certainly be a formidable figure indeed. If he becomes President of the United States the politics of the country may never again be the same.

If it were possible in America to defend oligarchy in public (and if a modern chronicler be permitted the license taken by the ancient historians), this is what party leaders might say:

"The danger is not so much Carter himself. We believe we can manage him well enough. The danger lies in the system that made his victory possible. Let us speak frankly for a change. It is not because the American people are judicious and wise that the American

Republic for two hundred years has been so little plagued by demagogues. It is not because Americans are free of envy and class hatred that American politics has enjoyed greater freedom from class warfare than any republic in history. It is because we, the leaders of both parties, are in firm control of the avenues to renown and have the power to keep from the high road to office dangerous men of wolfish ambition. The educated classes of America have no idea, not an inkling, of what they owe to party leaders, to the 'pols' whom they affect to despise. At the very least we give you peace of mind. It is because the leaders of the two parties do not practice an officious partisanship, do not contest with unseemly zeal even half the elected offices in the country, that popular passions do not sweep away the sanity of legislative bodies, that the folly and greed of the mob are not regularly turned into laws. We bring the country the blessings of domestic tranquillity, though we get precious little thanks for our pains.

"Now that tranquillity is menaced as never before in our history. Unless the political landscape is drastically altered, the path to the mighty office of the presidency stands wide open to men of the most dangerous stripe, exploiters of popular passions and founders of popular parties, men like the Gracchi or Juan Perón, who bring nothing but grief to republics. The blessings of political tranquillity, to say no more, would be lost forever to the country. In every district and precinct of the country our party—our two cozy, circumspect syndicates—and the tribune's party will be struggling for every office, vying for every vote, carrying the dregs of society into the voting booths and pouring the vilest passions into the public arena.

"To keep such wolves from the White House has been the grand task and labor of the party establishment. That duty we cannot fulfill unless the road to the White House is once again under our control, and we cannot regain that precious power until we have persuaded the American people that presidential nominations are safe only in our experienced hands, that a tribune of the people is not a hope but a curse. In a word, should Jimmy Carter become President we must see that he fails and fails badly. Fails so hideously that the very word 'outsider' becomes a hissing and a warning to the American people. Only then can we regain our power and, more important, our legitimacy as the guardians of the greatest office the world has known since the age of the Roman Emperors.

"We do this in our own political interest, it is true, but not our own interest exclusively. We do it for the sake of the American people, whom it is our honor and our duty to preserve from their greatest enemy. We mean, of course, themselves."

One week after the bicentennial the Democratic National Convention meets in New York City to nominate Jimmy Carter for President, strives mightily to allay any public suspicion that the party leadership and its triumphant antagonist are in any way at odds. "Unity" is the theme of the convention as speaker after speaker, following instructions, affirms, proclaims and vows that the Democratic Party stands united as never before behind the first Democratic presidential candidate whom the party leadership has opposed. After the nominee's speech of acceptance, the Democratic Party chairman, Robert Strauss, carried away perhaps by the imp of perversity, begins calling up a huge swarm of party officials to share the stage with the nominee. Within minutes the crowd of Democrats grows so large that the nominee and his family are almost entirely hidden from view. The curious and embarrassing little scene eloquently prefigures the fate that awaits Jimmy Carter—to be buried alive by his own party.

2.

DIXIE-DALEY

"I felt I was taking office at a time when Americans desired a return to first principles on the part of their government." The thought occurs to President-elect Jimmy Carter as he sifts, in his methodical way, through all the Inaugural addresses ever delivered. The awakened democracy is exacting, all too exacting, and has almost cost Carter the election. When independent voters began seeing the tribune of the people rushing around the country embracing Democratic Party leaders, they had deserted his banner almost en masse.

So the President-elect—a suspect tribune now—knows well enough what the great bulk of the American people expects of him: They want the democratic movement to go forward. What else is an outsider President for? The real question facing Carter, the terrible nightmarish question, is, What will the Democratic Congress allow him to do? Suppose party leaders in Congress give him no support at all? What then? "It was bad enough," says Hamilton Jordan, the President-elect's chief political aide, "that they didn't know him and had no stake in his candidacy, but to make matters worse, Carter had defeated their various darlings in the battles around the country." When Carter meets, postelection, with Democratic congressional leaders in Georgia, fear and hostility, fear masked as hostility, seem to roll off Carter in waves. "You'd sit at a meeting with Carter," Representative Morris Udall recalls some six months later, "and he felt the compulsion to remind you that he also had your constituents as his constituents and that he wouldn't hesitate to take Congress on. . . . It was almost like he felt a compulsion to do this, as though he felt it was inevitable, or looked forward to the conflict, or thought it was unavoidable."

"I can get to your constituents faster than you can by going on television," Carter reportedly warns the visiting party leaders. A dire threat indeed, an empty bluff, never to be carried out, but already necessary, for the first hostile shots have already been fired. Nine days after the election—Veterans' Day—the Committee on the Present Danger makes its first public appearance with a declaration of war against Carter's hopes for arms control and improved relations with the Soviet Union. "The principal threat to our nation, to world peace and to the cause of human freedom," goes the martial declaration, "is the Soviet drive for dominance based on an unprecedented military buildup"—in fact, a 3 percent average increase yearly since 1970, 2 percent since 1974, but America's "will"—and America's oligarchy— can be strengthened only by "massive understandable challenge."

The committee members, it is said, form a "who's who of the Democratic Party establishment." Chairman and founder is Eugene Rostow, Lyndon Johnson's Under Secretary of State, head of the foreign-policy task force of the Coalition for a Democratic Majority, some twenty of whose members have become Present Dangerists. "We started over, but with the same people and the same ideas," explains Rostow. To discredit the democratic reforms in 1972; to discredit détente in 1976. The same "ideas" indeed: rule by the few, oligarchy restored, one way or another. Cochairman of the Present Danger is Lane Kirkland, secretary-treasurer of the AFL-CIO and "heir apparent" to its president, eighty-three-year-old George Meany; heir to the votes of 14.5 million powerless union members; heir to trade unionism's unswerving devotion to the Democratic machine and the endless Cold War; oligarchy revived, one way or another. Chief counsel of the Present Danger is Max Kampelman, once one of the chief political advisers to Hubert Humphrey, now gravely concerned, among other worries, over the excessive "power of the press." The nine-man executive committee includes Dean Rusk, Secretary of State under Kennedy and Johnson, one of the first American officials to argue that a President's authority as Commander-in-Chief of U.S. forces allows him to make war at will. What loathing of liberty burns in these hearts! What scant love of truth! Chairman of the committee's "policy studies" is Paul Nitze, former Deputy Secretary of Defense under Kennedy and Johnson, arms control negotiator for Nixon, who quit in "disgust" in June 1974, now a member of Team B, the tumorous appendix to the CIA. Nitze has lived for twenty-five years in an atmosphere of ever-present danger: principal author in 1950 of a momentous State Department warning to President Truman that unless the U.S. embarked at once on the largest military buildup in its peacetime history, the Soviet Union would launch its drive for world conquest around 1956—Nitze's "year of maximum danger"; principal concocter of the fictitious "missile gap" in 1957; principal author in 1972 of the newest present-danger: Allied "perception" of Soviet nuclear superiority will bind them in terror to the Soviet will unless the U.S. demonstrates *its* "will and resolve" with a renewed race for nuclear supremacy.

The board of directors of the Present Danger includes a large and varied collocation of trade union leaders, bankers, financial speculators and retired officials of both parties: John Connally; William Casey; Sol Chaikin, president of the International Ladies' Garment Workers' Union; and Richard Mellon Scaife, generous supporter of right-wing causes. Also several future "neoconservatives" from the Democratic Majority: Norman Podhoretz; his wife, Midge Decter; Seymour Martin Lipset, the Stanford University political scientist who demonstrated in a 1970 work that the greatest menace to political liberty in America is its exercise by ordinary people. And Jeane Kirkpatrick, that busy tongue of Hydra-headed oligarchy, now convinced that the millions of Democratic primary voters who form a pernicious "elite" have gone one step further into evil and now generate a spirit of appeasement, and even, says colleague Podhoretz some months hence, a "culture of appeasement." Appeasement, in fact, is the leading "idea" of the Present Dangerists. "We are living in a pre-war and not a post-war world," says Rostow. "Our posture today is comparable to that of Britain, France and the United States during the

Thirties. Whether we are the Rhineland or the Munich watershed remains to be seen." The Soviet Union is Hitler's Germany on the verge of launching a war; the United States, like pre-war Britain, is stewing in fear; détente is cowardly appeasement, Senator Jackson is a second Churchill crying in the wilderness (or so readers of *Commentary* are told). It remains only to demonstrate—such is the Present Danger's grand object—that Prime Minister Chamberlain, weak, self-deluded appeaser of Hitler, who returned from Munich in 1938 announcing "peace in our time," has been reborn as—Jimmy Carter. The opening salvo has been fired.

The second salvo is more subtle, but far more deadly. On December 6, Democratic legislators assemble on the floor of the House of Representatives to organize their immense 149-seat majority into a vast burial ground for democratic hopes, vast burial ground, too, for a Democratic President. The meeting is open, the first party caucus in history in which bitter defeats, insidious betrayals, momentous decisions will not be safely hidden from prying public eyes. The first order of business at the Democratic caucus is the uncontested election of Thomas P. "Tip" O'Neill, Jr., of Boston to the great office of Speaker of the House. A bonhomous man is Tip O'Neill, supple, crafty, intensely loyal to the party establishment, otherwise treacherous in the extreme, a parliamentarian who "knows how to strangle without leaving fingerprints," as the *Times* puts it ten years hence. A Speaker, in short, for any season, but especially suited to this season of secret stranglings, mysterious legislative defeats—the Reaction at work.

No Speaker in sixty-five years has wielded as much power as O'Neill will exercise in the forthcoming Ninety-fifth Congress, for the old autocratic committee chairmen are gone, wiped out in the democratic awakening. The great new power of the Speaker, however, must be applied to the entire party contingent—or not applied—by the Majority Leader, as yet unchosen, the choice momentous, life and death, in fact, for the democratic cause.

Two liberals are the leading contenders for Majority Leader: Philip Burton of California, openly disfavored by "Tip," and Richard Bolling of Missouri. The Californian is a reformer still resolute; the Missourian is a reformer repentant, a founding member, in fact, of the Coalition for a Democratic Majority. A third candidate, who stands no chance whatever, is John McFall, also of California. The fourth candidate's chances, too, appear dim. He is a Texas "moderate," leader of the fight against reform of the national party at the turbulent 1968 convention, a man whose election would restore that bane of congressional reformers, the old "Boston-Austin axis," paralyzer of Congress for decades. Jim Wright, it quickly appears, has at least one very influential friend. The man who puts his name in nomination and delivers a furious harangue in his favor is Dan Rostenkowski, "Mayor Richard Daley's ambassador to Washington," as Drew of the *New Yorker* describes him. A delegate from the Philadelphia machine seconds Wright's nomination. The Texan's candidacy is becoming intriguing. In a brief speech, Wright describes what he takes to be the proper duties of a Majority Leader and his candidacy becomes still more intriguing. "Even when patching together a tenuous majority he must respect the rights of honest dissent, conscious of the limits of his claims on others." A somewhat Delphic utterance. Does Wright mean that if elected he will deploy the great powers of the Speaker as sparingly as possible? Obviously so. Does he mean that if he is elected, House Democrats will be free to desert "tenuous majorities" at the expense of the new Democratic President? To the wise, the Delphic utterance suffices. But it will take "a lot of figuring," Toby Moffett of Connecticut tells *Time* magazine a year later, before younger House members like himself "learned that it's really no big deal for a Democratic congressman to oppose a Democratic President." They will have to be taught. In the meantime Jim Wright has yet to be elected.

On the first ballot the new Speaker ostentatiously marks his secret ballot for McFall, who has been put up, obviously enough, to keep Burton, his fellow Californian, from gaining a possible first-ballot victory and disaster for the nascent Reaction. First-ballot results are: Burton, 106 votes; Bolling, 81; Wright, 77; McFall, 31. "Liberals" outnumber "conservatives" 187 to 108 at the very least. If "Boston-Austin" is to be restored, truly shameless effrontery is called for—and will not be found wanting.

McFall withdraws from the contest. The second ballot's results are: Burton, 107 votes; Wright, 95; Bolling, 93; or 200 "liberals" versus 95 "conservatives." The time for effrontery has arrived. By way of preparation Bolling's "liberal" supporters had "speculated all along that Burton might attempt to aid Wright to eliminate Bolling," *Congressional Quarterly* reports. Now they vow to do to Burton what they pretend Burton has done to Bolling. They throw their "liberal" support to Wright, and lo, with Bolling out of the race, mirabile dictu, Jim Wright is elected Majority Leader, 148 to 147. Thus Mayor Daley, iron champion of iron party discipline, bequeaths to the House of Representatives—two weeks before his death—a Majority Leader who vows to exert no discipline at all. The incoming President's legislative program will not meet walls of defiance. It will fall victim to "party anarchy," die in the "breakdown of party discipline," a "breakdown" preconcerted by the iron discipline of the big-city-machine delegates to Congress and their ancient southern allies. In broad daylight in this age of reform, the "Dixie-Daley alliance," the "bosses and the boll weevils," the ancient party machine has taken an iron grip on the House. It quickly appoints loyal henchmen to all the key positions in the leadership claque.

"You have never seen democracy shown like it was today," O'Neill hastens to inform the press, lest reporters suspect that what they just saw was "the never-ending audacity of elected persons." Nobody contradicts the Speaker; where the inner life of Congress is concerned, the members keep silent; the great cockpit of party power is shrouded in darkness by a tacit vow of *omertà,* and woe to the bringer of light.

When the Ninety-fifth Congress convenes on January 4, Senate Democrats—sixty-one strong—make analogous preparations for the "outsider" President. They, too, must elect a special kind of Majority Leader. To "smooth the way for legislation formulated by a Democratic President," notes *Congressional Quarterly,* is the traditional role of a Democratic Majority Leader. Hubert Humphrey, reelected to the Senate, would dearly love to play it; it may be the "last hurrah" for the old hero of the party. "Beloved by all" is Humphrey, but his chances are nil. The former Vice President is no man for the game now afoot.

He is much too decent, much too old-fashioned, has too much of the "executive" viewpoint. He would actually try to "smooth the way" for Carter when what is required is obstruction and treachery and knives wielded in the back alleys of Capitol Hill, where the Democracy, of necessity, must do its fighting. Three hours before the Democratic Conference is scheduled to vote, "beloved" Humphrey, deserted by nearly all, sadly withdraws his name. The majority leadership goes uncontested to "a little-known parliamentary technician" named Robert Byrd, "a moderate conservative," self-styled, from West Virginia, who strongly favors costly weapons systems, strongly opposes internal Senate reforms and has previously opposed civil rights for black people.

To President Carter, Majority Leader Byrd will appear a man of the most exquisitely touchy pride. "Sometimes he refused even to discuss with me other matters of importance which he thought could be safely postponed. Sensitive about his position, he made certain I paid for my mistake whenever I inadvertently slighted him." The Senate, on the other hand, knows Byrd as a laborious lickspittle, "your spear carrier," he calls himself, brought up in direst poverty, referred to by his colleagues as Uriah Heep, so *Time* reports a year hence. A more Heepish legislator has perhaps never been seen in the United States Senate. Early in his senatorial career Byrd was the hanger-on and errand boy of the eminent Senator Richard Russell, whom he addressed as "Senator Russell" in true 'umble Heepish fashion. When Senator Teddy Kennedy became the Democratic whip to demonstrate *his* humility, it was Byrd who did Kennedy's drudgework, but not without thoughts of revenge. Like 'umble Uriah, Byrd smiled and groveled and waited his chance. In 1972 he turned on Kennedy and challenged him for the whip's position. A party prince versus the party's toady, and the toady gained the palm. Now Humphrey has fallen to Heep, for the Democratic oligarchy knows that whatever needs to be done, no matter how shameless, no matter how treacherous, Byrd will do it. "Our problems," says the new Majority Leader, "will be as great in many ways now that we have a Democratic President as they were under a Republican President." Nothing Delphic about that. Byrd's "leadership," notes *Time*, "allows senators to follow their own convictions and accentuates the independence of the Ninety-fifth Congress." There will be no "smoothing the way"; obstruction, rather, and deadly postponements and many a quick-flashing knife blade.

Senate Democrats move at once to strengthen Byrd's hand. Defeated for Majority Leader, Humphrey, the well beloved, would like to be chairman of the Democratic caucus; small honor, indeed, for so tireless a party champion, but Humphrey, cancer devouring his life, loses again. The chairmanship is given to Byrd. Liberals would like the party caucus to name the members of the Democratic Steering Committee, the powerful body which gives out the committee assignments, making and breaking careers. The appointive power is given to Byrd. Liberals would like the caucus to have final control over scheduling legislation; the scheduling power is given to Byrd. There are things which must be done—tricks, treacheries, stabbings—which sixty-one Democrats cannot safely discuss in a body. Best leave it to Heep and turn a blind eye.

Thus, in the very heart, or conning tower, of the Democratic Congress, the organization of the Reaction swiftly moves forward. The Central Intelligence Agency, too, collapses before it. On December 26, the *New York Times* reveals Team B's crushing victory over the agency's intelligence analysts. "New CIA Estimate Finds Soviet Seeks Superiority in Arms." A closely held secret now blared to the world, the estimate "was more than somber—it was very grim," an intelligence source tells the *Times*. "It flatly states the judgment that the Soviet Union is seeking superiority over the United States forces," a speculation about Soviet intentions which the CIA had carefully eschewed in the past. "The insiders shifted 180 degrees," a Team B member crows to the *Times*. Confronted by Oligarchy's "experts," the Agency has turned belly up. The new Estimate, says the *Washington Post*, "is a high barrier for the Carter administration to overcome" in its pursuit of arms control. "Even if the Carter administration disagrees with the new National Intelligence Estimates on Soviet strategy, it cannot be readily rewritten. It will appear in two or three volumes that serve as a reference for policy-makers across the top echelon of the government."

That is the point of the whole enterprise—to transform Present Danger alarms into the new official orthodoxy—at the expense of the outsider President, at the expense of the revived Republic.

Still in Plains, Georgia, still awaiting inauguration, Carter is already a strangely isolated figure. "Press interviews and other statements made it obvious that the overwhelming Democratic majorities in both Houses were not about to embrace me as a long-awaited ally in the Executive Branch."

The AFL-CIO is openly hostile. This winter the national ward heelers produce, in partnership with right-wing lobbyists for U.S. nuclear supremacy, "The Price of Peace and Freedom," a film depicting the Soviet military threat, the folly of détente and the menace of arms control. On January 10, the union chieftains assail the President-elect for neglecting the poor in his "economic stimulus" package. The Right and the poor are the unions' upper and nether millstones, between which they hope to grind Carter to a pulp—not to the advantage of the poor.

The Washington press is as hostile as it dares to be and sends out light skirmishers for the preliminary assault. "Before we arrived in Washington some of the society page editors were deploring the prospective dearth of social grace in the White House and predicting four years of nothing but hillbilly music, and ignorant Bible-toting southerners trying to reimpose Prohibition on the capital city. The local cartoonists had a field day characterizing us as barefoot country hicks with straw sticking out of our ears, clad in overalls, and unfamiliar with the proper use of indoor plumbing."

There is also the matter of reorganizing the Executive Branch. The authority to do so, subject to a one-House veto, has been granted without demur to Presidents Truman, Eisenhower, Kennedy, Johnson and Nixon. Carter has talked *ad nauseum* during his election campaign of reorganizing the Executive Branch and has been asking House Democrats to give him the authority to do so since the November meeting in Georgia. Thus far, the Democrats have refused. Jack Brooks of Texas, chairman of the Government Operations Committee, considers one-House vetoes unconstitutional. Speaker

O'Neill disagrees, but supports the chairman, whereupon 290 other Democrats fall in behind the Speaker. As a result, when Congress convenes, a terrified Carter, envisioning a "highly publicized defeat" on his first day in office, cannot find a single Democrat willing to introduce his reorganization bill to the House. "The breakdown of party discipline" only occurs on command. "A hair-raising experience," Carter calls it, and so it is meant to be.

There is the matter, too, of Theodore Sorensen, President Kennedy's former aide and Carter's choice as director of Central Intelligence. On January 13, the appointment, seemingly unexceptionable, runs into "unexpected difficulties," reports the *Times*. The Senate Intelligence Committee has been shown two Sorensen affidavits concerning the celebrated "Pentagon Papers"—the classified documentary record of U.S. involvement in Vietnamese affairs. The affidavits say what every member of the committee understands perfectly well: that the classification system is grotesquely overblown, that high-ranking officials, Sorensen included, routinely use "top secret" files in writing their memoirs; that the Pentagon Papers had posed no threat whatever to national security. Fury, nonetheless, sweeps through the Intelligence Committee. Pentagon Papers no threat? Liberals join hands with conservatives, with the John Birch Society, with every rabble-rouser of the Right they can muster, to block the appointment of Sorensen.

The President-elect in Plains, Georgia, knows nothing of this until January 15 when Senator Byrd, at his regular Saturday press conference, announces that Sorensen's confirmation faces "considerable difficulty." What is more, he tells the press, he doesn't think he will endorse Sorensen either. Heep's knife quivers in the director-designate's back. Carter says a few words in Sorensen's defense, but the President-elect has no stomach for this fight. On Monday, January 17, the first day of the confirmation hearings, Sorensen, "with trembling hands," reads to the committee a "strident" defense of his character against "scurrilous and personal attacks," against "outright lies and falsehoods." He defies those "who wish to strike at me, or through me at Governor Carter." Upon saying which he withdraws his name from consideration as director of Central Intelligence. The Reaction has scored another victory over liberality of mind and draws first blood in the destruction of a President. To gauge the full measure of the victory—and of Carter's stunning defeat—parliamentarians delve into the archives and report that only eight Cabinet-level appointees have ever been rejected in the entire history of the United States. The last time a Senate of the President's own party had done such a thing was in 1925. Byrd "just wanted to teach Carter a lesson," a "junior" Democratic senator, nameless, explains to *Time*. And the lesson is: How feeble is a president with no party to support him.

3.
JACKSON'S REVENGE

All that stands between partyless Jimmy Carter and a nightmarish term of office is the esteem of the American people. On Inauguration Day, President Carter, the suspect tribune, begins a two-month campaign to regain it. The campaign begins not with, but after his Inauguration address, which is brief, cautious and speaks scarcely at all to the democratic yearnings of the country. For those yearnings, which Carter well understands, he has prepared a stunt or stratagem which electrifies and delights the hungry democracy.

The new First Lady, a woman intensely devoted to a husband entirely wrapped up in himself, describes the occasion well: "After a light lunch at the Capitol following the Inauguration, we climb into the waiting limousines and drive outside the grounds in perfect formation. Then the cars stop, to the great surprise of everybody but the Secret Service and our family. The word spreads down the parade route. 'He's out of the car!' people yell. 'They're out of the car' . . . and we keep walking and walking, smiling and laughing, warm as we go through the snow and ice in the subfreezing temperature. All along Pennsylvania Avenue are people wearing green-and-white woolen Carter hats, left over from the primaries in New Hampshire and Wisconsin. . . . I didn't realize the impact the walk would have until we stepped onto the street and began to hear all those voices. Just as we want to be close to the people, they want to be close to us. 'Hello, Jimmy. Hello, Rosalynn,' they call again and again. 'Good luck. God bless you.' Some are crying, standing in the cold with tears running down their cheeks. I can't feel the cold at all!"

The promise of republican simplicity, how powerful an appeal it makes! In swift succession Carter enrolls his daughter, Amy, in a local Washington public school, places a ban on the playing of "Hail to the Chief" and "Ruffles and Flourishes"; offers a Lincolnian pardon to Vietnam draft-resisters; holds a "fireside chat" in a cardigan sweater, attends town hall meetings, answers questions from the floor, answers questions from the entire country on a live, call-in radio show, promises equity, fair play, a "government as open and honest as it can be"—"setting a style of leadership now," *Newsweek* well puts it, "so that he will in fact be able to lead later on." Carter's "approval rating" soars to the 70 percent mark and stays near there for months.

On television, Capitol Hill cannot compete with the White House and does not try. It has its own select audience, however, the Washington press corps, quite strategic and superbly pliant, made pliant by the code of "objective journalism," a code which boils down to this one fundamental rule: "Thou shall not think for thyself, seek instead a high-ranking source." Two is evidently being added to two; the result, say administration officials, is almost certain to be four. Whether this result is intended has not yet been confirmed. Under the code of objective journalism, news is not only what the powerful do; its purport is what the powerful say it is. The code thus performs a daily political miracle: It prevents reporters from corrupting the news so that the news may be corrupted by the newsmakers.

It is imperative that the Washington press not suspect Capitol Hill of aiming at a President's ruin. Grounds for suspicion, however, already abound. For one thing, harsh mockery has greeted Carter's economic-stimulus package. Even the dimmest reporter, with head full of cant, might wonder what has happened to this outsider President's "honeymoon" with Congress. Reassurances must be supplied at once. "I don't think there's the slightest possibility Congress is going to war with the President," says Senator Long of Louisiana, a chief general in the war. What of Carter's stunning defeat in the Sorensen affray? "Nobody declared war on Carter. The honeymoon isn't over," replies Senator Howard Baker, Republican Minority Leader, as eager as any Democrat to keep from objective journalism—and the American people—the destruction of a Democratic President at the hands of a Democratic Congress: Collusion keeps secrets well.

It is the White House that attacks us, insults us, assails us, congressional leaders complain to the minions of objective journalism. Frank Moore, the President's inexperienced liaison with Congress, is singled out for particular attention. Day after day "veteran legislators" take reporters aside to tell them what a "laughingstock" he is, how "downright offensive" he is, what a "confrontational attitude" he has. "At the rate it's going now he's not going to last. He's going to be the first sacrificial lamb," a veteran legislative aide tells *Congressional Quarterly.* "He's a good boy. He's getting a helluva lot of criticism he doesn't deserve. Somebody's got a knife out for him."

The Speaker's knife has been busy since the Inaugural. Hamilton Jordan sent him, he claims, some inferior back-row seats for an Inaugural celebration, which may or may not be so; Jordan himself adamantly denies it. "I said to Jordan," the Speaker tells reporters, " 'when a guy is Speaker of the House and gets tickets like this, he figures there's a reason behind it.' " According to the Speaker, the President's chief political adviser then replied: " 'If you don't like it I'll send back the dollars.' " To which incredible insult to the most powerful man on Capitol Hill the Speaker tells the press he replied: " 'I'll ream you out, you son-of-a-bitch.' " Such is bonhomous Tip's story, word for word, as it appears in the *New York Times Magazine* on July 24, 1977, by which time it is a twice-told tale destined for a not-insignificant place in the history books. After the Speaker has been insulted so grossly, is it any wonder that virtually no important piece of legislation submitted to Congress by Jimmy Carter is destined to pass? Meanwhile, like Pavlovian dogs, the Washington press corps is being conditioned to bark on Oligarchy's cue.

On February 1, a four-page memorandum circulates anonymously in the Senate Armed Services Committee, where Henry Jackson, untiring foe of arms control, chairs the subcommittee on arms control. The memorandum is the work of one Penn Kemble, executive

director of the Coalition for a Democratic Majority and a "close adviser" of Jackson's; assisting Kemble is one Josh Muravchik, an aide of
Jackson's newest Senate ally, Daniel Patrick Moynihan of New York,
who eloquently laments the "erosion of political authority in
America." The memorandum's immediate object is to attack an
alleged "unilateral" disarmer, Paul Warnke, Carter's choice for chief
arms negotiator. Its larger object is to help dislodge a galling impedi-
ment to the further advance of the Reaction.

In November 1974, the United States and the Soviet Union had
reached a strategic arms control agreement, initiated by Nixon, negotiated by Kissinger and supported by Congress and the Joint Chiefs of
Staff. With a few outstanding difficulties unresolved or postponed
these "Vladivostok Accords" can be quickly transformed into a formal
arms control treaty, commonly referred to as SALT II. This is just
what Carter intends to do and just what the Reaction is desperate to
prevent. It will give the new President a striking popular triumph, will
strengthen détente and "the culture of appeasement," will weaken,
perhaps fatally, the American "will." The revival of fear, the iron discipline of the Cold War, the destruction of Carter, the stifling of
democracy: All that Oligarchy so urgently seeks could be wiped away
in one cheap victory—provided by Nixon, who loathed everything the
awakened democracy stands for. The irony of it incites added fury in
the ranks of the Reaction.

The situation, however, is far from hopeless; Jackson is much too bold
and crafty to be discouraged so early in the game. It takes thirty-four senators to block ratification of a treaty. Suppose all the friends of the
Present Danger and all the enemies of popular government join forces
against Paul Warnke and amass forty votes—this is Jackson's goal—
against his confirmation as arms control negotiator? What would Carter
do then? Would it strike fear in his not so lion-heart? Warnke's confirmation hearings will be conducted by the friendly Foreign Relations
Committee, but Warnke must not be allowed to appear untarnished
before the Senate. This shocking anonymous memorandum, says
Jackson, raises so many important issues that his Armed Services subcommittee, too, must subject Warnke to the closest scrutiny.

First, however, Carter must be told what unslumbering Power expects of him. At a breakfast meeting a few days after the memorandum appears, Jackson tells the President he must not sign a SALT II agreement, must demand of the Soviets, instead, deep reductions in their nuclear arsenal to save U.S. Minuteman missiles from hypothetical "vulnerability" to suicidal attack. Carter as yet is unimpressed. At his first press conference, on February 8, he calls for "quick agreement" on SALT II. Carter's refusal to surrender triggers the onslaught on Warnke. Before the Senate Foreign Relations Committee the next day, Paul Nitze, of the ever-present danger, harshly denounces his opinions and character. Once the two men had been friends, but Warnke has become a turncoat to democracy, has attacked the "fiction that protection of our interests implies a global military mission," has likened the nuclear arms race to "two apes on a treadmill." This equating of totalitarian Russia and democratic America is peculiarly loathsome to Americans warring against a democratic America, to enemies of the republican revival, enemies of popular government. There is a "peculiar, almost venomous intensity in some of the opposition to Paul Warnke," writes Anthony Lewis of the *Times*. "It is as if the opponents have made him into the symbol of something they dislike so much that they want to destroy him." Great is the fury of men of bad faith. While Nitze rails in the Senate against Warnke's "screwball, arbitrary and fictitious" ideas, Representative Larry McDonald of Georgia, John Birch Society member, accuses Warnke of "setting in motion the chain of events which allowed Daniel Ellsberg to steal the Pentagon Papers."

Liberal scurrility and right-wing scurrility join forces to blackguard Warnke and put fear into the presidential heart. At the Washington address of the Coalition for a Democratic Majority, a new Emergency Coalition Against Unilateral Disarmament enlists in Jackson's campaign against Warnke a few days after Nitze testifies. Leaders of the Coalition include one Howard Phillips, head of the Conservative Caucus, a Capitol Hill "grass-roots" lobby financed by Joseph Coors, Governor Reagan's chief backer; one Paul Weyrich, head of the Committee for the Survival of a Free Congress; and several colleagues of one Richard Viguerie, the direct-mail rabble-rouser. The trio call themselves "The New Right," having come into political existence in 1974, like looters preying on the wreckage of the Republican Party. This "New Right" wastes no time boring people with balanced budgets and laissez-faire doctrines. The New Right takes up, instead, the battle cry of George Meany and Jackson, of Professors Bell and Lipset and of editor Podhoretz, "the Jackson wing of the Democratic Party." What the fuglemen of the Democratic establishment have been saying since 1972—that the Democratic Party has been "taken over" by a pernicious "elite" of scheming professors, ferocious feminists, homosexual corrupters, despisers of ordinary values, champions of "acid, amnesty and abortion," to quote "Scoop" Jackson himself—the New Right says in scabrous, inflammatory direct-mail letters to people who think they are fighting "the liberal power structure." This is the New Right's self-appointed task: to urge Americans who loathe the old ruling Democratic oligarchy to wage war against its *enemies*. The New Right leaders are the rabble-rousers of the Reaction, Oligarchy's computerized street-corner agitators. Their ad hoc alliance with the Democratic leadership will continue until the Reaction is safely in command of the presidency.

In the meantime the campaign against Warnke needs all the help it can get, for it is no easy task to amass forty Senate votes against a new President's distinguished appointee, especially after tearing to shreds one distinguished appointee already. On February 12, therefore, Majority Leader Byrd tells the press he will "not be drumming up votes for or against" Warnke. "I might vote against him" myself, says Byrd, plunging his knife into Warnke's back, plunging his knife into Carter's, inciting talk at the White House that Carter may have "to go public" or Congress will devour him. This is dangerous talk, liberating talk, tribunician's talk requiring quick nipping in the bud. Tip O'Neill moves quickly to stop it. On February 17, at a party given in his honor, the Speaker takes the occasion to deliver a truly extraordinary threat to the President of the United States. If he tries to go over the head of Congress, says O'Neill, it will be "the biggest mistake Mr. Carter could ever make." Condign punishment awaits the outsider President if he dares tell the American people about his perfidious party. Not even Richard Nixon sunk in official turpitude had been threatened so coarsely by a congressional leader. Is this not the very moment "to go public"? To pick up the Speaker's gauntlet and hurl it back in his teeth? So far Carter has been extremely loath to do so, for all his brash talk back in Georgia in November. At the President's press conference on February 8, a reporter had given Carter the perfect opportunity to speak out against his congressional antagonists. "Mr. President, House Speaker O'Neill complained yesterday that some of your top officials seem to have adopted an attitude of confrontation regarding Congress, and this is only the latest of several complaints from the Democratic leadership that you haven't consulted with them enough." To which the President had meekly replied: "I have given them cause for some of the complaints, inadvertently."

If he does not protest now against the Speaker's threat, when will a protest be timely? Not yet, at any rate, Carter decides. In his defense there is this to say: His situation is extremely obscure. What is the exact political strength of an elected President of the United States who lacks any organized political support? Our history provides no clue. What would happen if an outsider President attempted to rally the electorate against Washington "insiders"? Would he precipitate a constitutional crisis of unparalleled danger? Or perhaps win a quick, painless victory over party hacks engaged in a giant bluff? What Carter needs is the fresh, penetrating mind of a Bonaparte, but alas, all the democratic awakening can rely on is the conventional mind of Jimmy Carter, an earnest, intelligent man carried by excessive ambition into a political nightmare.

Strike back at Congress he must, for "very quickly I realized that the Congress was treating me like I was still governor of Georgia." But he will not do it in public fashion, openly confiding in the electorate. Instead, Carter gathers a number of advisers around him, including Bert Lance, his close friend and budget director. They review 320 dams, canals and other water projects currently in the federal budget, mainly rewards to lawmakers for fidelity to the congressional leadership, which Presidents, by common understanding, leave entirely in the leadership's hands. No longer. On February 21, Carter sends a message to Congress recommending that nineteen of the most wantonly wasteful, environmentally damaging water projects no longer be funded by Congress when it votes on a revised budget for Fiscal Year 1978. The Chief Executive's hand has intruded itself into the congressional "pork barrel," threatening the ancient system whereby the powerful few in Congress use the people's tax money to corrupt their elected representatives. Whether Carter's assault on the ancient prerogative will give Congress pause remains, like so much else, to be seen.

It does not mitigate the assault on Warnke. For two days in late February the former Assistant Secretary of Defense is subjected to "withering cross-examination" in Jackson's arms control subcommittee. Jackson and Senator Sam Nunn of Georgia pound away at Warnke's contention, shared by Kissinger among others, that nuclear superiority confers no political advantage. Warnke gives ground, is then attacked for yielding it. In the meantime, 600,000 letters, stirred up by the New Right, pour into Senate offices demanding a vote against Warnke, champion of Ellsberg and unilateral disarmament. When the three-day Senate debate opens on March 4, Jackson's subcommittee supplies the Senate with all the ammunition it can muster against Warnke, whom the Senate Foreign Relations Committee has in the meantime approved. Warnke had been asked to submit to Jackson a copy of testimony he had given in 1972 about the political insignificance of a nuclear advantage. An ambiguous comma is missing in the submission. Jackson accuses Warnke of tampering. Warnke denies the charge and stands by his original testimony with its original comma. Jackson says Warnke is lying, vehemently calls on the Senate to "judge whether a man capable of such deceit can be entrusted with two appointments and such serious responsibilities." Nunn declares that with a man this deceitful in charge of arms control, "then I think the chance of having a SALT II agreement is diminished." Tempers flare, fists pound on senatorial desks. Hubert Humphrey, leading Warnke's defense, deplores Jackson's scurrilous tactics. Senator Kennedy calls them "irresponsible and reprehensible." Senator Goldwater, too, deplores them, although not their object.

Carter urgently telephones senators, begs them to consider that a vote for Warnke is a "vote of confidence" in the President. He is fighting to keep the nay vote total below thirty-four. Senator Byrd, for his part, reminds the Senate that the Majority Leader is still utterly indifferent to the way Democrats vote. Senator Moynihan says Warnke cannot be trusted to fathom the "motives" of the "evil" Soviet rulers. An ingenious and supple mind has New York's freshman senator. As a supporter of Robert Kennedy's presidential ambitions in 1968, Moynihan had described the antiwar movement as an admirable expression of "the democratic process." In a place-hunting memorandum to President-elect Richard Nixon eight months later, he described Johnson as "the first American President ever toppled by a mob." He calls the democratic awakening "America's crisis of confidence"; calls the new moderate foreign policy "liberal cowardice and appeasement"; calls the "oppositionist" press during Nixon's presidency a threat to our "capacity for effective democratic government"; means by "effective democratic government" democracy with *demos* effectively gagged. Among the myriad mislabelers who wait upon Oligarchy as its shadow, Senator Moynihan is far from the least adept. The "Jackson wing of the Democratic Party" already regards him as a fine prospect for President once Carter is finished off. What hatred of democracy burns in these hearts!

Forty nays, claims Jackson, will reduce Warnke "to the point of uselessness." When the acrimonious debate ends on March 9, Warnke is confirmed 58 to 40. Byrd consolidates Jackson's victory by warning the President that he, personally, will resist any effort by the administration to lobby for ratification of a SALT II treaty. The Democratic Majority Leader forbids the President to speak with senators! Such is Carter's political condition after seven weeks in office: A lickspittle treats him with sovereign contempt. After the vote, the President calls once again for "rapid agreement" on SALT II, but he speaks with his heart in his mouth.

The day after nullifying Warnke the Senate roars in outrage against Carter's recommendation that Congress delete funds for nineteen worthless water projects. Senators falsely accuse him—for how can they tell the truth about the "pork barrel"?—of threatening the impoundment of funds in despotic Nixonian fashion, cry out in rage against "government by executive," accuse Carter with utterly shameless effrontery of violating the Constitution and the law. Urged on by Senators Long, Byrd and Edmund Muskie of Maine, the Senate votes 65 to 24 to prohibit the President from carrying out his figmented assault on the U.S. Constitution. "An overwhelming rebuff to the White House" and its "hit list," reports the press, which watches these brazen antics as uncomprehendingly as four-year-olds watching Punch and Judy in the park.

Carter knows exactly what Jackson and the Senate mob want of him: abandonment of the Vladivostok Accords; substitution of a one-sided U.S. demand that the Soviets sharply reduce their strategic arsenal to safeguard from fictive danger America's invincible deterrent—a proposal which the Soviets will certainly reject, a proposal which, when suggested to President Nixon in 1974, he had called "an insult to everybody's intelligence and particularly to mine."

Must Jackson be propitiated? Apparently yes. "Who wants to get beat over the head by a well-respected, tough senator saying, 'You've bargained away our security to the Russians'?" So says a very high-ranking administration official after the Warnke vote. The State Department thinks otherwise, but alas for the democratic cause, the Secretary of State is a milksop, one Cyrus Vance, a "pillar of the New York foreign policy establishment," which is not an establishment at all, but rather a glorified typing pool full of well-bred appointees and appointees-in-waiting. "Cy was extremely deferential to the President; he had a way of very pleasantly blinking his eyelashes to indicate agreement and deference." Thus writes Zbigniew Brzezinski, Vance's deadly rival for control over Carter's foreign policy, a Polish émigré who serves as the President's national security adviser. A founding member of the Coalition for a Democratic Majority, a secret follower of the Present Danger, Professor Brzezinski "has spent years putting a progressive coat of paint over his old [anti-Russian] instincts," says an academic colleague. Were that all there is to Brzezinski he would count for little; in fact he counts for much. Early in his advisership Brzezinski writes in his journal: "I will try to sensitize [Carter] to the need to have somewhat more tough-minded a group in security and arms control–oriented areas." Late in his White House career he will hail Carter's landslide defeat as the welcome presage of "a policy of assertive competition" with Russia, the ancient enemy of his country. In the innermost citadel of the White House, Brzezinski is the Reaction's secret agent, ready to betray the President to his enemies if it will help them overthrow détente. Such is the treacherous intriguer who meets with Carter each morning at eight and often four times a day. Already in State Department circles "dark rumors" are afloat that Brzezinski is meeting secretly with Jackson's aide, Richard Perle, to lay the "deep cuts" trap for Carter.

On March 10, at Brzezinski's bidding, the National Security Council's Special Coordinating Committee holds its first serious discussion of deep cuts in the Soviet arsenal. With this bureaucratic machinery set in motion, Brzezinski sweetens the pill of surrender he wants the President to swallow. Carter has called for "real arms control." Why not attempt it now? Why accept the stale leavings of Kissinger, Nixon and Ford? On March 12, a frightened Jimmy Carter helps the Reaction encompass his ruin and the ruin of prospects far more important than his own. At a meeting in the Cabinet Room the President tells his chief advisers that he has grown impatient—since March 9—with "merely staying within the Vladivostok framework." Brzezinski, presiding, declares the Accords a dead end; urges deep Soviet reductions to safeguard Minuteman missiles from a hypothetical vulnerability to a surprise attack which Carter and everyone in the room—Vance, Warnke, Secretary of Defense Harold Brown and others—know to be a doomsday bogey. "Good, let's do that," says Carter, for Jackson is not a doomsday bogey.

Only Warnke has the courage to demur. Deep-cut proposals are a deadly political trap; they will not propitiate Jackson, they will strengthen his hostile hand. "If they're shot down and we end up with a compromise then we'll be criticized for retreating." And "shot down" they will be. The proposal Vance takes to Moscow calls upon the Soviet Union to cut their nuclear deterrent almost in half, in return for which the United States—with 2,100 Minuteman warheads aimed at Soviet missile silos—will vow not to replace them with the new MX missile, the most powerful weapon ever devised.

State Department officials are stunned by Carter's decision—"flabbergasted and dismayed," says one of them. Brzezinski, the secret agent, is gleeful. The Reaction has been saved from imminent disaster. The Soviets, he writes in his journal, are "likely to reject and ridicule our proposals," perhaps finishing off détente at one fell stroke. The trap works perfectly, leaving the Secretary of State shattered and "traumatized." On March 30, the Soviets angrily reject Carter's arms proposal, which the White House angrily defends. It would seem, says a Soviet negotiator to his American counterpart, that Senator Jackson "has an invisible chair at these talks"—and so he has. In the immediate aftermath of the Moscow debacle, the Committee on the Present Danger rushes forward to praise Carter's diplomacy. There is only one reason why the Soviets have rejected the President's "equitable deal," ever-present Nitze explains to reporters. They are bent on world domination. The same day—April 3—Majority Leader Byrd and Majority Leader Wright strongly urge the President to stand firmly behind his deep-cut proposals and give not an inch to the Soviets, thereby increasing their weight as a bludgeon with which to smash, and smash again, the head of their rattled victim in the White House.

4.
CORPORATE COFFERS

The April 1977 issue of the *Conservative Digest*—newest house organ of our "New Right," which carried an article by George Meany in its first issue—contains an essay filled with portentous consternation. The author is a former speechwriter for trodden-down Nixon, Patrick Buchanan, who dreams fierce, vengeful dreams of the day when another "conservative" President shall take up Nixon's fallen banner, shall "declare war on the Congress," shall "conduct siege warfare against the bureaucracy," shall use the great resources of the Chief Executive to humble the too-powerful press, subdue the federal courts and reign supreme as a truly democratic President, albeit of the elective-despot variety. The object of fierce Buchanan's April strictures, however, is the *Fortune* 500 and their laggardly political ways. The great corporations of America have done nothing, have done much worse than nothing in the great struggle against the "liberal power structure"—alias the revived Republic. At the very least, says Buchanan, they must cease and desist their current practice of subsidizing with billions of advertising dollars "our common adversary—the networks and the national press."

Strong minds are thinking alike these days. Buchanan is not alone in urging the great economic interests of the country to enlist in the war against the awakened democracy. On the pages of the *Wall Street Journal,* Irving Kristol—a "new conservative" two steps ahead of his fellow liberal intellectuals—urges America's corporations to enter the political arena against the "new class" of envious intellectuals, spiteful professors and college-educated activists who fly the "ideological" banner of "egalitarianism" to mask their "class struggle with the business community for status and power" and to conceal their "hidden agenda" of red, socialistic hue.

Truly, strong minds are thinking alike. The deadly enemies of *capitalism,* according to I. Kristol's mock-Marxian arguments, are exactly the same as the enemies of "traditional liberalism" as depicted by the "Jackson wing of the Democratic Party." So much the same that Ben Wattenberg, "leading theoretician" of the Democratic Majority, a "traditional liberal," a former Humphrey speechwriter, lauds "new conservative" Kristol as the man who "put spine into the business community." Mark the convergence of this spectrum-straddling Reaction: New Right, New Conservatism, Traditional Liberalism all want corporate America to help them strike and smash and crush the common democratic enemy, the menace of which Big Business, that giant dwarf, cannot quite grasp.

Nevertheless, it cannot be denied that Big Business is well worth enlisting in the ranks of the Reaction. Its enormous wealth, poured into the campaign coffers of Capitol Hill, can make elective office so costly that independent spirits and dissenting voices would be hard put to enter the political arena—a shrinkage and walling off of the public realm absolutely essential to the restoration of Oligarchy. Poured into the hands of congressional leaders, it can provide them with handsome private slush funds for redistribution to the faithful, strengthening yet further Oligarchy's legislative hand. Corporate America's vast army of publicists, lobbyists and professors, allowed to press with impunity upon the Legislative Branch, can help our newly restored Dixie-Daley Congress alter the general course of legislation and with it, perhaps, the general political atmosphere.

Active recruitment, however, is called for, hence Buchanan's railing and I. Kristol's preaching. Corporate America is politically timid, more so than many imagine. "Business didn't even want to try to fight against something with a consumer handle to it," says a Chamber of Commerce lobbyist, recalling the days before the great corporate recruitment, now about to commence. Moreover, Corporate America is highly suspicious of glib-tongued, perfidious politicians. It will not pour wealth into political coffers without fair assurance of recompense, will not press publicly on Congress without the promise of immunity from political attack—nobody in America *likes* the Money Power, to put it mildly. Only the Democratic congressional leadership can make the payment and provide the immunity. As for doing so, Dixie-Daley is nothing loath. Far from it.

Even while it gave ground to the awakened democracy, the party establishment took care to punch loopholes or gunslots for counterattacking later on. In the midst of much-admired efforts to *reduce* the influence of money in federal elections, Congress in 1971 actually undermined a 1907 statute forbidding any corporate contributions to federal elections. Under the new law, corporations and trade unions were permitted to use their treasuries for "the establishment, administration and solicitation of contributions to a separate, segregated fund to be utilized for a political purpose." In short, Congress had legalized the corporate political action committee—a loophole of the utmost importance, but at first of mere pinhole size, for the 1971 statute forbade any corporate body from setting up a political action committee if it held a government contract, which effectively excluded the *Fortune* 500 and thousands of lesser beings. As of 1974 only eighty-nine corporate PACs existed, a miserable showing, of virtually no use to Oligarchy.

Never-ending, however, is the audacity of elected persons. Under cover of radical new legislation that provided for federal funding of presidential elections, Congress, in the very throes of democratic reform, turned the pinhole into a giant funnel for corporate wealth to pour through. At the "suggestion," it was said, of the trade unions, the Democratic Congress lifted the ban against government contractors organizing political action committees. "Labor," it seems, did job training for the government and fretted over the legality of its political action committees. Behold the flimsy pretext. The AFL-CIO's job-training activities are so overwhelmingly important in the grand scheme of things that opening the political arena to a tidal wave of corporate wealth seemed a *small* price to pay for it. "Labor pulled business's chestnuts out of the fire," a campaign finance "expert" is supposed to have said—expert in not calling a spade a spade. What actually happened was simple: The "party of the people" had pulled "business" into the political arena and put "labor" forward as its "liberal" alibi. A pitiful, transparent lie; why bother to tell it? Because objective journalism demands a high-level answer—what kind matters not to objective journalism—or it will doggedly seek its answer from a low-level "source," who just might blurt out the truth, for the truth sometimes escapes even from the darkness of Capitol Hill.

So suspicious is Corporate America, so craven and mousy, that the new huge loophole or gunslot or funnel did not work as expected. By 1975 there were still only 139 corporate political action committees. Then the Federal Election Commission put heart into the timorous Money Power when the commission—three Democrats, three Republicans, six lapdogs of Oligarchy—ruled emphatically that the political action committee of the Sun Oil Company was perfectly legal. Only then did Corporate America begin to organize. Even then, Representative Guy Vanderjagt, chairman of the Republican Congressional Campaign Committee, had to spend most of 1975 rushing around the country urging corporations to establish political committees. "Wake up, America," he would urge preoccupied industrial magnates—America's *popolo grosso*—"wake up. There's a war going on—a war that will determine the economic future of the country—and you're not involved." By the end of 1976 there are 433 corporate political action committees, and general PAC contributions to congressional elections have increased from $12.6 million in 1974 to $22.6 million in 1976. The direct result of Oligarchy's arduous efforts to undermine democratic reform, this "growth" of corporate PACs is now attributed to the "*unintended consequence of reform,*" for the trashing of democracy is ever the business of Oligarchy's ten thousand busy tongues.

Even these 433 corporate political bodies are a paltry affair, however. The Reaction requires far more from the *Fortune* 500. The Dixie-Daley Congress, which is bent, in any case, on Carter's ruin, has to cope with a slew of legislative proposals by no means easy for the popular party to send to perdition. On March 22, the Carter administration introduces a number of electoral reforms "with considerable fanfare and high hopes for speedy passage." One of the measures is "universal voter registration," intended to rid the country of our "antiquated and overly restrictive voter registration laws." It will allow voters to register even on Election Day, will bring the poor to the polls, and will be of such obvious advantage to Democratic office seekers that Tip O'Neill must vow "to work to the utmost to see that we can get that enacted as soon as possible," while he figures out how to strangle it without leaving fingerprints, for there is scarcely anything Oligarchy wants less right now than a large increase in social dregs voting. The second proposal is even more exasperating. It aims at public financing of congressional elections in order to nip in the bud the "growth" of PACs, which Dixie-Daley has worked so hard to plant and to nourish. *Newsweek* predicts swift passage for the bills because both parties are "caught up in the drive to restore public confidence" by extending democracy's sway. They were "ideas whose time has come," a number of Republican senators complain ruefully to Paul Weyrich, whose Committee for the Survival of a Free Congress promises to fight Oligarchy's fight, Dixie-Daley's fight—New Right and Traditional Liberalism joining forces yet again—for the revival of an expensive, bought and slavish Congress.

Then there is Carter's Consumer Protection Agency bill, providing representation for consumer interests in the deliberations of government agencies, another embarrassing proposal for the Dixie-Daley Congress to defeat. Both Houses of Congress had passed the same legislation in 1975, despite a Republican President's *opposition*. More than shameless effrontery will be required to explain how it could go down to defeat in 1977 despite a Democratic President's *support*. There are other irksome defeats on the Dixie-Daley agenda. Carter proposes to use general revenues to help "rescue" the Social Security fund, a truly repulsive prospect. The Social Security tax has been made deliberately oppressive to the lower orders—it is the most regressive tax in the civilized world—so that they will not lightly demand greater benefits; a healthy discipline, which the ravenous poor undoubtedly need, or so America's leaders since Roosevelt have thought. Then there is Carter's proposal, an idea of Kennedy's, to authorize federal agencies to defray the expenses of less affluent people and groups who wish to testify at government hearings, an example of the dangerous new "class struggle," in the view of I. Kristol, to deprive full purses of their natural right to speak louder than empty ones. And there is Carter's promise of "comprehensive" tax reforms such that, he tells a Clinton, Massachusetts, town meeting, "you will feel that everyone is paying their fair share," another repulsive prospect, for the Reaction cannot afford to let even the idea of fairness flourish, must crush it to the ground, and will soon enough.

All these proposals further the democratic awakening, advance the democratic cause. For that reason alone, Dixie-Daley would work for their defeat. Their passage, moreover, would revive the suspect tribune, establish him as a genuine democrat in the White House, which establishment is not to be thought of, must be stopped at all costs. Let us, says Dixie-Daley, kill not two but three birds with one stone. Let us kill off every single one of these democratic proposals, let us wreck Carter's best chance to look like an able democratic leader, and let us invite Corporate America in on the kill, let it taste blood, let it see that Dixie-Daley, the popular party, will protect it from political attack. Then, and perhaps only then, will the giant dwarf, throwing timidity to the winds, fully enlist in the cause of the Reaction.

On April 5, House Democratic leaders hold an "unusual meeting" with the chief executives of ten giant American corporations. The ten are "deans" of the Business Roundtable, a five-year-old organization composed of the heads of two hundred of the largest corporations in America, who would like, if granted immunity, to lobby personally against a number of Carter administration proposals. The discreet little conclave is later described as a "get-acquainted meeting" by *Congressional Quarterly,* a summit conference between Boston-Austin and Business Roundtable that "set the tone for the Roundtable's participation in legislative deliberations: an articulate advocacy of a limited agenda by top business leaders." The language of *Congressional*

Quarterly, usually clear and forceful, tiptoes and squirms uncomfortably. These are deep waters of corruption, too deep and dark for that estimable weekly journal. What Speaker O'Neill and Majority Leader Wright have done this April day is exactly what the Reaction requires: They have invited the heads of the largest corporations in America to walk into the offices of congressmen, make free of Capitol Hill and direct all the influence they can muster to kill off any legislation they do not like; a "limited agenda" which will leave the "outsider" President without a single democratic reform to his credit and which will alter, in due course, the political atmosphere of the country.

How is the partyless, nerve-rattled President to govern? He makes his National Energy Plan the single major domestic enterprise of his first year in office, magnifies its importance to the utmost, makes his ruin as a President a delicate problem for the Dixie-Daley Congress.

The soaring price of oil had brought on a global recession, had spread panic and fear through the boardrooms and Cabinet rooms of the industrial world. America must reduce its precarious dependence on foreign oil, so thoughtful people agree; must curb its profligate, energy-guzzling habits, personal and industrial. After long wrangling in Congress in 1975, however, almost nothing has been done. Mighty Jackson has deplored the energy "deadlock"; Jim Wright, too, has deplored it; so, too, has every expert who testified before Congress during January hearings on the energy crisis.

On national television, broadcast from the Oval Office, the National Energy Plan is launched on April 18. "With the exception of preventing war, this is the greatest challenge that our country will face during our lifetime," the grim-faced President warns. "The alternative may be national catastrophe." Two days later, before a joint session of Congress—an immense solemnity this—the President outlines the various regulatory, tax and pricing measures which make up the administration's complicated, comprehensive energy plan. Like a gambler at the racetrack, fatigued with petty calculations, Carter bets all his official prestige on the legislative success of this single enterprise. What is more, the White House wants everyone aware of the magnitude of the bet. "This will be a measure of Carter's ability to lead the country. It is a greater test of his leadership than any other single issue." So Hamilton Jordan advises the press. A few days before, Senate Democrats had harried Carter into withdrawing, in humiliating fashion, his proposal to give every taxpayer a fifty-dollar rebate as an economic stimulus. The energy program, however, cannot be trifled with so readily, cannot be strangled without leaving fingerprints. If it is killed it must be done in full view of an alerted electorate. Defeat the President here and the White House is an empty shell. Such is the White House message. The energy program is both a gamble and a dare.

As Carter enters his fourth month of office he even appears to be growing less rattled. In early May, arms control talks are resumed at a more negotiable level; something may yet be salvaged from the deep-cuts trap. On May 22, at Notre Dame, the President warns against excessive preoccupation with the Soviet Union. He instantly relieves of his Korean command Major General John K. Singlaub, after contumacious Singlaub tells the *Washington Post* that the President's plan to withdraw U.S. troops from Korea by 1982 will inevitably lead to war. He refuses to yield in the water project battle, threatens to veto any public works appropriation which preserves any of the projects he opposes.

Is it possible that Carter is losing his abject fear of the Democratic establishment? Congressional leaders are wary, have good reason to be: Destroying a President is a dangerous business, and quite as unprecedented for the doers as for the done to. "I've got a little feeling," an unnamed House leader tells Elizabeth Drew in mid-May, "that somewhere along the line they would like to have a test, that he's champing at the bit a little to take one to the country."

Meanwhile Dixie-Daley keeps testing the President's resolve. By June, electoral reform is dying in committee; public financing of public participation in regulatory hearings meets "surprisingly tough" opposition in the House. Using general revenues to rescue Social Security is dismissed out of hand in the House Ways and Means Committee, killed off a month later in Senator Long's Finance

Committee. The Boston-Austin-Roundtable axis has distorted the Consumer Protection Agency bill beyond recognition. "It's a good bill," says Representative Frank Horton, a New York Republican. "I've never seen a bill maligned as this one's maligned." Where is the great Democratic majority that passed the bill a mere two years before? Has it lost its tongue entirely? Not at all. Liberal Democrats tirelessly belabor Carter for his fiscal conservatism, fall mute when "conservative" Democrats kill off his democratic legislation. "Even Nixon had his partisans here," says an anonymous House Democrat in May, "but you never hear anyone saying, 'Let's do it for Jimmy.'"

On June 7, O'Neill keeps the Consumer Protection Agency bill from the floor to prevent its defeat at the hands of the Roundtable; sheds a crocodile tear as he does so. Consumer advocates are downcast; Roundtable lobbyists delighted; O'Neill has given them more time to lobby. Carter at once urges Byrd to salvage the bill by bringing it up in the Senate, which had passed it in 1975 by the strong margin of 61 to 28. But the Majority Leader, nonsmoother of the way, curtly turns down the President. "If it doesn't pass the House we cannot waste time on it," says Byrd, tightening the screws another notch. How difficult it is to be a leader when nobody who matters will consent to be a follower! On June 9, a House Ways and Means subcommittee and a House Commerce subcommittee tear the National Energy Plan to shreds in devastating "tentative" votes, testing, perhaps, how far Carter can be pushed before he "takes one to the country."

With energy program and "leadership" both tottering on the brink, Carter threatens to go "more and more public" if Congress continues to "chip away at individual component parts of the package." So he tells a delegation from the Magazine Publishers Association, but he rests content for the moment, merely belaboring "lobbyists"—nobody in particular, the most harmless of targets—for which he is belabored in turn by Byrd. Then, on June 14, a curious thing happens on the floor of the House of Representatives. An amendment that would eliminate all the water projects opposed by the President demonstrates "unexpected" strength, despite anti-Carter votes in two committees, despite the Democratic leadership, despite all the furious denunciations that had swept across Capitol Hill. Jim Wright, nonbuilder of "tenuous majorities" for the President, applies intense pressure, "something stronger than the gentle art of persuasion," to build a tenuous majority *against* him, averts a Carter victory by the unpleasantly narrow margin of 218 to 194—50 Republicans and 144 Democrats, the bulk of them young, have voted for frugality and freedom from the "pork barrel" tyranny of their elders.

Much is revealed herein to eyes that can see. The partyless President has far more potential strength than he seems to imagine. If he stands fast behind an honest democratic cause it is Dixie-Daley which will find itself beleaguered and the President who will gather support. If Carter realizes his strength (for a sense of weakness is his chief weakness) the Reaction is seriously endangered. Parliamentary machinery goes quickly into motion. The day after Carter's surprising moral victory a Senate Appropriations subcommittee votes to eliminate nine of the eighteen water projects opposed by Carter, a bid for a compromise which the President is fully expected to veto, is almost honor-bound to veto—adding that much more to his stature as a leader of strength and conviction. Some days later, however, Carter gets a telephone call from the Speaker asking him to accept unvetoed that very compromise. "I thought for a few seconds, considered the progress we had made in changing an outdated public-works system, decided to accommodate the Speaker and then agreed to his proposal."

A trifling concession, seemingly, but Carter, looking back, knows better, many years too late, alas. A "timid" decision he calls it; what frightened him he does not say, but it is not difficult to guess: If he does not "accommodate the Speaker" (and betray those who bravely stood by him on June 14), the House leaders will destroy his energy bill. "I regretted it as much as any budget decision I made as President." But why such deep regret for so small a matter? Because the decision "was accurately interpreted as a sign of weakness on my part." A fateful sign indeed. At the height of his power as President, when the Dixie-Daley Congress has good reason to fear him, he has revealed to the gimlet eye of Oligarchy that he still trembles before it. The Reaction has little further to fear from Carter. Oligarchy can do with his "leadership" whatever it likes whenever it needs to. It can even pass his National Energy Plan in the House and gain lasting credit for "loyalty" to the President. It should gain lasting credit, also, for the Speaker's power to drive legislation through the House, but this power will be utterly forgotten by the end of the year. Objective journalism is also not permitted to *remember* for itself. In late June, tentative adverse committee votes are wonderfully reversed, difficult measures win full committee approval; young members line up dutifully behind the Democratic leadership. How easy it is to be a "leader" when your party leaders support you! How swiftly do difficulties evaporate! On August 5, the National Energy Plan, not greatly altered, passes the House of Representatives. Although nobody has actually said that a political war has been raging—Carter taking pains to deny it—everybody in Washington knows that peace, or at any rate a "truce," has broken out. "The long-expected, much-feared collision between Congress and the President had not occurred," notes *Time,* "and as Congress recessed relations between the two branches of government had considerably warmed." *Time* predicts that the Senate, too, "is likely to act favorably" on the National Energy Plan.

Even in early August this is excessively sanguine. In the Senate, the tax portions of Carter's energy legislation will fall under the sway of Senator Long, a hostile party oligarch who has just joined forces with Republicans to protect a three-day filibuster that effectively kills off public financing of congressional elections—"David's victory over Goliath," exclaims topsy-turvy Viguerie, who credits the New Right with this triumph of power and wealth over the democratic "Goliath." "See what a great dust I kick up," cry these street-corner agitators for Oligarchy, like Aesop's fly on the chariot wheel. The entire nontax portion of the National Energy Plan falls to Senator Jackson's Energy and Natural Resources Committee, which enjoys this enlarged jurisdiction because Jackson has requested it—not to enhance Carter's reputation for "leadership."

The Majority Leader's hostility to the White House, moreover, has intensified, grown venomous, seems by late July almost half-mad. On July 7, Carter had proposed one-House approval of the sale of advanced radar equipment to the Shah of Iran, whom the Dixie-Daley Congress overwhelmingly favors. On July 22, notwithstanding, Byrd orders Carter to withdraw the proposal on the trumpery pretext that the Senate has only another week to consider it. He whines, he pleads, he begs his fellow Democrats to back him against intolerable presidential arrogance; persuades Senator Baker, who strongly favors the sale, to oppose it; gets three "senior" House Democrats on the International Relations Committee—all of whom strongly favor the sale—to vote against it; gets several Republican members of this House committee, who also favor the sale, to absent themselves on the day of the vote, whereupon the committee, which overwhelmingly favors the sale, "confounded nearly all expectations" by voting against it, compelling a humiliated Carter to withdraw the proposal, humiliating the Shah in turn. Heepish spite and malice, stored up in a lifetime of laborious groveling, Byrd vents upon Oligarchy's victim, political duty and psychic impulse beautifully congruent in our senatorial Heep.

The President, nonetheless, is rapturous with joy and relief—true measure of his secret fears: The Democratic establishment has chosen not to destroy him! The nightmare is over! "I've been deeply grateful at the spirit of cooperation and harmony that has evolved because of the leadership in the House and the Senate," he tells ABC News, which has come to Plains, Georgia, on August 10 to interview the President, surprisingly victorious, not least to himself. "I feel more and more like an insider," says the former champion of the people against the insiders. "I feel part of the Washington government now, not in an embarrassed way, but in a natural way. And I believe there's been a restoration of harmony and cooperation and national purpose between the White House and the Republicans and Democrats in the Congress, which is very healthy for the country."

How great were Carter's terrors and how measly and self-regarding are his hopes! And how utterly baseless as well.

5.

THE DEADLOCK MACHINE

"Traditional liberalism" this summer begins to trickle into the Republican camp, shrunken and unpopular though it outwardly appears. In August, Ben Wattenberg, champion of the blue-collar worker, becomes a senior fellow at the American Enterprise Institute, hitherto known in the national capital as "the Republican Party in exile." Our Democratic Majority "theorist" and onetime adviser to Senator Jackson will help enlarge the institute's political networks, will edit a new institute journal, *Public Opinion,* with coeditor Lipset, another traditional liberal now looking elsewhere for the revival of Oligarchy. On the magazine's editorial board sit Herbert Stein, economic adviser to Republican Presidents, and David Gergen, a Ford White House aide. In one of the first issues, Senator Moynihan and Henry Kissinger, interviewed jointly, belabor the "American elite" for its failure of nerve—its retreat before the democratic upsurge.

Trickling into the Republican camp, too, via American Enterprise is Penn Kemble, of the Warnke memorandum, leaving the Democratic Majority minus a director in order to become a "research assistant" for the Republican Party in exile. Also trickling through is Michael Novak, founding member of the Democratic Majority and Washington newspaper columnist, who becomes the institute's "scholar-in-residence" and in due course a lay Catholic defender of "traditional values" and severe critic of the Catholic Church's insufficient faith in the "free market."

How wonderfully does the Reaction girdle the "political spectrum," which is in truth spectral, ghostly, unsubstantial; having almost nothing to do with the one great question—who shall rule in this democratic republic, the sovereign many or the usurping few? When New Yorkers in 1968 demanded full local control of their public schools, much of the Left denounced them for "union-busting"; liberals detected "anti-Semitism" (the central school bureaucracy being dominated by Jews) and William Buckley from the Right declaimed against this outburst of "Jacobinism." That is the short course in the American political spectrum.

Do these tricklers matter? Only in the sense that weather vanes matter. They indicate the way the wind blows and very accurately do they do so. The truth is, the leaders of the Democratic Party, who care nothing for, indeed fear, the party's thirty-six governors, thirty-seven state legislatures and its overwhelming congressional majorities, are also looking to the Republican camp to salvage the political establishment and secure it firmly from the democratic menace.

Opportunity to strengthen the Republican Right, fiercest of democracy's enemies, beckons the party of the people on August 10, the day the President of the United States pronounces himself grateful to be a "part of the Washington government" (which part he will enjoy for perhaps one more month). The administration has achieved "an agreement in principle" on a treaty which will make over the Panama Canal to the Panamanian government by the year 2000. This completes negotiations begun in 1964 by Johnson, pursued by Nixon, nearly completed by Ford, supported ardently by the Catholic Church, the National Council of Churches, the Southern Baptist Conference, large American business interests, David Rockefeller's Council of the Americas, the Joint Chiefs of Staff, senior military men: Generals Matthew Ridgway and William Westmoreland; elder statesmen: Averell Harriman, Dean Rusk, Henry Kissinger, Melvin Laird; as well as the AFL-CIO, most of the press and John Wayne, a friend of the Panamanian dictator Omar Torrijos.

Weighty political considerations unite this elite mass of endorsers. The Panamanians are boiling over with fury at the canal's perennial insult to their national sovereignty; have rioted in the past, been shot down by American guns; will riot again and be shot down again, a prospect extremely displeasing to the Joint Chiefs, among others. The entire underdeveloped world looks upon the canal "as the last vestige of a colonial past which evokes bitter memories and deep animosities," says Sol Linowitz, treaty negotiator. Besides, the canal is "obsolescent"; only 11.4 percent of U.S. maritime trade goes through it. Failure to ratify the treaty, on the other hand, will leave blood on the head of the United States Senate, will shatter the President's power to conduct foreign policy. The White House, taking no chances, has done all in its power to remove any possible pretext for nonratification. There has been "an unprecedented amount of prior consultation," Senator Baker admits. There have been senatorial trips to Panama under State Department guidance so that senatorial eyes can see for themselves the physical vulnerability of the canal, and the vehemence of the Panamanians. There have been meetings upon meetings at the White House where civic leaders from thirty different states hear the President speak eloquently of the virtue and necessity of the treaties—"a masterful selling job," says a reporter attending a briefing. The White House has even left room in the treaties for "cosmetic" changes, should a senator find it necessary to show off his keenness to his constituents. In a word, the partyless President has devised a nearly foolproof scheme for gaining a quick, striking victory for enlightened leadership in foreign affairs. Even the Present Danger feels compelled to support the canal treaty, lest their increasingly vocal attacks on Carter's arms control negotiations seem merely ill willed and obstructive. "Carter would like to make a battleground of the new Panama Canal treaty," notes shrewd old "TRB" of the *New Republic,* "in hopes of trouncing his foes quickly and using the momentum for tougher tests yet to come."

There is one difficulty in all this: "Giving away" the Panama Canal is unpopular, very unpopular indeed. The canal is no "colonial vestige" to Americans of middle years. It is one of the glories of the national school history: how the canal locks work, how Walter Reed conquered tropical disease; how Yankee ingenuity triumphed where feeble Europe failed—all this is as vivid as the first Thanksgiving, Valley Forge, Lincoln's log cabin, Betsy Ross. When Governor Reagan in 1976 tried to attack Ford's détente foreign policy he ran into difficulties, sounded too bellicose, but when he said of the Panama Canal, "We bought it, we paid for it, it's ours and we're going to keep it," audiences roared in exultant approval. It was as if Americans, reconciled to a smaller, saner role in the world, were determined to salvage something from the expansive past and that something was the glorious storybook canal. For every three Americans who tepidly thought the treaty was probably the sensible thing to do, there were five Americans who thought it an infuriating thing to do. Anti-treaty sentiment is perhaps the only spontaneous mass opinion expressed in nearly two decades that does not serve, can be used to damage, the democratic cause. And Governor Reagan is the only public man of great political importance reckless enough to exploit it.

New Right and Old Right are eager to help him do so. A popular cause is the one thing Reaction is ever in need of, being by its nature for the few against the many. "It's not just the issue itself we're fighting for. This is an excellent opportunity for conservatives to seize control of the Republican Party." So says a leader of the American Conservative Union, which organizes in late August the Emergency Coalition to Save the Panama Canal, which will shortly produce a documentary film for television entitled "There Is No Panama Canal . . . There Is an American Canal in Panama." "Win or lose," says Viguerie, "the conservatives will benefit by this. We will raise America's consciousness about national security. It will bring hundreds of thousands of people who had not been previously involved into the conservative movement." Governor Reagan's man in the Senate, Paul Laxalt of Nevada, calls the canal treaty "the best political issue that could be handed to a political party in recent history": He means by "political party" the former governor of California, no more, no less. What New Right, Old Right and Reagan men need is time, as much time as possible to mail inflammatory letters, show inflammatory films, send out inflammatory "truth squads" to "stem any erosion of anti-surrender sentiment among the general public," says Howard Phillips of the Conservative Caucus.

Time to denounce the treaty as another "Munich," as craven "appeasement" and abject surrender to Soviet dominion. Time, in short, to turn
sentiment and nostalgia into a political force.

What the President wants is quick action, preferably in 1977, while
the great mass of eminent endorsements retains its freshness and
strength, before the Right has a chance to turn the tremendous trifle
of the treaty into the acid test of "the resolution and the will of the
American people," as the American Enterprise Institute calls it in its
Defense Review issue this August. Will Senate Democrats bestow a
minor victory on the Democratic President or a major victory upon
the right-wing enemies of all that the party has for so long represented? Is the party leadership so base, so perfidious, so utterly indifferent
to avowals, professions, pledges, platforms, past Presidents, ten thousand orations, New Deal, Fair Deal, New Frontier, Great Society, the
common man, equal opportunity, compassion, the rights of labor, that
it will take steps to strengthen New Right, Old Right and Reaganite
prospects? Carter cannot imagine this: In any case his "hopes of
trouncing his foes quickly" rest entirely on his failure to imagine it.
For the Democratic Party leaders are exactly as base and perfidious as
its chief victim cannot imagine them to be.

The canal treaty "faces an uphill battle," says Majority Leader Byrd
within twenty-four hours of the "agreement in principle." He intends
to do nothing, let the White House be advised, to rush the treaties
forward. The Senate, says Byrd, must have its floor clear for energy
legislation. Nor will the Majority Leader endorse the treaty; nor will
Senator Frank Church, second-ranking Democrat on the Foreign
Relations Committee and Carter's presidential rival in 1976; nor will
some fifty other senators, let the Harrimans and Rockefellers, Joint
Chiefs and high churchmen opine as they will over the tremendous
trifle, thirteen years and four administrations in the making.

Before the Right even begins its campaign of rabble-rousing, a half-
dozen congressional committees, Democratic-controlled of course, are
already in full cry *against* the treaty, arming the Right as best they can.
"Antagonistic House committees," recalls Carter, perpetual underesti-
mator of his party's baseness, held "public hearings even before the

negotiations were completed. That summer, a stream of witnesses and some of the committee members had paraded before the television cameras their arguments that the treaty was illegal, unpatriotic, a cowardly yielding to blackmail, a boon for communism and a threat to our nation's security." In the House International Relations Committee, a leader of the Veterans of Foreign Wars denounces the canal transfer as "a slow motion act of strategic self-mutilation." In a House Ways and Means subcommittee, investigating what it calls "Panama Canal ramifications," the chairman, Gene Snyder of Kentucky, publicly declares that "banking interests may be behind the canal giveaway," a populist element in the attack which the Right takes up with alacrity, for it badly needs a populist mask and finds it in "the treaty that Wall Street wrote," and in "the subversive penetration of the White House" by David Rockefeller's Council of the Americas.

"We did not fare well in the Senate Armed Services Committee," either, recalls Carter, possibly surprised that the chairman, old John Stennis, would try to weaken *his* presidency by providing "a forum for a few retired military officers" to declaim against Soviet threats to the Caribbean, when this self-same Stennis was so strong a champion of a "strong presidency" that he was prepared to lie through his teeth to conceal Nixon's impeachable offenses from the Senate and people of the American Republic.

Then there is the Senate Judiciary subcommittee which calls upon Governor Reagan as its "star witness" to testify on September 9 that "whenever the United States withdraws its presence or its strong interest from an area, the Soviets are ready, willing and able to exploit the situation. Can we believe that the Panama Canal is any exception?"

All this is mere preliminary. The axe falls on September 13, six days after the formal signing of the treaty, when Senator Byrd declares that there is virtually no chance whatever that the treaty can be dealt with in 1977. Energy legislation is no longer the reason. Byrd now claims that too many weeks of hearings will be required before the treaty can reach the floor, a floor which will stand virtually empty for almost two whole months in 1977. "Anyone who thinks I will bring it up before January is living in a dream world," Byrd says again on September 24.

The White House is downcast, the Right elated. At Viguerie's Falls Church headquarters, outside Washington, New Right agitators and twenty Republican senators, led by Laxalt, meet to discuss what to do "outside" and "inside" the Senate to exploit Byrd's precious gift of time. And what great gobs of time does our senatorial Heep provide the Right and the Reaganites! Not until February 21, 1978, will Senate debate on the treaty begin in earnest. Not until the tremendous trifle has consumed more Senate time than any foreign policy issue since the Treaty of Versailles will the debate cease. "We will have had the issue for eight or nine months," says a delighted Viguerie after the Falls Church meeting. "We will have rallied many people to our cause, we will have given our supporters an issue, a cause to work for," with the compliments, unavowed, of the Democratic Majority Leader and the Democratic Senate which stands behind him. For the Reaction not only moves on; it is pushing Right. The "traditional liberals" trickling into the Republican camp are not turncoats but scouts.

While these Panamanian preliminaries are being arranged, Carter's budget director is being driven from office and the Senate is tearing his National Energy Plan into humiliating shreds. The war against the partyless President suddenly intensifies, grows truly pitiless and cruel.

Bert Lance, the budget director, seems an unlikely victim. A large, jovial, outgoing person, Lance is respected, able and widely liked, perhaps the only person in this self-absorbed White House who *is* widely liked—though precious little good this will do him. He is also the President's dearest friend, perhaps Carter's only real friend; their relationship is very intimate, very intense. "It is difficult for me to explain how close Bert was to me or how much I depended on him."

In July 1977, scandalous reports appear in the *Washington Post* and the *New York Times* about Lance's loose, possibly illicit, activities as a fast-rising small-town Georgia banker. Massive overdrafts; personal loans to Lance from banks which, in turn, receive large deposits from Lance's bank; private use of a company airplane. On July 25, Lance appears before the Senate Governmental Affairs Committee and refutes, so it seems, the outstanding allegations, but the Comptroller of the Currency has ordered an inquiry, "prompted" by the news stories. On the evening of August 17, the White House receives an advance copy of the Comptroller's lengthy "interim report." "There appear to be no violations of any applicable laws or regulations," the report concludes. In 1975, Lance had used an overdraft from his own bank—the most serious charge—to help finance his failed campaign for governor; this could be construed as an "illegal campaign contribution" by the bank, but the Justice Department dropped the case. There is no evidence "that warrants the prosecution of any individual." Lance's loose banking ways "raised unresolved questions as to what constitutes acceptable banking practices." But surely it is not a banker's duty to improve the accepted ethics of banking? Or so it seems to presidential eyes dimmed by love and loyalty. The main thing is, the ugly press charges of crime and corruption are utterly false, or so it seems to a presidential heart burning with heaven only knows what resentments against the hostile, circumambient "Washington elite."

On the afternoon of August 18, Carter flies from Camp David to stand at Bert Lance's side in the Old Executive Office Building, where Lance will be holding a press conference. "I have reviewed the report of the Comptroller of the United States, both personally and also with the White House legal counsel, Bob Lipshutz, and my faith in the character and competence of Bert Lance has been reconfirmed." The President goes on to thank Lance for "going through this ordeal" like "a gentleman and man of complete integrity." Then as Carter turns to leave he says in full hearing of the press, "Bert, I'm proud of you." A folly inspired by loyalty and friendship, but partyless Presidents, marked for destruction by Oligarchy, cannot afford such lapses.

The press plunges in like a dagger. What? cries the Washington press corps, stiff with indignation. A President who talks of "honest" government is "proud" of a man whose activities "posed serious questions of banking ethics"? This is not to be borne. The Washington press corps dares not add two plus two by itself, but this is not to be borne; dares not compare today's official Heepish lie from Byrd with last week's lie from Heepish Byrd, but this is not to be borne. The President, says *Newsweek,* crowing not a little, has put "his vaunted morality at hazard." From August 18 onward every charge, rumor, allegation that can be marshaled against Bert Lance spreads itself across the pages of the press, leads off on the evening television news. "Not a single official allegation has been made against Lance," notes John Osborne of the *New Republic.* "It's been mainly a media exercise," much of it trafficking in "dubious trivia." But trivia that can enrage, like the private overdrafts enjoyed by Bert Lance's wife. At Carter's August 23 press conference, the ill will of the press corps vents itself in cruel stupidity. "What words in the Comptroller's report convinced you that Bert Lance should not resign?" a reporter asks the President about a man officially accused of nothing and whose official conduct is not even in question. To which Carter, severely self-suppressed as usual, replies that Lance has done nothing "contrary to normal practices that exist in the banking circles of this country." Then this question: "Mr. President, do you think the American taxpayer has reason to question the competence of a man in charge of the federal budget who, after he has taken that job, made seven overdrafts on his own account?" Hugh Sidey of *Time* can see no other interpretation of Carter's defense of Lance save that of being "either sleazily dishonest or grossly uncomprehending." Is there no inkling here of friendship, love or loyalty? No thought of what presidential "leadership" would look like if Carter threw his dearest friend to the wolves at the first baying for blood? No thoughts in the press, or much of it, but of blood.

Whence does the Washington press corps derive this savage strength? It is forbidden to think for itself; it is forbidden to remember for itself. Does anyone suppose it can *hate* for itself, can plunge itself into a President's heart by itself? The American people are not baying for Carter's blood, but somebody certainly is. Most revealing about the assault on Lance is that the *Washington Post* is manifestly its leader. "The *Washington Post* is conducting a vendetta against Bert," the President writes in his diary on September 1, "and has apparently ordered two front-page stories about him each day. This morning, for instance, they had nine separate stories about Lance—headline stories—throughout the paper. In contrast, the *New York Times* didn't mention him." When Drew of the *New Yorker* visits the White House to discuss the Lance affair, aides speak of themselves fighting, not the press, but "Washington" or, interchangeably, the *Post*. "If the *Washington Post* wins this one . . . ," an aide remarks to Drew, then shrugs and sadly nods his head. For the *Post* is no ordinary newspaper. It is as close to being the national organ of the Democratic establishment as circumstance and objective journalism will allow—and it allows much when Oligarchy nods.

The beginning of the end for Lance—and Carter—comes on September 5, when Senators Abe Ribicoff and Charles Percy, senior Democrat and senior Republican, respectively, on the Governmental Affairs Committee, call publicly for Lance's resignation, basing their demand on a convicted embezzler's baseless, self-serving charge that Lance was his partner in crime. The vile accusation is quickly given to the press, chipping away still further at Carter's public reputation—his only shield—as a man of honor and integrity, which reputation, in truth, is the main target of the assault on Lance, now being conducted by the press, a number of congressional committees and several executive agencies as well. For the second time in less than four years the White House is a fortress besieged by the Capitol. But mark the change: In 1974 the Capitol laid siege to a feeble tyrant; now it is besieging a feeble democrat—and abetting the tyrant's would-be avengers.

The National Energy Plan, Carter's gamble and dare, is the supreme test of Carter's leadership; Jackson takes up the dare. Deplorer of energy "deadlock," he creates, upon the return of Congress from summer recess, a new, invincible deadlock. On September 12, Jackson's Energy Committee declares it cannot support the Carter/House proposal to continue government control of natural gas pricing with prices set sharply higher. Senator Jackson and eight other champions of the "consumers" ardently support regulation but will not approve higher prices. Two Democrats and seven Republicans, champions of the "producers," will not accept continued regulation no matter how high the prices are set. This nine-to-nine "deadlock" among eighteen veteran extollers of half-a-loaf compromise and get-along, go-along has a remarkable parliamentary future before it, but Jackson has just begun his assault. Two days after the natural gas deadlock, Jackson's committee votes to "scrap" entirely the utility-rate provisions of the Carter/House energy program. On September 15, Jackson's committee votes to send Carter's National Energy Plan to the floor "without recommendation," thereby declaring that it has found nothing, absolutely nothing in the House-passed legislation even worth amending. Two days later Long's committee resolves not to vote for Carter's crude-oil equalization tax—"centerpiece," it is said, of the National Energy Plan—unless the revenues are rebated, not to consumers but to oilmen. On September 19—two days before Carter, with choked voice and tear-filled eyes, announces Lance's resignation—Jackson's committee votes 13 to 1 to urge the Finance Committee to kill the "centerpiece" tax outright, which the Finance Committee does on September 26. "President Carter's energy bill is on the verge of devastation," reports *Congressional Quarterly* in late September.

In October, it passes the verge. On October 4, the Senate votes 50 to 46 to deregulate new natural gas, a "major defeat" for the President, who had struggled for months to avert it. On October 6, Long's Finance Committee kills Carter's coal conversion tax, "as critical a blow to the Carter program as could be struck." On October 14, Long's committee eliminates all of Carter's energy taxes and the National Energy Plan has virtually ceased to exist in the Senate. It has been "gutted," "butchered," "junked" as openly, as thoroughly and as contemptuously as Capitol Hill can contrive it.

Parliamentary experts are puzzled, grope for an explanation of this "abrupt turn of events," this sudden "loss of momentum" since the House enacted the National Energy Plan in August. "The extent to which it has been pulled apart has come as a general surprise," Drew writes in the *New Yorker*. Objective journalism requires an explanation; Capitol Hill provides it: "The consensus on Capitol Hill appeared to be that the President and his team were themselves largely to blame for the current plight of his energy program," *Congressional Quarterly* reports. Congressional aides say administration briefings were "too little and too late," that "consultations" were inadequate, that Carter had not addressed the people on energy since April.

Capitol Hill buttonholes reporters; tells them that Carter has "yet to master the art of congressional relations," that he has "overloaded the congressional circuits," a picturesque disorder very popular with the press. If the National Energy Plan is a "greater test of his leadership than any other single issue," then Capitol Hill is nearly unanimous that Carter has failed. Objective journalism can only agree since the White House seethes in silence. Nonobjective punditry agrees as well. "Most of his difficulties are of his own making," opines the *New Republic,* noting the overloaded circuits. "Can Carter Cope?" asks *Newsweek* in blaring headlines; Carter's inability to "cope" having become the "fashionable gossip" now that two powerful party oligarchs have torn his House-passed bill to shreds. Carter's "skill, his credibility, even his competence have fallen under daily attack in the columns." Bonhomous Tip, the ever-treacherous, blames Carter for the senatorial slaughter, confirming the fashionable gossip; indeed making it fashionable, though not one whit less false. The fashionable gossip speaks of a one-term presidency; fashionable gossip mentions Senator Moynihan, "a favorite of the Scoop Jackson wing of the Democratic Party," for the presidency in 1980.

In this season of Lance and "gutting" and "loss of momentum," the House of Representatives begins leveling its own heavy blows at the President's "leadership." On September 20, the President's long campaign to eliminate the Clinch River nuclear-breeder reactor suffers a crushing defeat in the House. On September 29, his *successful* campaign to rid the budget of yet another prodigious boondoggle, the B-1 bomber, suffers a reverse when the House Appropriations Committee refuses to delete funds for its production although Congress has already voted to cancel the plane. Efforts to "save" the bomber, reports *Congressional Quarterly,* are mainly "a platform for members who charge that the administration has been too soft" in arms control negotiations with Russia.

Destructive reversals are the rule of the hour. In August, mackerel-bright Moynihan had praised Carter's welfare reforms as "superbly crafted"; on September 30, he testifies before a House committee that they are "grievously disappointing." The AFL-CIO supported Carter's crude-oil equalization tax in the House, opposes it now in the Senate. On October 19, an administration bill requiring that 9.5 percent of all imported oil be carried in U.S. ships, a bill passed by the House in 1974 and considered "certain" to pass again, goes down to crushing defeat—attributed by Capitol Hill to excessive lobbying by its maritime supporters. On November 1, the Consumer Protection Agency bill, also once-passed, is again pulled from the floor by the Speaker to prevent its defeat by intensive Business Roundtable lobbyists; intensive lobbying producing either victory or defeat, according to which Punch-and-Judy show Capitol Hill chooses to put on. Universal voter registration suffers a striking reversal, too. Back in March we must "work to the utmost to see that we can get this launched as soon as possible," said the mock-enthusiastic Speaker. But a Cook County Democratic official in Chicago calls the measure unwise, has not "found one responsible political leader from anywhere in the spectrum who wants any part of this," which ward-heeler wisdom prompts "southern and big-city Democrats" to urge Tip to keep it off the floor. Dixie-Daley cannot be seen voting against Democratic election victories or even Political Science might ask an awkward question. So the Speaker strangles the bill. He is loyal to Dixie-Daley, loyal to nothing else. The financing of public participation at regulatory hearings falls likewise into legislative limbo; public financing of congressional elections is "bottled up" in a House committee on October 25; the democratic cause is being butchered in the Democratic Congress.

The alteration of opinion between summer and fall devastates Carter with particular force on October 1. Back in July, the *New York Times* had hailed the President's efforts to reconvene the four-year-old Geneva Conference on the Middle East, a conference cochaired with Nixon's approval by the United States and the Soviet Union. In August, Arthur Goldberg, former Supreme Court Justice, had urged Carter to "proceed aggressively" with his Geneva plans. Senator Ribicoff, too, had advised him "to be very, very tough" in pursuing a Middle East settlement. More illustrious Jewish voices can scarcely be imagined, or so Carter believes. On October 1, the administration produces a joint U.S.-U.S.S.R. communiqué regarding the confer-

ence. The administration has won several Soviet diplomatic concessions which Carter regards as "an advance of unprecedented importance." He actually expects praise for his handiwork, receives, instead,
a torrent of nationally televised abuse. "The reaction was immediate,
intense and almost overwhelmingly unfavorable," says Jody Powell.
The innocuous communiqué, says Brzezinski, "set off a storm of
protest, bringing together traditional anti-Soviet forces and supporters
of Israel," the two conjoined by the pretext that inviting the cochairman to the conference has injected the Soviets into the Middle East.
George Meany, National Ward Heeler, roars in rage over Carter's
attempt to "undercut" Israel; Jackson, aiming at Carter's destruction,
says his Israeli policy could lead to his destruction. On October 4, an
influential "supporter of Israel," one Rabbi Schindler, threatens to
unleash the power of the pro-Israel lobby to delay the Panama Canal
treaty—in other words, help the Reaganites and the Right—unless
Carter relieves alleged pressure on Israel. Taking up Oligarchy's cry,
Professor Lipset, spanner of the spectrum, warns that Carter's mis-
treatment of Israel "will have a devastating effect on President Carter's
chance of reelection." The reaction to the October communiqué is, in
truth, the voice of the Reaction, which has now firmly recruited to its
growing coalition powerful pro-Israeli interests, those who look upon
an awakened American democracy as a threat to the security of Israel.
"Dejection and disappointment," says a Carter aide, sweeps through
the browbeaten White House.

One bold presidential act bears promising fruit. On this dismal
October 4, day of rabbinical threat and Senate defeat, the President
goes before the United Nations General Assembly to announce a
"breakthrough" in arms control negotiations. "We and the Soviets are
within sight of a significant agreement in limiting the total number of
weapons and restricting certain categories of weapons of special concern to each of us." Achieving such an agreement "will create a foundation of better relations in other spheres of interest." Alas, there are
no "deep cuts" in this preliminary outline of an agreement; Jackson
has been ignored. "There was no probability of support from Scoop
Jackson for any treaty which the Soviets were likely to sign," Carter

now realizes, six months too late. But Jackson, as Warnke has warned, is no man to trifle with; he leads a bipartisan clique in the Senate; heads a party "wing," is champion of the arms lobby; ally of the Right, promoter of Oligarchy and commander of many a glib oligarchic tongue. When a Republican wanted to run for Jackson's seat in 1976, Senator Jesse Helms, moneyman of the Republican Right, refused to give him a penny to challenge "Scoop," traditional New Deal liberal. Another short course in the "political spectrum."

Jackson is furious; Senate gang is furious. Present Danger, Democratic Majority, Republican minority all roar and bellow forth the question: How dare you, Jimmy Carter, abandon your enlightened and equitable demand that the Soviets cut their nuclear arsenal in half? Why has Carter "given away the store?" asks Richard Perle, Jackson's anti–arms control aide and Israel's chief agent in the Senate. Jackson's subcommittee demands an administration answer and gets one. Jackson calls it a "fabrication," Perle calls it "an outright lie." What Carter and his negotiators have done in this impending agreement is "a double—and therefore doubly disastrous—cave-in; they've surrendered their own earlier efforts both to reduce heavies and to put a meaningful cap on land-based MIRVs." So says Jackson, bludgeoning Carter with his March proposals just as Warnke had prophesied. Privy to negotiating secrets, Jackson leaks misleading versions to the press, which pours forth critical stories of cave-ins and surrenders; leaks them to Present Danger as well. On November 1, Paul Nitze makes the dramatic charge that by 1985 the Soviet Union, thanks to Carter's cave-in since March, will be able to destroy 90 percent of Minuteman missiles in a surprise attack, will have locked the United States into "a position of inherent inferiority," paving the way for Soviet world domination. On November 2, the Coalition for a Democratic Majority, quiescent these many months, springs into vigorous life, links both "traditional anti-Soviet forces and supporters of Israel" by charging Carter with betraying pledges to Israel and making "unbalanced U.S. concessions" to the U.S.S.R.

What the *New Republic* calls "a swelling band of anti-détentists" has fallen on Carter's modest outline of an arms agreement like a pack of rabid dogs. "They released classified materials," says beaten-down Vance. "They made false charges about U.S. 'concessions'; they published unsubstantiated and incorrect allegations about Soviet cheating on the SALT I agreement; and they attacked the administration for not solving fundamental strategic problems, such as the alleged ICBM 'window of vulnerability.' " The Dixie-Daley Congress is stirred to action by an article in the December *Reader's Digest:* "Arms Control— The Russians Are Cheating," by former Defense Secretary Melvin Laird. At once House and Senate committees call upon the administration to answer Laird's magazine allegations that the Soviets "repeatedly, flagrantly and indeed contemptuously" cheat on the 1972 Anti-ballistic Missile Treaty and the SALT I interim agreement; they subject administration officials to withering cross-examination, order U.S. negotiators to demand stringent verification procedures—else they negotiate in vain. On December 6, the "swelling band of anti-détentists" demonstrates its power in the House, which votes to keep the B-1 bomber alive, after voting to cancel it in early September. The *New Republic* detects in December "a hawkish ascendancy that threatens to defeat the SALT treaty."

In the meantime the Dixie-Daley Congress has devised a truly devilish, black-comedy fate for the National Energy Plan. The House having enacted the plan and the Senate having enacted an antiplan, differences must be resolved in a House-Senate legislative conference. Normally each House appoints as conferees only supporters of its bill, but this conference, this "test of Carter's leadership" conference, is founded on quite different principles. Deregulation of natural gas, voted by the Senate despite the House and the President, is the great divisive issue; all agree that until it is resolved no bill whatever should issue from the conference. The Speaker has called deregulation "totally unacceptable," but of the twenty-six legislators he names to the conference, thirteen favor deregulation. Jackson adamantly opposes deregulation, but the Senate's conferees are none other than the eighteen exquisitely divided members of his committee. What kind of House-Senate conference has Dixie-Daley contrived? The answer is: a deadlock machine. And what does this forty-four-man, flesh-and-blood machine produce with remarkable clockwork efficiency? Ironclad, unbreakable deadlock, day after day, week after week, month after month. Get-along, go-along, half-a-loaf compromise, where have these grand parliamentary mainstays fled this autumn, this winter, this coming spring and deep into the summer of 1978? "An unusually uncompromising mood prevailed," notes a nonplussed *Congressional Quarterly*, "as conferees haggled day after day making almost no progress on the most controversial parts of the plan." Especially obstructive are the Jackson eighteen. They are "evenly split 9–9 and could not agree among themselves on anything," will remain 9–9 until next August 18, when they all agree to—deregulation, just what Carter opposed. How marvelously efficient, how ductile, how superbly manageable is this Dixie-Daley Congress, when once its real intentions are divined!

As if to dramatize the President's failure of his own "test of leadership," Capitol Hill on November 4 falls into a prolonged state of suspended animation. Activity virtually ceases in House and Senate (this Senate too busy to take up the canal treaty) as Congress waits with baited breath for the deadlock machine to *not produce* a National Energy Plan. The President had planned an overseas trip to last from November 22 to December 3; congressional leaders persuade him to cancel it in order to "work more closely" with the House-Senate energy conference. It is the first such cancellation in seventeen years; "an embarrassment to the entire administration," writes *Time,* "since it contributes to the impression of a Chief Executive who is losing control of events." Shortly after Carter decides he must stay in Washington, however, the conferees decide to leave it. They recess from November 18 to 28, or seven of the eleven days which the President would have been away had he not embarrassed the entire administration by canceling his trip.

What possible illusions can Carter have left by now? He is partyless, friendless, isolated, besieged. The Democratic establishment defeats him, insults him, betrays him, traps him, treats him with unexampled contempt. It has driven his dearest friend from office, has defeated administration bills which Congress had passed when a

Republican President opposed them. He knows that Democrats are making "strange combinations" against him. He knows that the Chamber of Commerce and the AFL-CIO "were each working to kill our [energy] legislation," that "their efforts were concerted in the Senate." He knows that Jackson is "doing everything possible to defeat the [arms] agreement even before its final terms could be known," knows that Jackson is the key to the humiliating House-Senate energy deadlock, knows "they've never gotten one senator to change a position even when repeated efforts to put forth a compromise have been made," as he bitterly complains to a business group, but not to the people at large.

To public and press Carter has pretended that all is well. He has appeased and propitiated the party leadership, called them his "friends," insisted to every press questioner that there is no "schism between the White House and Congress," has claimed at news conference after news conference that "our relationship with Congress has been good" when everybody thinks it as bad as it can possibly be, given no palpable reason for its being bad at all. As the year 1977 draws to a close, all that he has reaped from appeasing, truckling and pretense is a bitter harvest of insult and injury. "He has played it quiet," a political consultant named David Garth shrewdly remarks in December. "He has tried trade-offs and nothing has run. . . . He came up against Congress and nothing happened. And there weren't any appeals to the outside. Nobody knows exactly what is happening. Nothing is coming through [Congress] and nobody is getting yelled at."

The White House "plays it quiet" but Oligarchy does not. Is objective journalism puzzled by "the glacial pace of Congress this year" and the sorry legislative record of the outsider President? Oligarchy will provide the reason, Oligarchy and its ten thousand tongues. Let objective journalism consider this: that, so *Time* puts it, "as a result of reforms, power in Congress is so widely dispersed that a President can no longer strike his bargains with just a few barons." Our baron-bereft Congress is becoming "unmanageable to its leaders," a wild "Brahma bull." Never mind that the Speaker pushed the National Energy Plan through the House with juggernaut force this July; objective journalism can remember only what the powerful choose to recall. Let objective journalism consider, too, that Congress is still "rebelling against the imperial presidency" (though it appears to be kicking a dead horse). And then let objective journalism consider this above all: that the new system of nominating Presidents robs them of any "natural constituency in Congress." In short, let objective journalism clearly understand that the first President of the United States ever elected without the approval of his party's leaders is the victim of nothing whatever except an excess of democracy in America. Thus Oligarchy opines and thus objective journalism reports, having no contrary "source" to quote in rebuttal. The mere silence of the White House damages the democratic cause.

Why does Carter not "appeal to the outside"? That is the question of the hour and of much more than the hour. "This fellow Carter, he really puzzles me," says Alfred Landon, defeated by Roosevelt in 1936, now in his ninety-first year. "He tells Congress he's going to take his case to the people, but he smiles when he says it." Old Landon is one of the very last survivors of the last great rebellion against political oligarchy in America; had fought the old Kansas Republican machine; had fought with Theodore Roosevelt against the national Republican machine in 1912; knows it is not a matter for smiles. When you strike at an oligarchy you must strike it down—"politics is not the nursery." But Carter will not strike. His aides, it is rumored, have asked him to do so, have begged him to become once again "the old Jimmy Carter fighting for the rights of the outsider." But Carter will not fight the party establishment, has not the lion-heart required, nor does he understand with the absolute clarity required for high and dangerous deeds that the timid alternative is utterly futile.

"We've had a very productive year," says the appeaser President, referring to routines and trifles, as the first session of the Ninety-fifth Congress draws to a close "with more of a whimper than a bang." Congress is to be lauded for its "hard work, dedication and courage." Vice President Mondale is to be sent to Capitol Hill with a personal message of commendation from the President. When Congress adjourns on December 15, Carter tells the country how "very pleased" he is with his "legislative record." When the deadlock machine decides on December 22 to adjourn until January 23—after the Senate conferees vote 16 to 2 against agreeing to anything—Carter swallows his bitter disappointment and puts a good face on failure. It is "very good and very healthy" that Congress should act slowly, he tells a national television audience on December 28; his "biggest mistake" as President was expecting it to go faster—a sad and contemptible pretense.

After such outpourings of praise and deep satisfaction, how can Carter ever turn upon his tormentors and accuse them of tearing his presidency to shreds? The time for that has come and the time has now gone by. No memorial marks the moment, but it is a historic moment just the same, for in casting the die for appeasement Carter has sealed the fate of the democratic cause. It remains only to discover how much the Reaction can extract from the President before it completes his destruction and tosses him aside.

6.

QUACKERY

Bitter defeat in endless procession is what Oligarchy metes out to the partyless president in Year Two of the Reaction. "Tax law reform: Killed. Labor law reform: Dispatched to die in committee. Consumer Protection Agency: Killed. Hospital cost containment: Gutted. The crude-oil tax in the energy bill: Stalled." The litany is recited by *Time* in its issue of August 7; 1978. The full list of defeats is appreciably longer. Welfare reform: Strangled by the Chairman of the Ways and Means Committee, Al Ullman, after a select subcommittee *approves* it. Election reform: Dead in committee or killed on the floor. Regulatory reform: Lost, heaven knows where. Wasteful water projects deleted by "compromise" in 1977, defiantly restored in 1978 despite a "taxpayers' revolt." Insult, as always, added to injury. On April 20, a group of senators holds a birthday party to celebrate with jeers the first anniversary of the National Energy Plan, still locked inside the deadlock machine, which now operates in secret sessions—juniors excluded—to conceal from the public the twiddling of thumbs.

Victories are few but more costly than defeats. Carter's successful fight in the Senate to sell jet fighters to Saudi Arabia as well as to Israel proves so bitter, fills the air with such poisonous charges of White House "anti-Semitism" that Carter resolves never again to pit his weakened presidency against the power and ill will of the pro-Israel lobby. The ratifying of the Panama Canal treaty is so long protracted, the opposition so bellicose, the President so visibly weak that it "effectively catalyzed latent public fears of retreat and withdrawal," says a White House aide engaged in the treaty fight. To limn more sharply the image of presidential weakness—to make it the personified image of national "retreat," to etch it, engrave it, carve it into the national mind—"uncommitted" Democrats force Carter to beg and truckle and openly bribe for last-minute votes. "Christmas on Capitol Hill," crows the press, growing more stupidly cruel as Oligarchy grows more brazenly vile and Carter more stupidly meek. Ratification ends up a victory for the Reaction, a defeat for the President. "Carter is turning into an indispensable ally in our effort to revive Republicanism," says Reagan's fugleman, Senator Laxalt, truthfully enough.

What is the explanation, asks *Time*, of this extraordinary series of humiliating defeats? And asking, *Time* answers: "a dramatic new development in Washington: the startling influence of special-interest lobbyists." They are "swarming in Washington" in unprecedented numbers, reports *Time*, building up organizations of unprecedented size, operating with unprecedented impunity, and enjoying unprecedented success imposing their will on a Congress ostensibly Democratic. Congress is suddenly bowing to the corporate swarm; Congress is suddenly thinking as the corporate swarm thinks. There has been "a dramatic swing in economic and political philosophies in Congress," notes *U.S. News and World Report* in July. Commercial reasons, commercial pretexts, the commercial *idea* of America, more or less subdued for nearly half a century, have suddenly revived in the summer of 1978.

Not by happenstance, nor popular will, nor yet by inner prowess does the corporate swarm appear. By invitation only, the invitation first extended at the little "get-acquainted meeting" April last between Dixie-Daley leadership and Business Roundtable "deans." The lobbyists swarm because Dixie-Daley wants them to swarm. The great corporate magnates who ardently supported the Panama Canal treaty did virtually nothing to secure its ratification. Swarming *for* Jimmy Carter is no part of the arrangement with Dixie-Daley. The corporate swarm gains sudden sway in Congress because Dixie-Daley welcomes its sway. The corporate "philosophy" is becoming the dominant "philoso-phy" because Dixie-Daley enacts it into law. Great, indeed, is the influence of Power over Thought, or what passes current for thought in the public realm.

In the general progress of the Reaction, mark this as the latest stage: the deliberate demise of the Democratic Congress as the spokesman and champion of ordinary citizens. The country is to be handed over to wealth and privilege, and the rule of business, in a word, to "revived Republicanism," whether the country likes it or not. Dixie-Daley has decreed it, has no real choice in the matter. Even a nominal party of the people hinders the progress of the Reaction, so nominal popular party the Democratic Party ceases to be. In three legislative acts, the party leadership on Capitol Hill makes it known to the agents of "Republicanism," as yet unrevived, that the Democratic Party aegis has ceased to protect, even by mere word of mouth, the rights and interests of plain people.

On February 8, the ten-year struggle to give consumers a voice in the deliberations of government agencies goes down to a well-prepared defeat, 227 to 189, 101 Democrats "deserting" the President, who had made the measure his "top consumer goal." Invited to swarm, the Chamber of Commerce swarms, no longer fearful of anything with a "consumer handle to it." Its avalanche of "grass-roots" anticonsumer mail is said to be instrumental in the fatal outcome, which kills much more than a bill. "The House has dealt a decisive blow," reports *Congressional Quarterly*, "both to President Carter and the consumer movement." First blood for corporate America, the decisive blow launches in earnest the corporate swarm. It launches, too, demands for counteraction, not least by Ralph Nader, leader and virtual founder of the consumer movement, now suddenly tottering on its last legs. "The corrupting influence of big business contributions, promised or with-drawn, has never been more clear than in the past few days." Speaker O'Neill agrees, butter not melting in his mouth, that though he has "been here for twenty-five years, I have never seen such extensive lob-bying." Surely something will be done in the Democratic Congress to moderate this "corrupting influence."

The sums which political action committees spend on congressional elections have begun to soar. The total was $12.5 million in 1974, will reach $35 million this year, and corporate wealth has scarcely been tapped yet. The total will reach $190 million by 1982. The number of these political committees has doubled since 1974; the number of corporate committees has quintupled since 1974 and will triple again in the next few years. The remedy for this money pollution (which Republican Senator Charles Mathias will one day call "the worst thing that's happened in politics in my lifetime") has been moldering in committee since last spring—the public financing of congressional elections. It is favored by the voters, ardently championed by nearly a hundred young lawmakers. It is an "idea whose time has come," an idea which the unprecedented corporate swarm is making more timely than ever.

Hard-pressed indeed is the Dixie-Daley Congress. To curb "the corrupting influence of big business contributions" means no further corporate swarms, no private slush funds for the leadership, no pricing of independent spirits out of politics, no doing all that can be done with corporate millions to strengthen the hand of Oligarchy. It would mean a signal victory for the democratic cause: a severe setback for the Reaction.

To defeat public financing, whose time has come, shameless effrontery is once again called for and once again will not be found wanting. This March the House Administration Committee concocts a parliamentary ruse. It draws up a bill curbing the amount of money which political parties and political committees may contribute to individual candidates, a measure calculated to hurt only Republicans. To this so-called partisan bill the committee adds public financing as an amendment. The object of this display of "partisanship" is perfectly plain: to give twenty-five or so Republicans who dare not oppose public financing openly an excuse to cast a "partisan" vote against the committee's "partisan" concoction. Wondrous indeed is partisanship in America's complicitous two-party system. On March 21, public financing is killed in a procedural vote by 209 to 198 with 140 Republicans unanimously lined up on the nay side. A "dirty, sullied-up vehicle" has been used by the leadership to drag public financing down to defeat, charges Abner Mikva, an Illinois Democrat so angered by the coarse sabotage he breaks the vow of *omertà*—197 of his colleagues keep their mouths tightly shut; that is the true measure of "party discipline" in Congress.

An enlightening defeat—to privilege, if not to the people—is this defeat for public financing, unimpeachable testimony to Dixie-Daley's devotion to the Reaction, a strong eradicator, therefore, of lingering corporate suspicion. "The days of being concerned over a Democratic majority are over," declares a corporate lobbyist named Pat Walker a few days after the defeat is secured. Let the signal go forth to corporate boardrooms, says Walker: "The Democrats have seen the business point of view." Seen and embraced it, and will embrace it for years to come. What will not be seen is the *nonbusiness* point of view. With dramatic suddenness it virtually disappears from public discourse after Congress transforms Carter's tax reform bill—the third leg of this legislative odyssey—into a revived gospel of wealth and privilege.

Carter's bill, pivot of the counterrevolt or *coup de main*, is a modest proposal put forth on January 20, 1978. Its object is to mitigate somewhat the gross injustice of the American tax system—a "disgrace to the human race," Carter had called it during his election campaign. The bill's chief feature is a $24.5 billion tax cut which benefits 94 percent of all households—"with special emphasis on low- and middle-income taxpayers." What "significantly improves the progressivity of the tax system," says the Carter tax message, is the administration's replacement of the $750 individual tax exemption (which most benefits the affluent few) by a $240 tax credit for each household (which most benefits the nonaffluent many). Six million families below the poverty line would be removed, thereby, from the tax rolls, a much-needed relief in a country where the total taxes paid by Americans include levies so harshly regressive—property taxes, sales taxes, excise taxes, the Social Security tax, among others—that the poor actually pay a higher percentage of their income in total taxes than anybody else. The "progressivity" of the federal income tax is the chief instrument for mitigating the entrenched injustice of the overall tax burden.

It has been used to do so by the popular party, as a matter of official policy, since the tax was introduced in 1913. How can the party fail to support Carter in this? How indeed.

The second element in Carter's "improved progressivity" of the tax system is the "elimination of some of the most glaring tax preferences and loopholes," in particular a provision which allows wealthy investors to shield nearly 65 percent of their capital gains from any taxation, "a benefit which is grossly inequitable," notes the tax message, "when most workers are taxed on every cent of their wages and salaries." Proposed is a very small reduction in a very large tax privilege, for capital gains are said to be "perhaps the greatest single source of unfairness in the American tax system." Under the tax code, one-half the profit made from the sale of property held for six months or more is tax-free, need not even be reported as income. The benefit is not widely shared. Only 10 percent of American households report any capital gains; a mere 3 percent of the population collects 65 percent of the benefits. The richest one-tenth of 1 percent of the populace receives 37 percent of the benefits. Capital gains drives the search for tax loopholes and tax shelters, subsidizes speculation in real estate and unproductive investment in general and will be eliminated in the tax act of 1986. Carter's own proposals are the most modest of entrenchments on privilege, "not a sweeping revision," notes the *New Republic* in early February, "just a solid improvement, composed of ideas that have been debated many times over." *Congressional Quarterly* expects "almost certain approval." *U.S. News and World Report* predicts that the President's proposal for a big tax cut this election year will swiftly arrest his decline in the polls. Behind the President's tax measure, too, stands the electorate's deep conviction that the loophole-ridden tax system favors the rich. The unfairness of the tax code "puts the whole concept of citizenship in jeopardy," says Senator Moynihan (though not in Year Two of the Reaction), "and that is the one irreplaceable resource of this Republic."

In the "whole concept of citizenship" the Republic lives; without it the Republic wanes, fades, matters not. The concept of the citizen is the great stumbling block to privilege, for citizens are equals in rights and in burdens—or meant to be. It is the perpetual menace to Oligarchy, for citizens are public beings with a voice in their own governance—or meant to have, citizenship being a standard and a principle of judgment, without which American bearings are lost. The citizen-idea, in short, is an obstacle which the Reaction must remove from its path. To let it be strengthened by Jimmy Carter is not to be thought of, is thought of by nobody who matters. The Carter tax bill is dead the day it reaches Capitol Hill. The only question pondered is how the Reaction would fare if America's unjust tax code were made even *more* unjust than before. Such is the *coup de main* being contemplated in the powerful Ways and Means Committee of the Dixie-Daley House.

Little is heard from the committee for almost three months after Carter submits his foredoomed tax bill. The Ways and Means leaders are waiting, perhaps, for reassuring signs—presidential weakness, popular apathy, the progress in Congress of "the business point of view"— before they attempt their counterrevolt, which is not unattended with risk. A free hand to work with, the Speaker has given them, having "predicted" on national television in late January that Carter's tax reforms would have trouble in the House, that baron-bereft body, in which he has become, he says—and who dares contradict him?—a mere hapless bystander. The President's own voice in the country is growing ever more feeble, less and less heeded. How can it be otherwise when his one consistent policy in speech after speech, briefing after briefing, news conference after news conference is to conceal from the people the perfidy of their leaders, not wanting, he says, to undermine "confidence," undermining, thereby, himself, for surely we did not elect an "outsider" President to protect the powerful from the people.

The very evening before O'Neill strangles his "top consumer goal," Carter hails the Speaker as his "closest friend" in Washington. After this betrayal he says not a word of complaint or rebuke. "The frustration I feel is a good thing," Carter tells a town meeting in Bangor, Maine, a few days later; the defeats he suffers at the hands of Congress are to be understood as a tribute to America's system of checks and balances, an alibi not without grace, but false and futile nonetheless.

When "the idea whose time has come" goes down to defeat in late March there is no presidential demur. Does the former popular tribune not care about "the corrupting influence of big business contributions"? Apparently not. When a Democratic commission hands down new rules for nominating Presidents which curtails the chances of "outsiders" and strengthens the hand of the party regulars, Carter does nothing even here—at the very touchstone of his own presidential career—to stay the progress of the Reaction, so desperate is he to appease the party leaders. The champion of "open" government becomes the first President to formally authorize secrecy agreements for government officials; enforces lifetime censorship of CIA officials, a truly vile seed of the tyranny to come; begins the restoration of the surveillance system, yet another deadly seed of oppression. Brutally betrayed by his party, Carter is becoming the betrayer as well.

At the urging of Brzezinski—and against the fervent pleas of Vance—Carter and his aides spend months repeatedly denouncing the Soviet rescue of Ethiopia from invasion by neighboring Somalia, call it a "violation" of détente, vainly demand Soviet and Cuban withdrawal. The object of this worse-than-futile effort, the national security adviser explains to the *Washington Post,* is to "prove we weren't soft." The result—as Vance feared and treacherous Brzezinski hoped—is the further strengthening of the "swelling band of anti-détentists," the further weakening of support for an arms control treaty and the spectacle of a President whose foreign policy is becoming a shambles, whose solemn avowals are losing credibility to an electorate growing increasingly bewildered, sour and inattentive.

Such is the general state of things when the Ways and Means Committee makes its first move in early April. A Republican committee member named William Steiger proposes that instead of restricting the capital gains preference, the preference be increased. The wealthiest investors now pay a maximum of 49.1 percent tax on their capital gains. Steiger proposes to reduce the maximum to 25 percent. The rich are not rich enough! "Investors" are overburdened. "We have swung too far toward egalitarianism," says a proponent of this massive tax relief for the wealthy. "It's time to swing back and increase economic growth." The American economy is suffering from excessive *equality*, although the poor bear the heaviest tax burden and 2 percent of the population owns 54 percent of the national assets, while countries with higher taxes and less inequality outstrip us in economic growth. Facts no longer matter. Quackery suddenly rules, as if by decree.

Wondrous indeed are the virtues of this increase in the capital gains privilege. On the Ways and Means Committee, twenty-five Democrats and twelve Republicans listen respectfully to a study which purports to show that a $2.2 billion capital gains tax cut given to the richest 0.4 percent of American households will provide 440,000 new jobs and reduce the federal deficit by $16 billion. Chief propagator of these factitious studies is a curious organization called the American Council on Capital Gains and Estate Taxation. The chief economist on the board of this Council is a young Californian named Arthur Laffer, now a protégé of Governor Reagan and his retinue. Ways and Means listens all ears.

Opposed to the capital gains tax cut, among many other economists, is the chief economist of the Treasury Department, who says of the Steiger proposal that "there is not a shred of evidence it will produce any economic stimulus," let alone 440,000 jobs. The huge privilege solves a feigned problem: "There has been no shortage of investment," says the eminent economist Lester Thurow. The idea is merely a "bogey." Opposed to the Steiger proposal, too, is Secretary of the Treasury Michael Blumenthal, who calls it "the millionaires' relief act of 1978." Ways and Means heeds not, half of it, at any rate, organized by an obscure Oklahoma Democrat named Jim Jones, a former appointments secretary to President Johnson.

On April 17, President Carter warns that the committee is tampering with the foundation of civic virtue, nothing less. "Tax reform is not just economic," says the President. The tax code is "the measuring stick by which citizens can judge the effectiveness of their own government, and the fairness of their own government, and evolve, therefore, trust in their own government." Exactly so. The *coup de main* is not "just economic" either; in fact, it is scarcely "economic" at all. Ways and Means heeds quackery in order to justify privilege, to justify an assault on tax justice, and subvert, thereby, "the whole concept of citizenship." And with it the grand principle of equality, what Lincoln called the "stumbling block to all who in after times might seek to turn a free people to the hateful paths of despotism." Quack economics masks the political object; quack economics is thus in demand, suddenly reigns in the councils of state. "By the time the liberal economists reassembled their forces and challenged [these studies] in the various tax journals," writes Robert Kuttner of the *New Republic,* "the political battle was over."

"Bipartisan" support for this blow to the Republic understandably "surprises" *Business Week,* is "surprising," as well, to *Congressional Quarterly.* Nobody can anticipate the audacity of this Reaction-in-progress, or its power to span the political spectrum. Among the directors of the oddly influential American Council on Capital Gains and Estate Taxation, alongside Laffer, are the illustrious figures of aged Clark Clifford, grandest of the grand chams of the national Democratic Party, and Edward Bennett Williams, deepest of all the Washington lawyer-intriguers in the national Democratic Party. "There is a crossing of party lines," says the chairman of the Council, Charls Walker, "an ignoring of party lines"—in the common assault on the revived Republic. Walker, champion of tax privilege, is also treasurer of the Committee on the Present Danger; the Reaction is one, however disparate its elements may seem.

The counterrevolt, however, does not carry in a day. Liberal Democrats on the committee are too infuriated, some "moderates" are as yet too frightened to follow Jim Jones into the camp of "revived Republicanism" and strangled republicanism. On April 24, therefore, Chairman Ullman abruptly stops work on the tax bill (after stripping it of Carter's reforms) and waits for an opportune moment to strike anew. The Senate has no such difficulties. In May, sixty-two senators led by Long sponsor a massive capital gains tax relief for "the people who invest"—quackery's new term for the rich; new alibi for privilege. The weakened President struggles in vain to halt "this surprisingly strong movement" in favor of "the business point of view."

The key to the success of the *coup de main,* however, lies in the

House, the popular, tax-originating branch. And the key to House approval lies in a California referendum scheduled for June 6, 1978.

California homeowners are in an angry mood. They pay the highest property taxes in America—a "highly regressive" tax at any time, now increasing in California at a "skyrocketing" rate. In Los Angeles there are families earning $15,000 a year paying $2,500 a year in property taxes on their jerry-built bungalows. The whole California tax system is galling in the extreme. Requests for small property tax reductions have been rejected repeatedly by the state legislature, leaving the local tax base overburdened and the state treasury with an infuriating surplus of $5 billion. As the final galling element, the local property tax in California supports the one social expenditure which a majority of Americans actively dislikes; namely, the welfare rolls, 2.2 million strong in California.

On the California ballot is a referendum—Proposition 13—which would cut property taxes by almost 60 percent and require a two-thirds vote of the electorate to approve any new local taxes. "Revenge," it is said, "is in the air." On June 6 Californians troop to the polls and cast 65 percent of their vote for this immense reduction in the property tax. Attention at once is riveted on the state. What does this massive, angry vote signify? More to the point, who will have the power to say what it signifies, for power in America is often just this capacity to determine what a popular vote means, what "message" it sends, what "mandate" it supplies.

The proponents of Proposition 13 want California anger seen as a popular mandate for curtailing government in general; they have exploited the anger for that very purpose and in truth for no other. "We have made a new revolution. We are telling the government, 'Screw you,'" says Howard Jarvis, a crabby, quarrelsome old businessman who led the fight to get Proposition 13 on the ballot. The California vote is a "public reaction against our overgoverned society," says the famed economist Milton Friedman, a champion of Proposition 13 and of minimal government interference in the market. The reaction, says Friedman, is "nationwide" in extent.

No opinion poll supports such claims. Republican lawmakers facing electoral competition this fall do not campaign on a platform of curtailing public services. It is the "liberal" press which tends to agree with the Right, the *New Republic* flatly declaring that "suddenly" the great body of the American people has "thrown aside whatever generous impulse may have made them support public services in the past." The Dixie-Daley budget makers agree with the Right, declare a nationwide "taxpayers' revolt" and "aimed our meat axe at elementary education, at aid for the elderly, the handicapped and the poor," complains Silvio Conte, a Massachusetts Republican on the House Appropriations Committee. Capitol Hill's sudden passion for "thrift," however, does the President no good. Nothing does him any good. The Clinch River breeder reactor, a $2.6 billion rathole, is once again saved by Congress; last year's deleted water projects are insultingly restored; a $2.2 billion nuclear aircraft carrier, rejected by the administration, is defiantly added to the defense budget. Carter's bill to curtail soaring hospital costs is "gutted" in the House, "rejected" in the Senate, "a stunning loss for the President." "When the proposed savings appeared to be at the expense of the powerful health-care industry, thrift went out the window," says *Congressional Quarterly,* endlessly chagrined by this mystifying Ninety-fifth Congress.

What then does the California vote mean? Only what Dixie-Daley says it means. Does the "taxpayer revolt" signify a general wish for a tax reduction? Surely yes, says common sense. No, says Ways and Means, and demands that Carter *reduce* his tax reduction request to $15 billion. Californians have voted against an overburdened regressive property tax; is that an outcry against "an unjust tax system designed and continued by selfish special interests," as Senator George McGovern contends? That is the *one* meaning of the California vote which has no political support at all. The one thing Proposition 13 will not mean, is forbidden to mean, is decreed not to mean, is the one thing it most obviously means: that Americans would like a just tax system. Justice is not to be thought of, decrees Dixie-Daley. Tax justice—justice in one of its most basic forms—must be blotted out of public life. The "tax revolt" is a cloud, a fog, a cover, a vast confusion, under which, among other things, the *coup de main* can now be delivered.

Carter, to his credit, struggles hard against it as it begins to gather overwhelming force in the Ways and Means Committee, after being tempered somewhat by Jones. At a press conference on June 26, Carter lashes out at the committee's work. Neither he nor the American people, he says, in a rare exhibition of manly anger, "will tolerate a plan that provides huge tax windfalls for millionaires and two bits for the average American." Strong words, but Carter's words count for nothing now on Capitol Hill. The President is "irrelevant," says a Republican lawmaker, and he is right. By the middle of Year Two of the Reaction the party establishment in Congress has taken charge of the country, ruling unchecked. The Coalition for a Democratic Majority is talking of a new Democratic presidential candidate in 1980, someone, says editor Podhoretz, "who can help mobilize the [anti-Soviet] sentiment that is stirring in the country." Senators Byrd, Jackson and Dole and National Ward Heeler Meany demand suspension of the arms control talks. "Liberals" blame Carter for every defeat the party gang inflicts on his liberal programs. The people are baffled, "ask what's going on," says TRB, in the *New Republic,* and get no answer, with what effect on their poise and self-assurance, sense of unity amidst diversity, it is difficult to say, but harmful to self-government the effect must be.

How can Carter bear the agony of so much failure and defeat? What it is like to be reduced to irrelevance in the greatest office in the world is likewise beyond imagining. The President soldiers on, appears calm, endures; hopes for one big "victory" that will save his presidency. The unprecedented notion of *personally* negotiating a peace treaty between Egypt and Israel, decided on July 31, is born of that desperate, tenacious hope. Carter's aides do not have his power of self-suppression. In this season of defeats bordering on debacle, press secretary Jody Powell sinks into despondency so deep, he says, it is nearly "clinical." Seeing the grim, despairing look on Powell's face, a small-town reporter asks him if he intends to resign. Despondency is punctuated by rage. "They resent us," says Powell, unnamed, to a *U.S. News and World Report* interviewer. "If Hamilton Jordan went up and groveled at the feet of every member of Congress it still wouldn't

change their minds." "Paranoia" afflicts the White House, retort the
pundits of the press, as if to warn Carter of what he can expect by way
of denunciation should he dare accuse party leaders of savaging the
first President ever forced on them by the people.

On July 27, the Ways and Means Committee, by a vote of 25 to
12—the twelve being angry "outgunned" liberal Democrats who
pleaded in vain for the Speaker's support—report out a tax bill which
gives the lion's share of a $16 billion tax reduction to the wealthiest
5 percent of the country, now referred to as "the middle class"—the
vast middling population of the country, once the nation's pride,
being suddenly demoted to the lower orders in this season of quackery
and sudden change. An almost total defeat for President Carter, the
tax bill provides the 37,000 richest households with a capital gains tax
reduction of $25,000 a year, a gross dispensation of privilege now
described as "increased incentives for risk-taking and job-creation."

"Outrageous," cries the outspoken Abner Mikva, for $25,000 is
more than what 90 percent of American families earn in a year.
"Revolutionary," say jubilant Republicans when the House passes the
tax bill by the immense margin of 362 to 49 on August 10. The
Democrats have given up at long last their efforts to "redistribute the
wealth," say Republicans, for mitigating the gross unfairness of the tax
system has suddenly become—in this season of quackery—an assault
on the deserving rich. They have accepted by overwhelming vote the
old "trickle down" doctrine that the riches of the rich are the blessings
of the people. "We've turned around the whole thrust of what tax
reform was two years ago," says a Republican senator, have turned it,
in truth, inside out. Republicans have reason to be jubilant. The popular party has openly abandoned tax justice, abandoned equality of
rights and burdens, abandoned citizenship itself, has proclaimed by
overwhelming vote that America is an economy suffering from republicanism—the innermost idea of the American Right, its pith, core
and essence—and so paves the way for its rule. The American people
will have to follow as best they can.

Suddenly in this season of Democratic self-demise and "trickle
down" revival, "supply-side economics" becomes a household phrase,

gets cried up by our jubilant Republicans, turning Arthur Laffer into the celebrity of the hour. The chief progenitor of this new economic theory is described as a "wizard" and not unjustly, for magical thinking is what he traffics in, and moral transformations of the fairy tale sort. An immense tax reduction is his wizard's wand, soon to be wielded by a wizard incomparably more potent than Laffer.

High taxes, according to the new Laffer-Republican economics, have turned once-virtuous Americans into a nation of reckless spendthrifts, the worst in the industrial world. They have made us debt-ridden abusers of credit cards, eaters of junk food, buyers of snobbish labels, nonmenders of clothing, noneaters of leftovers, nonrepairers of broken fixtures. But give this corrupted American people an immense reduction in taxes (a 30 percent reduction is proposed by legislators Kemp and Roth) and Americans will be transformed into a nation of toilsome scrimpers and laborious savers—as virtuous as our thrift-loving forebears. Banks will suddenly bulge with our new scrimp-and-savings, working yet another moral regeneration. Our giant corporations, bloated with overpaid "executives" and made rigid and shortsighted by the need for a 16 percent return on new investment, will become as flexible and venturesome as a nineteenth-century toolmaker. A marketplace that has scarcely known price competition in fifty years will inspire, nonetheless, a new nationwide entrepreneurial spirit. Our chief executive officers, trained in finance, marketing and bureaucratic infighting, will be transformed into inventor-engineer-industrialists; Henry Fords and John Deeres will once again flourish in the land. Our financiers will concentrate, as they have never concentrated before, on long-term "productive" investment instead of profitable short-term "deals," mergers, agglomerations, monopolizations. With workers and capitalists thus regenerated, America will become a horn of plenty so copiously flowing that the U.S. Treasury, depleted by hundreds of billions of tax dollars, will be replenished within a few years. No social programs need be repealed. Americans can eat their cake and keep it, too. This is the heart and soul of the supply-side magic: edible, keepable cake. Its validity is demonstrated with scientific precision by the Laffer Curve, much talked about this summer, said to have been drawn first on a cocktail napkin, the divine afflatus at work in a restaurant. It is a bell-shaped curve which illustrates the proposition that if you work for no reward you will not toil very hard and if you work for a handsome reward you are certain to toil harder and save more. No entrenched habits of consumption, no entrenched defects in the economic machinery, no social reality whatever mar the scientific simplicities of this geometric demonstration of a futile tautology. "The Curve as a pedagogical device was immense," says one Jude Wanniski, chief drum-beater for supply-side economics, with the *Wall Street Journal* providing the drum. "It saved years. You could, in drawing the Curve, persuade someone."

But not honest economists of whatever school or stripe. Even at the American Enterprise Institute in this season of "revived Republicanism," economists shake their heads skeptically. "There can't be two or three times more bang in a Kemp-Roth tax cut than we have had with any other," says Rudolph Penner of the Institute. "The U.S. is not yet at high enough tax rates to produce anything like the severe explosion Laffer is predicting. I think he is wrong," says a former adviser to Gerald Ford. Americans pay lower taxes than anyone else in the industrial world, despite which they save much less; the whole relation between low taxes and high savings being dubious, concocted, wishful, no more. The supply-side tax cut will produce "a huge surge in demand that will overwhelm our supply capacity and soon generate soaring deficits," says Walter Heller, economic adviser to President Kennedy, voicing the near-unanimous professional belief that whatever else "supply side" achieves it will not transform Americans into scrimp-and-savers.

How then can deficit-denouncing Republicans, champions of the balanced budget, embrace this new quack economics which promises nothing more certain than a mountain of deficits? Yet they do. "The Republican National Committee, united by the most complete agreement on an economic issue in modern Republican history, is about to take the issue of a badly needed meaningful tax cut for all Americans directly to the people," proclaims party chairman Bill Brock this July. Republicans plan to charter a jetliner—"The Republican Tax Clipper"—to carry party leaders around the country to preach the new supply-side gospel. What has happened in this summer of Democratic demise to the ancient Republican fear of *deficits*? "Inflation comes from the government spending more than it takes in. It will go away when government stops doing that," says Governor Reagan, but this summer he, too, embraces immense tax cuts and duly boards the "Republican Tax Clipper" with Gerald Ford and Senator Baker. Alan Greenspan, Republican economist, denounces deficit spending, but he also embraces Kemp-Roth and the Laffer Curve. Our infinitely supple neoconservatives embrace it as well. Irving Kristol is actually the first "intellectual" to promote it, calls it "the last, best hope for democratic capitalism in America." Even traditional liberals of the "Jackson wing" find it meritorious. "Supply-side economics?" says Ben Wattenberg, moving left and right simultaneously. "The numbers may not work, but economics is symbolic. Forget the numbers. It's growth economics. That's New Deal economics."

There is no mystery about supply-side economics. Its object is to overcome the single greatest obstacle to the final triumph of the Reaction—the sheer vote-repelling ambitions of the Republican Right, with its laissez-faire sharks, its minimal government for the powerful and excessive government for everyone else, with its deserving rich and its ill-concealed elitism. The supply-side fairy tale is "the necessary first step in the renaissance of the GOP," says Wanniski, and so it is. "The Democrats offer the voters a menu of soup, salad, fruits, wines and beef," says Representative Jack Kemp of Buffalo, first "supply-side" congressman, while "Republicans have said, 'Come to our table and we'll tighten your belt' . . . that's not a very appetizing menu and I want to change it"—from vote-repelling Old Right candor to New Right demagoguery. Kemp's proposal for a 30 percent tax cut "has given Republicans a new argument, a new style, and it's delightful," says jubilant Senator Richard Lugar in this season of Republican jubilance.

One thing only makes this transparent demagoguery politically feasible: the assured complicity of the Democratic Party establishment. Supply-side economics is not just a false promise of plenty; it is a sinister mask for deprivation. The American people are told that they can enjoy a huge tax cut without loss of the "welfare state"—by sworn foes of the welfare state. They are told they can devour the fisc with impunity by champions of a shrunken fisc. They are told they can eat their cake and have it, too, by those who want that cake devoured and gone forever. Expose the supply-side hoax, and shark's motives stand exposed. Lay bare the real intentions behind the new quackery, and Reaction's triumph would be immensely complicated. Republicans, however, have complete faith in the popular party now. The *coup de main* has supplied the earnest. "The Democrats have seen the business point of view." And so the Reaction rolls on.

7.

KENNEDY

On January 22, 1979, the "liberal wing" of the Democratic Party bursts into fury at Jimmy Carter, mutters of rebellion and "testing" the President in 1980.

Target of liberal fury is Carter's "lean and austere" budget for 1980, which takes tiny nips from the social-spending agenda, pandering to inflation-bred demands for reduced budget deficits. It cuts $600 million from Social Security's $129 billion annual cost, chiefly by eliminating several small programs arguably needed only by the poor, argued in any case by Carter; cuts $400 million from the school lunch program, again by confining it to the needy alone; altogether cuts $2.1 billion from operating social services, counterbalanced by a $1.2 billion increase in expenditures on food stamps, child welfare and social welfare. Along with this petty cheese-paring is a 3 percent increase in military spending, a sop to the Present Danger mob in the Senate, which will have Carter's arms control treaty at its mercy sometime later this year. Thus the "lean and austere" budget proposed to Congress by the partyless President and greeted this January 22 with well-prepared "howls of protest from liberal groups."

"I'm not going to allow people to go to bed hungry for an austerity program . . . no way," says furious Tip O'Neill, who lifted not a finger to remove 6 million poor households from the tax rolls last year. The President's budget is "a major attack on the living standards of the average American," further widening the gap between the "haves" and "have-nots." So bellows the AFL-CIO, champion of guns, now championing butter, but always championing just one thing—party interest, party power, party oligarchy.

"Human needs and national priorities have been sacrificed to political expediency," cry Americans for Democratic Action a few days later, as they call for a "budget coalition" to combat the cheese-paring President. Forming liberal coalitions is the rule of the hour this furious hour in the capital. Douglas Frazer, president of the United Auto Workers, announces the formation of a new "Progressive Alliance"—some eighty liberal organizations to be mobilized by the union to scotch the "austerity" menace. A former Cabinet official in the Johnson administration, Wilbur Cohen, announces a "budget coalition" of his own to defend the Social Security system from Carter's one-half of 1 percent invasion. No one thunders against Carter more loudly than Senator Edward Kennedy, who calls the Carter budget "heartless." No one's word is heeded more closely, for in the past few months Kennedy has "emerged as the unquestioned leader of the liberal bloc."

Party rebellion is in the air this angry January day, as Meany's political henchman, one Al Barkan, head of union "political education," circulates among the Washington "activists" whispering that the AFL-CIO might not be endorsing Carter in 1980. Let the activists make of this what they will: the archenemies of party rebellion and party activists whispering to activists of party rebellion. Strange business is afoot in the Capitol this January.

Watching the liberal clamor, a White House aide shakes his head ruefully: "Don't they realize that there are people who would put a bullet behind the ear of these programs?" As if to underscore the point, Ronald Reagan visits Washington on this day of liberal fury. Shepherded by Senator Laxalt, he meets Republican senators, assures them that he is not "a terrible right-wing person," has even favored a more progressive income tax—just look at his record in California. He detests the idea of "Big-Brother government" spying on the American people, has just sent out a public letter to that effect under the auspices of his personal political organization, Citizens for the Republic.

Fortunately for Reagan, only the electorate will believe him. Reagan dines, too, with the leaders of the Present Danger, is invited to join their great crusade to rebury the Republic in the imperial sepulcher—and does. He has "tête-à-têtes," reports a Washington columnist, "with people who once paled at the mention of his name." Now they are flushed with high hopes.

Reagan and the Republicans are still jubilant, although revived Republicanism barely revived in the 1978 elections and supply-side economics, foisted on candidates by the national party, fell on deaf ear, magical thinking and demagogue effrontery holding little appeal for a people not yet reduced to a credulous mob—not yet, but soon to be. Despite inflation running at 10 percent, despite a near-vacuum in the Democratic White House, despite a Democratic Congress which has become a vast, intricate, mystifying obstruction, all that revived Republicanism managed to gain were three seats in the Senate and twelve seats in the House. Even this meager showing bears the stigmata of Democratic connivance, and the deeper imprint of the Reaction. One Republican Senate gain came with the unexpected defeat of Iowa's Dick Clark, author of the amendment barring intervention in Angola, now the very epitome and symbol of the "culture of appeasement." A low Democratic turnout in heavily Democratic Duquesne—index of ward-heeler perfidy—and the refusal of a major union to endorse him—an even surer sign of party perfidy—combined to bring Clark down. Another Republican victory in the Senate was the even more unexpected defeat of New Hampshire's Thomas McIntyre, the only member of the Armed Services Committee who dared defy Jackson, whose New Right allies made McIntyre their primary "target" in 1978. Of the twelve new House Republican seats, seven belonged to representatives of the democratic awakening—Democrats elected in 1974—defeated, reports *Congressional Quarterly,* by unusually low Democratic turnouts—ward heelers not ward heeling—and in some cases by campaign funds in remarkably short supply. So the Republican Party has reason to remain jubilant. With the popular party ridding itself of its democrats, defeating popular measures and simultaneously inciting a "liberal" rebellion, Republicanism is bound to revive in due course. At the Republican Party conference in early February, the leadership boldly deplores "the decay of American influence and the decline of American military power," calls for abandoning "traditional bipartisanship in foreign policy," meaning—for politics in the Age of Reaction is chiefly conducted in code—that Senate Republicans will join forces with Senate Democrats against the Democratic President.

Where stands the "liberal bloc" in all this? It stands like a giant gun aimed at exactly the wrong target. "Their real adversary," notes shrewd old TRB, "is not Carter but Congress"—a Democratic Congress which spent two locust years defeating liberal measures, strangling democratic proposals, which found welfare reform too expensive to waste on the poor and tax reform too "egalitarian" to inflict on the rich. Yet it is Carter, victim of that Congress, which the "liberal bloc" attacks. Dixie-Daley it does not attack; arms-mongering, fear-mongering, Cold War–mongering "labor" it does not attack; perfidious congressional leadership even presumes to lead it.

Peaceful coexistence is the relation between the angry "liberal bloc" and the illiberal Democratic Congress. The two go their separate ways, having different party tasks to perform. On January 23, second day of the liberal clamor, the House Democratic Caucus actually gives Jim Jones—chief Democratic architect of the "millionaires' relief act of 1978"—a coveted seat on the Budget Committee. Is this not a clear signal that *betraying* liberal principles is the high road to success in the new Ninety-sixth Congress, that forming "conservative" combinations with Republican lawmakers is just what Dixie-Daley wants from the Ninety-sixth Congress? Of course, but of this the "liberal bloc" says nothing. What business is it of the "liberal bloc" if Dixie-Daley betrays liberal principles? No business at all. The new Ninety-sixth Congress, attentive to leadership signals, is already truckling to the corporate swarm, is already parroting the latest corporate quackery. In this very hour of liberal protest, the idea has "taken root" in Congress, so *Congressional Quarterly* reports, that government regulation of business, costing an alleged $150 billion a year, represents a prime source of our unnerving inflation. The Ninety-sixth Congress arrives at this figure by omitting, one eye closed, the cost of nonregulation; calculates the price of health, forgets the price of illness. Thus, while ADA blathers about "national priorities" and Speaker Tip blathers of "hunger" and National Ward Heelers blather about "living standards," cost-without-benefit analysis—costly beyond reckoning this new Cooked Bookkeeping will prove to be—has become a "fad" and a "vogue" in the new Democratic Congress, which spreads corporate quackery over the country like a metastasizing cancer.

What, then, does this January outburst signify? What is its purpose, who stands to gain? It is a Washington outburst, for one thing, a hue and cry raised by national Democratic leaders and their national adjuncts. It is a beating of drums and shouting of slogans to spur local activists to start up a "draft" for Kennedy, the drafters to "provide him with a way of being able to say the party called him rather than his being represented as trying to usurp an incumbent President," explains a founder of the Draft Kennedy movement, one Joanne Symons, who believes she is saving liberalism and succoring the needy. History will not judge too harshly this kindhearted folly, except to note once again that politics is not the nursery, republican politics perhaps least of all.

The January clamor is a signal, too, to state and local party officials that this liberal rebellion is no insurrection against the party oligarchy, but oligarchy's dearest, if not quite avowable, wish. Most important, it is a great pushing forward of Senator Kennedy, half-willing, half-wary, into that most difficult of enterprises—attempting to wrest the nomination from a sitting President, something no elected President has had wrested from him since Franklin Pierce in 1856. And a dubious enterprise as well, difficult to explain to ordinary people, as Kennedy is uncomfortably aware. At a secret meeting with his closest advisers in early February, Kennedy asks Sorensen to devise a "rationale" for challenging Carter in case he decides to make the running.

And what is Dixie-Daley's object in pushing Kennedy forward as the leader of a great, destructive liberal insurgency? To make certain what is far from certain in 1979, that even a battered Jimmy Carter will be beaten in the 1980 elections. The last time an incumbent

President was defeated for reelection after his party had held the White House for just four years was back in 1892. The last time the Right put up a presidential candidate he lost by 16 million votes. Kennedy must "take on Carter," explains Douglas Frazer to the political writer Garry Wills, or "I may have to live with him for another four years." So the party drums have begun beating for Kennedy—bearer of a great name, a great "legacy" and no mind of his own—and will continue to beat louder and louder until he is safely ensnared in the coils of rebellion.

While the liberal drums beat for Kennedy, a propaganda of panic is launched upon the country. Month after month the fear-mongers of the Reaction—anticipating the SALT II treaty—warn Americans of nuclear annihilation pouring through our infamous "window of vulnerability" to a surprise nuclear attack, warn of the U.S. held ransom to Soviet missiles in "a limited nuclear war"; warn of Soviet "nuclear blackmail," of America's shameful nuclear inferiority, vile fruit of "appeasement" and loss of "resolve." This January "The Price of Peace and Freedom," the AFL-CIO's contribution to fear-mongering, begins to play on television and will play 852 times by June. The American Conservative Union's film "Soviet Might, American Myth: The United States in Retreat" will play over 370 stations during the same span. The newly formed Coalition for Peace Through Strength, chiefly Republican, enlists the Democratic Majority among its fifty affiliates, enlists Jackson's man, Perle, for its speakers' bureau and its campaign for a massive military buildup, while the Committee on the Present Danger, newfound friend of Reagan's, soon to be richly rewarded, warns with deepest foreboding that America is "becoming number two" to would-be world conquerors.

Never mind, fellow citizens, that America and its allies command an economic machine seven times more productive than the Soviet empire's. Never mind that we and our allies outspend the Soviet bloc in the sinews of war, far outspend it in many a year, that Soviet weapons procurement has been "flat" since Carter's election. Never mind that *one* Poseidon submarine, so Carter reminds the country in his State of the Union message this January, "carries enough warheads to destroy every large and medium-sized city in the Soviet Union." Never mind that the U.S. nuclear arsenal of 9,200 warheads is three times more lethal than the 6,000 warheads of the Soviet Union. Never mind that the vulnerability of our land-based missiles is merely a "theory," as the Pentagon itself says in 1981, a "worst-case scenario," a doomsday fantasy. Never mind that "nothing has been put forward," the conservative *Strategic Review* reports (also in 1981), "which technically supports the belief that we (or the Soviets) could, with any degree of confidence, expect to hit one silo at ICBM range, let alone a thousand of them." Never mind that the poisonous Present Danger blather about nuclear "blackmail" is an idea "too incredible to warrant serious debate," so former Defense Secretary Robert McNamara argues in vain. The propaganda of panic and doomsday terror is a stream of lies and sophistries, poisonous to a free people's inner repose, destructive of their "supreme confidence in themselves," destructive, therefore, of the one great barrier, so Walt Whitman warned, against tyranny entering "upon this country." To turn the American people into a headless, terrified mob is perhaps the chief object of the Reaction as the 1980 election approaches.

Assailed from the left and right wings of the party establishment—two giant pinions of an ancient bird of prey—Carter struggles to provide some semblance of leadership, to gain some kind of grip on affairs, struggles ever more desperately, for time is fast running out on him. He proposes that labor and management voluntarily hold wage and price increases to 7 percent or less in 1979; Meany vows to violate his guidelines at the first opportunity. He proposes a novel system of tax compensation for workers heeding the guidelines should inflation exceed 7 percent; Congress contemptuously strangles it at birth. The press has become Oligarchy's tame dog, barking at Carter as if on command. "If he did something popular," recalls Powell, "he was pandering to public opinion. If he defied the popular mood he was trying to combat his wishy-washy image by looking tough. If he defied Congress with a veto he was preparing to run against a Congress controlled by his own party and blame it for his problems. If he compromised it was a play for backing in some key states." In January, the Shah of Iran falls to one of the most massive uprisings in modern history. Carter is blamed for the "loss" of Iran, pleads vainly that Iran is "not ours to lose." Liberalism accuses the President of supporting a vile tyrant too long; conservatism accuses Carter of abandoning a staunch ally too soon. No real difference in that distinction, merely two wings of the bird of prey nesting in unison: America is declining, America is endangered, America, above all, is leaderless, always that.

On March 4, Carter decides on an "act of desperation," as he rightly calls it. He will fly to Cairo and Jerusalem to negotiate a peace treaty between Israel and Egypt—a desperate effort to recapture the lost glory of September 17 last, when Carter had come down from the Catoctin Mountains with Egypt's Sadat and Israel's Begin at his side. In hand was a signed "Framework of Peace in the Middle East" and a signed "Framework for the Conclusion of a Peace Treaty Between Egypt and Israel," both negotiated by Carter himself, a deed without precedent in our history. He had been the "born-again President" back then, rising phoenix-like from the ashes of defeat and failure. But the "frameworks" had led to no accords. Begin had balked and quibbled, obstructed and obfuscated, had publicly demanded $3.5 billion as the price of his signature, and then, adding injury to insult, had refused to sign anything. Euphoria by now has turned to despair; the glory has vanished utterly; the personal triumph of September has become just another defeat in the grim procession. By late February, Carter's advisers are convinced that Begin wants Carter defeated in 1980. His "real purpose was to hurt Carter politically by being deprived of a much-needed foreign-policy victory." So State Department officials have come to suspect, not wrongly. The Reaction and the Begin government are pursuing the same end, and not by mere happenstance. They are deeply and closely allied.

On March 4, Carter flies off on his Middle East "act of desperation" while the Capitol cuts the ground from under him. "Presidential credibility," so highly prized in mendacious props of oligarchy, is now of no concern to our leaders. On March 7 and 8, for sixteen hours, the Senate reverberates with attacks on Carter's formal recognition of

Communist China the previous December. Having done so, Carter, perforce, has terminated the fiction that "China" lies compact on the island of Taiwan. The "China card," thus played at Brzezinski's urging, is meant to please Senate "hardliners." Instead, Carter is assailed once more for appeasement, retreat and surrender—the Reaction's litany beating down incessantly on the national mind. "When are we going to start acting like Americans? We had better start today," brays Republican Senator Charles Percy on March 8, while the President is in Cairo conferring with Sadat.

Three days later, while Carter is in Jerusalem struggling to persuade Begin to sign a treaty advantageous to Israel, the *Washington Post* puts out a shockingly scandalous story: A former warehouse worker at the Carter family peanut business, one Jimmy Hayes, says that he and the President's brother, Billy, had falsified business records to conceal a $500,000 debt to Bert Lance's National Bank of Georgia—a criminal act if true. On March 13, within hours of the President's address to a hostile Israeli parliament, Senator Baker demands—and will get—the appointment of a special prosecutor to investigate the possible criminality of the President of the United States. Shall Carter be spared what Nixon was not, the Republican Majority Leader demands to know? Is there to be "a political double standard in American life"? There already is, for where are all the staunch advocates of a "strong presidency" now? Where are all those glib tongues of oligarchy fearful of a "weakened presidency" in a dangerous world? How silent they fall when Oligarchy is bent on a President's destruction. On the contrary, this "Goobergate" scandal, says *Business Week,* provides a "golden opportunity to chip away at Carter's reputation for integrity, the quality for which he consistently scores highest in public opinion polls."

On the fourteenth, Israel finally consents to sign the peace treaty, but no trumpets blow for Carter. No phoenix rises this time; instead, belittlement and scorn and praise as deadly as knife thrusts. The peace may well cost the taxpayer "10 billion over the next few years and be the single most costly effort in American history," CBS News reports on the fourteenth. Carter's last-minute success "was orchestrated by Jerry Rafshoon [Carter's media adviser] to make it look as though the

President had performed a miracle," adds CBS, citing unnamed Israeli sources. Diplomacy as cheap showmanship; diplomacy as arrant bribery. A bribe well worth the price, say the nation's leading politicians, damningly praising the President. "The Price of Peace; Treaty Seen Costing U.S. $5 Billion in Aid," proclaims the *Post* on the front page the next day. No foe of aid to Israel, far from it, the *Post* now questions whether the peace is worth the price Carter paid for it. "Treaty Seen as Straining U.S. Relationships with Other Arab Countries." Do the interests of Israel conflict with the interests of the United States? The point is not normally driven home to Americans. Virtually taboo on Capitol Hill, it is temporarily de-tabooed. Senator Jacob Javits of New York, second to few in his devotion to the Jewish state, demands to know whether Carter has signed a secret "mutual security" agreement with Israel— Israel's highest desideratum, for the fulfillment of which President Reagan and the Reaction will be praised to the heavens. Senator Frank Church, champion of Israel and now chairman of the Foreign Relations Committee, asks, "Why should we pay for the peace?" Reviled for two years by pro-Israel interests for excessive partiality to Arabs, Carter is now derided, his triumph made to sound vaguely disgraceful, for excessive aid to Israel—by pro-Israeli interests. Where is the rhyme and reason in all this? *Carthago delenda est.*

Democracy in America had awakened from a half-century slumber and now, a few years later, ferocious, vengeful Oligarchy, bent on its own restoration, has turned our politics into a quagmire of hypocrisy, quackery and lies.

On April 5, Carter makes one last effort to fight free of the quagmire before slumping back, bludgeoned and broken and ripe for betrayal. The Iranian upheaval has disrupted the world's oil supplies: "The energy crisis is real." Carter feels vindicated, makes a major address to the nation, in tone unlike any he has given before. "We are dangerously dependent on uncertain and expensive sources of foreign oil," warns the President. To reduce that dependency he will gradually "phase in" over twenty-eight months the decontrol of domestic oil prices, mandated by Congress in 1975. As redress for this "painful step" he calls upon Congress to impose a 50 percent "windfall profits tax" on the oil companies, calls for it angrily, vehemently; denouncing the oil companies as "cheats" and "price-gougers," challenging the lawmakers to act. "Every vote against it [the tax] will be a vote for excessive oil company profits and for reliance on the whims of the foreign oil cartel." He calls on the American people to lobby Congress in support of the tax, defying, for the first time, O'Neill's warning against appealing directly to the voters. What manner of temerity is this? Carter publicly angry? Carter defiant? Carter boldly bidding to regain the leadership of the country?

This the Democratic Party cannot, and does not, allow. Senators Jackson and Kennedy move at once to balk the President, call on Congress the very next day to fight against the decontrol of oil, claiming that a windfall profits tax can never pass Congress. The truth is exactly the opposite. The windfall profits tax cannot be defeated; repeal of the oil decontrol law commands twenty-five Senate votes at the most, by *Congressional Quarterly*'s reckoning. There is no truth in our politics now, no probity. To attack oil decontrol is to attack and discredit the President—how many Americans know that Congress, not Carter, has decontrolled oil prices? Thus reasons Kennedy, hero of the party "activists," thus reasons Jackson, champion of the party "regulars," the two leaders working in tandem, lying in unison, inciting a "liberal" outcry against Carter's "hypocrisy."

Back to the quagmire, Carter must be bludgeoned—once and for all. An arms control treaty—always popular, always impressive—looms in the very near future. Reagan still trails battered Carter by fourteen percentage points in Gallup's latest presidential preference poll, one reason, perhaps, why the New Right's newest recruit, a television preacher named Jerry Falwell, launches his "Clean Up America Crusade" from Capitol Hill this April 27. "We are going to single out those people in government who are against what we consider to be the Bible, moralist position, and we're going to inform the public," cries the evangelist, plunging into the stream of the Reaction. Falwell's goal, say his New Right allies, is to "mobilize at least two million Americans to work for pro-God, pro-family policies in government." Revived Republicanism, barely reviving, scours the country for the "winning coalition"—Viguerie's phrase—a congeries of sour, single-issue sectarians, into which the American people, alas, are fast dividing as the democratic tide recedes and the citizen idea weakens.

For Carter's head, in any case, Capitol Hill has bludgeons in abundance. The Panama Canal treaty must be implemented in the House; there, for months on end, the treaty issue is fiercely reagitated, reviving last year's accusation of surrender, retreat and appeasement, the Reaction's never-ending litany. An "extended nightmare," Carter calls the implementation fight; his whole term of office is one extended nightmare.

The handiest bludgeon, however, is the administration's plan for emergency gasoline rationing, a plan coaxed out of Carter by Congress back in February, now ready to be smashed over his head.

The President's plan seems simple and sensible enough. In the event of a severe energy shortage, it would allot the same amount of gasoline to every automobile, but permit private trading in ration stamps, a "white market" substitute for heavy-handed bureaucracy, in perfect keeping, it seems, with the "mood" of Congress. On April 25, nonetheless, a House committee defeats Carter's plan by four votes—this despite a strong public appeal from the President. On May 1, the committee defeats the plan by one vote, this despite yet another public appeal from the President. A change in the plan is required, says Jackson, our tireless bludgeoner-in-chief. States that use more gasoline per capita must be formally accommodated in the plan or the administration is "dead in the water." Vacillation is said to be Carter's main failing; let him dance a veritable dance of vacillation.

On May 7, the administration, dancing attendance, submits a revised plan, making a 50 percent allowance for historical state rates of fuel consumption. On May 8, the Jackson committee rejects the revision by two to one, demands rationing based solely on historical rates of consumption. Wanton quibbling is calling this humiliating dance: At stake is a few gallons of gas per vehicle *per month* contingent upon a national crisis. At 3:30 P.M. the same day, the administration, facing a legislative deadline, rushes yet a third plan to Jackson's committee. The issue is now in the limelight, for gasoline lines have formed in

California and the idea of rationing stirs the public mind, not favorably. The third plan, too, is thought to be in trouble. "We've been operating by trial and error—mostly error," Jackson tells the press. "It's an open secret we've been in a hell of a mess." In the crowded committee hearing room, reports *Congressional Quarterly,* "television crews, strung together by wires like caterpillars, noisily pressed close to the action, swinging microphones over the senators' heads." What television viewers see and hear is senators tearing the third plan to shreds, haggling and whining over a few gallons of gasoline, indifferent to the common good, contemptuous of citizenship, contemptuous of patriotism, determined to appeal to nothing that binds a free people together; the whole action a call to pettiness, a small contribution, but a clear one, to the making of a mob and the unmaking of a President.

Carter's revised and carved-up rationing plan passes the Senate on the ninth of May, but it is merely a target set up for destruction. On May 10, the House sends standby gasoline rationing to a resounding, humiliating defeat, 246 to 159, chiefly on the grounds that a much-revised plan must be a poor one. Why is it not an improved one? Ask not such questions. We are governed by fiat and arbitrary decree. "Carter was wobbling on the issue," lawmakers explain to the press, the attack on Carter's leadership being the entire point of the exercise, the entire point of the "extended nightmare."

The White House is stunned. This much wanton hostility compressed into a quibble not even Carter has seen before. The vote is a "shock to me," Carter tells newsmen, calls them into the Oval Office just to say so. It is "a very severe setback—an embarrassment, indeed, a shock to me," he tells visiting editors the next day. The shock, perhaps, is the terrible truth of his plight: Nothing he says or does or proposes can stay the bludgeoning hand of the party establishment. He is utterly at the mercy of those he appeased, at their mercy because he appeased them, having forfeited by that very appeasing the confidence of the people. A great many Americans suspect, says a Wisconsin Democrat named David Obey, that "Carter is being worked over as a good man in a sinful world," but worked-over Carter confirms no such suspicion. "Is it a problem with the party or something like that?" a high school student asks the President during a call-in radio show, the raw youth seeing what all of punditry cannot see. And Carter in reply complains of "the influence of the oil companies on the Congress of the United States." What about the influence of the Democratic Party on the Congress? Not to be talked of, least of all with the party drums once again beating loudly for Kennedy.

"Teddy Comes on Strong," says the message blazoned across the cover of *Newsweek* on Monday, May 21, 1979. The senator's latest announcement of comprehensive medical care for all from "womb-to-tomb" is "fueling the corrosive gossip in the Capitol that the President is in danger of being dumped by his own party." Fueling the gossip, too, is a "draft-Kennedy guerrilla movement at work in at least fifteen states," reports *Newsweek,* half-reporting, half–drum-beating. Powerful party officials fuel the gossip, too. The New York State Democratic Party hints it may nominate Senator Moynihan as its "favorite son" candidate in 1980. The Cleveland or Cuyahoga County Democratic Party holds a draft-Kennedy convention, the first of its kind. On this drum-beating May 21, five liberal congressmen announce their change of allegiance from Carter to Kennedy; electrifying news of this "gang of five" is carried across the country by CBS, the Democrats' network, more or less. A "Kennedy bloc" has formed in Congress, reports the *Christian Science Monitor* on the twenty-third—lawmakers urging Kennedy to run against Carter, including Al Ullman of Ways and Means and the *coup de main.* What manner of "liberal" rebellion includes this champion of the oppressed investor? Mainly a hollow-hearted rebellion-from-the-top, so hollow that the House Democratic Caucus votes on the twenty-fourth to conceal the hollowness with a ringing 138-to-69 vote for retention of oil price controls, a demonstration of party support for Kennedy and party hostility to Carter, a "rebuke" it is called, and an "uprising." A "stinging blow for Carter," says *Congressional Quarterly,* "though it has no legislative status." On this very same day of liberalism rampant, Democrats quietly kill public financing of congressional elections, which Carter had called for, not without eloquence, in his last State of the Union message. Defeat, says *Congressional Quarterly,* is compassed by a coalition of Republicans, "veteran northern Democrats," "southern Democrats," lobbyists for "conservative groups," lobbyists for the Chamber of Commerce and a fierce lobbyist from the Cook County machine, Representative Rostenkowski—in a word, the party oligarchy, wings beating in unison as usual. What says the "liberal bloc" to this illiberal defeat for Carter, this triumph for the money pollution and the onrushing Reaction? Nothing of consequence. The "liberal bloc" rebels, not against Oligarchy, but in its service, whatever "draft-Kennedy guerrillas" may think they are doing.

Drum-beaten Kennedy still remains wary of running, his advisers advising against it, but Carter has been bludgeoned back into the quagmire, sinks more deeply into it than ever, reports *Newsweek* on May 28, "The consequence of what has become a daily battering in Congress, the polls, the press and the corrosive back-chatter of Washington," which chatters loud enough for the whole country to hear that the President sits in the Oval Office deciding who will and who will not use the White House tennis courts. Among the corrosive back-chatterers is the Speaker, who "has lately reverted," reports *Time* in late May, "to his old habit of calling Carter's man Hamilton Jordan, 'whatzisname—Hannibal Jerkins.' " Thus, our bonhomous "old pro" Speaker, whom one of today's "gang of five" will accuse five years hence of colluding with President Reagan.

On June 14, the President is scheduled to fly to Vienna to sign the long-awaited SALT II treaty. Never was a President so ripe for the plucking. "The Democratic Party seethes with cabals against Carter." Congress has smashed his every attempt to lead the country. The administration is a shambles: "Our backs are up against the wall." So says a White House aide in late May. Carter himself seethes in self-pitying rage, having "had a bellyful," says Powell, "of being blamed for the irresponsibility and shortcomings and failures of others." The treaty holds the promise of political salvation, renomination, reelection, vindication despite every betrayal, failure and defeat. So Carter thinks at any rate. "I have one life to live on this earth," Carter tells members of the Democratic National Committee on May 25. "I've got one political career. And I will never face an issue so important as getting SALT II ratified by the Senate." Alas, it can be defeated by thirty-four Senate votes. Partyless, achievementless and now threatened by a party rebellion, Carter is prepared to pay and pay dearly for the treaty, to deliver himself up body and soul to the Reaction, if that is what it takes. The drums are not beating for Kennedy in vain.

8.

COLD WAR

Truth and probity have gone from our politics: Now simple propriety is departing as well. Not even Carter's flight to a momentous summit conference this June 14 brings him surcease from political assault. Instead, Congress, in a "frenzy of defiance," tears at every piece of administration foreign policy it can reach out and claw. On the twelfth, the House threatens to scuttle the Panama Canal treaty. On the twelfth, too, the Senate, ignoring frantic appeals from the President, opposes economic sanctions against the white regime in Rhodesia. On the thirteenth, the House vents its spleen against military aid to Turkey, a NATO ally whose bases are needed to monitor compliance with an arms control agreement. On Carter's first day in Vienna, General Edward Rowny quits the SALT delegation to devote himself to discrediting the treaty. No fear of a "crippled presidency" now, chiefly fear of a President not yet crippled enough.

Jackson prepares a farewell of his own—a virtual declaration of war against Carter delivered on June 12 to the Coalition for a Democratic Majority, now streaming into the camp of the Right, "neoconservatives" ready to grovel at the very feet of despotism, so deep is their fear of liberty and self-government. Jackson thunders against "appeasement"; calls the SALT II treaty "appeasement in its purest form," put forth in "a misty atmosphere of amiability and good fellowship under a policy of détente." He warns—when does he not warn and alarm and cry up?—of "the Kremlin's political use of strategic superiority as an umbrella under which to pursue a series of probes to expand Soviet power and weaken the power of the United States." The American political atmosphere—the democratic awakening—he finds "ominously reminiscent of Great Britain in the 1930s," likens Carter to Chamberlain; likens his forthcoming meeting with Russia's Brezhnev in Vienna to Chamberlain's infamous meeting—umbrella in hand—with Hitler at Munich. Consumed by malice and thwarted ambition, Jackson rails against "appeasement" on and on, obsessively, before an audience that fears not Russia armed but the Republic revived.

The speech is a dagger plunged into Carter's back, reaching into his timorous heart. When the presidential plane alights at the Vienna airport rain is falling, but no umbrellas are seen—by Carter's order. "I'd rather drown than carry an umbrella." Fearful of a symbol, shying from a shade, Carter conducts himself at the summit like a puppet on the strings of the war party, for such, by now, the "swelling band of anti-détentists" deserve to be called. Arms control must not lead to delusive "euphoria," the war party warns, and so there will be no euphoria at Vienna. Chamberlain had spoken of peace in our time, so there will be no talk of peace at Vienna; instead "sharp exchanges" with the Soviet premier, bitter attacks on Soviet "adventurism" duly passed on to the press to prove that Carter is no dupe of "amiability and good fellowship," indeed scarcely a supporter of détente at all. The Vienna summit is grim, made grim by appeasement—Carter's craven appeasement of Oligarchy. The Soviets are scornful of our "politically wounded" President—who is not scornful of Carter by now? "We follow the polls," says a Soviet delegate to his American counterpart. "We read all your eminent columnists who write about the political ineptitude of this White House. We watch the House of Representatives threaten to liquidate the Panama Canal treaty. We see the administration, despite all its commitment to arms control, try to ingratiate itself to the military-industrial complex by deploying new weapons. We see it trying to ingratiate itself to cold warriors . . ."

Carter brings back to America not peace, not hope, least of all

110

euphoria. He brings back an arms control treaty which is solid, modest, meritorious—and with it a sword. The great merit of this SALT II treaty, proclaims the President before a joint session of Congress on June 18, is that it allows the United States to deploy the MX missile, the most destructive weapon in the world, each missile carrying ten independently targeted warheads, each warhead seventeen times more powerful than the Hiroshima bomb and three times more accurate than any warhead in existence. Two hundred of these missiles, 34,000 Hiroshimas' worth—will be targeted on Soviet ICBM silos, giving the United States "a unilateral first-strike capability [that] will increasingly endanger the strategic balance," warns Republican Senator Mark Hatfield of Oregon; which will "lock both sides into a new, much more dangerous and frightfully expensive arms race," warned Senator McIntyre until the New Right unseated him. It is the Reaction's weapon of choice, demonstrator of "our will to prevail," harbinger of a revived race for "nuclear supremacy" and of a revived Cold War. "A nauseating prospect," Carter calls the MX in private, and "a gross waste of money." But the Joint Chiefs of Staff demand it as their price for endorsing SALT II, are encouraged to do so by Brzezinski, who boasts that Carter complained "I was jamming a decision down his throat."

So the "nauseating" price is paid—mocking arms control, betraying détente—and buys nothing, except an appetite whetted for more. On June 27, Minority Leader Baker denounces the treaty for giving the Soviets "substantial strategic superiority." On June 28, Majority Leader Byrd warns Democratic senators not to commit themselves too soon on the treaty. Let Carter stew in suspense. Let ratification be dangled before his eyes like the grapes of Tantalus. Let us see what further payment, what deeper betrayal, we can extract from this ruin of a President.

And this ruin of a man as well. For Carter, who had endured the extended nightmare with a kind of passive Christian fortitude, reading the Bible in Spanish every night before bedtime, can bear the solitary strain no longer. He hurls himself at the feet of the Democratic establishment and begs its forgiveness for his sins. Such is the bizarre "domestic summit conference" which the President conducts for ten days at Camp David in early July—while gasoline lines spread from state to state "like an unseen plague," inciting panic and hysteria, inciting pettiness, incivility and violence—sad signs of mob-mindedness advancing.

Mornings and afternoons, day after day, helicopters take off from makeshift launching pads set up by the Reflecting Pool and the Washington Monument. They ferry to the presidential retreat a large assortment of mayors, governors and National Ward Heelers—Lane Kirkland and ilk; "old Washington hands"—Clark Clifford and ilk; fixers, power brokers, corporate executives, hostile columnists and congressional leaders whose knives have made a pincushion of Carter's back and a misery in his soul—Jackson, no less, and Byrd and ilk. And what does the President want of this ingathering of party wolves and sharks, of tormentors, enemies and betrayers? He wants them to tell him, with utmost candor, what *he* has done wrong as President! He sits with a yellow pad on his knee, taking notes on his errors and failings. Repentance is sweet, not painful. The conference gives Carter "a remarkable sense of relief," he says and it shows. "He seemed at times to savor the punishment," reports a visitor to the camp. And what do the wolves and sharks of Oligarchy tell the President? That "Congress doesn't pay any attention" to him only because his "approval rating" has sunk so low, as if they had not torn him to pieces when it hovered around 70 percent. From these mouths does anything ever issue save lies?

Carter, for his part, has something of importance for the wolves and the sharks to hear. He tells them that he became President by exploiting "the ignominious defeat that we suffered in Vietnam"—so *Time* reports him saying—and the American people's woeful lack of "confidence" in their betters. With brazen face and sinful pride he had told the people that they had been misruled by their leaders. Worse yet, more sinfully, he had wickedly told them they were better than their leaders. For this the President is penitent. Can Oligarchy not find it in its heart to forgive his former effrontery and spare him further disgrace and defeat? The bizarre conference is the President's

Canossa. The yellow pad full of lacerating criticism is Jimmy Carter's sackcloth and ashes.

Beyond the confines of Camp David, where the President has so inexplicably gone to ground, wild rumors circulate: The President is about to resign; the President has gone mad. The stock market plunges; Allied governments telephone the White House in panic. Rumors of madness are so rife that New Jersey's governor Brendan Byrne assures questioners after leaving the camp that "he's all right. He knows what he's doing"—not losing his mind, just bartering his faded tribuneship, a pearl of no value to Oligarchy now. The congressional leaders who promise the penitent President to "be more supportive in the future"—so Carter writes in his diary—keep their promise for a week, if that.

Even while Carter does penance, the whole pent-up fury of the Reaction—brutal, vindictive, contemptuous of truth—pours itself out on the SALT II treaty when Senate hearings begin on July 9. The treaty is denounced as appeasement and surrender, as Chamberlain's handiwork. "We gave concession after concession," charges General Rowny. "The Soviet Union bluffed and we folded." It is described as an American retreat, the very "image" of retreat, charges Admiral Elmo Zumwalt of the Present Danger, specialists in the subjective side of national security, the objective side being, alas, too deficient in danger to do Oligarchy much good. The treaty "can only incapacitate our minds and wills," charges Nitze, whose hour at last has come. Fear and false alarms stream from senatorial lips. The treaty is "becoming," says Brzezinski, gloating, "a catalyst for a more assertive posture." America's defenses are "weak and imperiled," utterly overwhelmed by "the most awesome military machine mankind has ever seen," shamefully neglected: "We've goofed off for ten years." Something must be done and done quickly to correct the "ominous tilt," to avert almost imminent disaster. An immediate massive arms buildup is the only solution, cries a Senate suddenly dominated, so a commentator says, by "bipartisan militarism." The cry begins coursing through the Senate, sweeping everything else before it of recent concern on Capitol Hill: reducing the deficit, combating inflation, appeasing the "taxpayers' revolt."

What are these compared with a revived arms race and the Cold War's revival, chief prop and foundation of our modern, war-nourished Oligarchy?

What must Carter pay now for SALT II, having already paid with MX in vain? It is left to young Senator Sam Nunn to set the price—an icy "fellow Georgian," second only to Jackson, and perhaps not even to Jackson, as Oligarchy's leader in matters of defense. The price for SALT II is a firm, inviolate "commitment" by the President to a 5 percent real increase in military spending to commence at once and continue for five years. So Nunn decrees: No massive arms buildup; no arms control treaty. The very gods could weep. But that is not all, not by a long chalk. Oligarchy demands, nay Oligarchy desperately needs, not only payment from Carter but betrayal as well, deep betrayal indeed. The President still insists that American power is second to none. Instead, says Nunn, the President must "alert the American people to the danger" of Soviet military supremacy, must "speak out" and tell the nation how weak and menaced it is. Senator Nunn demands "candor" from the President, meaning Present Danger lies. Carter must put himself at the head of the fear-mongers, certify their falsehoods, substantiate their sophistries, impeach his own understanding, or "I cannot in good conscience support ratification of the SALT II Treaty." An ultimatum, nothing less, delivered on July 25.

On this day of brutal ultimatum, and not unconnected with it, a news story appears in the *Washington Post* of more consequence than interest to the country at large: It seems that Henry Jackson predicts—not an endorsement, just a prediction—that Kennedy could wrest the nomination from Carter. The prediction is nicely timed to crop up at the President's televised press conference that day and does: "Mr. President, do you agree with Senator Jackson that your problems will force you to forgo any election plans and hand over the nomination to Senator Kennedy?"

On Sunday morning four days later, Jackson appears on the television program "Face the Nation" and says that Kennedy would be the strongest alternative to Carter in 1980. There is no mistaking these signals, and nobody who matters mistakes them. The coarse, baleful champion of the party establishment has given "the nod" to Kennedy—poor, dithering, dilatory Kennedy, who still cannot make up his mind to run, having no mind of his own to make up. The implacable foe of freedom in party politics has given approval to party rebellion, deems political civil war a boon to Oligarchy, paradoxical though it may seem to duller wits in the party. And, lo, the nod being given this late July day, let us behold the result: "Teddy-Mania" bursts forth in August. Suddenly, after Jackson nods, there is "an eruption of pro-Kennedy sentiment and statements across the country."

The mighty pinions of the ancient bird of prey beat once again in unison. Endorsements for Kennedy, open or nearly so, issue from party liberals: Senators McGovern and Cranston, state party activists, union officials. Discreet winks and nods from party illiberals: Senator Lloyd Bentsen, powerful Texas oligarch, "predicts" that Kennedy will run, while carefully nonendorsing Carter. New York governor Hugh Carey, creature of Brooklyn's squalid county machine, urges Kennedy to declare his rebel status. "Neoconservative" Moynihan does likewise, being no longer fearful, it seems, of the "erosion of political authority in America," if indeed he ever was. The tongues of Oligarchy wag for Kennedy: A few "neoconservative" pundits cease belaboring "outworn liberalism" to urge the hero of the "liberal bloc" to run, say it "widens the voters' options," say anything needful if Oligarchy needs it.

What the political oligarchy needs right now is Carter beaten into utter submission—enforcing Nunn's ultimatum being much on Oligarchy's mind and doubtless on many a neoconservative's mind as well. What Kennedy needs is the assurance—a complete illusion, the cruelest of traps—that the Democratic nomination is his for the taking. So the August of "Teddy-Mania" is also, contrapuntally, a season of nightmare for Carter, the season of the "Killer Rabbit" story, told and retold for weeks: The President, out fishing, flayed away in terror at an onrushing rabbit. Season of brutal cartoons: Carter depicted "as a bumbling gnome-like clown—short in stature, with comically big lips and teeth"—the summary is given by *Congressional Quarterly*— "wearing a bewildered expression on his face as he gets his foot stuck in a bucket or is trussed up with a rope by Teddy Kennedy."

The season, too, of surgical knifing, precise paring away of what little remains of Carter's strength.

Sunk low in the polls—32 percent, according to Gallup's August approval ratings—Carter still retains the sympathy of his fellow "born-again" Christians, whom the New Right and its new "Moral Majority" are trying to herd into the Republican camp. Into the well-springs of sympathy this August, the infamous Roy Cohn, a man steeped for a lifetime in bipartisan corruption, pours his poison. Attorney for two New York nightclub owners indicted for tax fraud in June 1978, he has them accuse Hamilton Jordan of taking cocaine at their club back in April 1978. On August 25, before even the Attorney General has heard of the scurrilous charge, it appears on the front page of the *New York Times* and continues a damaging scandal for nine months more. Meanwhile, Reagan goes around the country warning of the "vice of permissiveness" spreading "its deadly poison."

The President's reputation for probity remains his last personal resource, "Goobergate" proving a mare's nest. In late August, an unknown forger passes on to Jack Anderson, the syndicated columnist, a letter purportedly written on White House stationery showing Jordan and a close friend of Carter's, one Charles Kirbo, dealing with Robert Vesco, the corrupt fugitive financier of the Nixon years. The White House tells Anderson the letter is a fake; Anderson publishes it anyway. Before August is out, a grand jury is investigating crime at the White House, and Carter is being asked by reporters whether or not his Attorney General is engaged in a "cover-up." The shadows of Watergate pass over the White House. Nothing, it seems, is to be left to Carter.

The President still retains the goodwill of black voters. In this August of "Teddy-Mania" and licensed vileness, the Israeli government forces the resignation of Andrew Young, U.S. ambassador to the United Nations, the highest-ranking black man in the Carter administration, a truly sordid tale of the Reaction, worthy of a moment's scrutiny.

Back on July 26, Ambassador Young, as president of the Security Council, met in secret with the UN observer for the Palestine

Liberation Organization to arrange postponement, in Israel's favor, of a vote in the Council. Since it might be construed as violating a U.S. agreement not to talk to the PLO, Young had notified Israel's UN ambassador of the meeting, supposing Israel to be America's ally. On August 10, the postponement secured, Israel strikes: Informed Israeli "sources" tell *Newsweek* of the PLO meeting, let the magazine make of it what it will. *Newsweek,* to its credit, checks the story with the Secretary of State, who is told by Young, untruthfully, that the meeting was accidental. Such is the story relayed to the press on the twelfth, forestalling for the moment the well-organized outrage of the pro-Israel lobby. Israel, however, will not be denied its prey. In a hostile act, astonishing between friendly countries, the Israeli government on August 14 exposes Young's lie. The pro-Israel lobby and its many friends across the spectrum of Reaction roar in outrage, demand—and get—the resignation of Young, humiliating Carter and enraging black people, whom ABC News tries to infuriate further by reporting, without proof, that Carter had wiretapped Young's apartment. "The Israelis were after the President," not black people, says Young, and such is the truth: Israel is not merely an ally of the United States, government-to-government. More deeply, more intimately and far more consequently, it is the ally of Oligarchy in America, hence an agent, and a formidable one, of the onrushing Reaction.

Is America ripe *now* for magical thinking and demagogue effrontery? Reagan's campaign managers believe it is. So "Policy Memorandum No. 1" is produced in this month of "Teddy-Mania" and pitiless lying. Governor Reagan will call for a tax cut so large, so magically fruitful of economic growth, it will eliminate the budget deficit and wipe out inflation thereby. A huge tax reduction that balances the budget: edible, keepable cake.

Suddenly, over the Labor Day weekend, furious alarm bells go off. Danger "pretended from abroad"—manna to Oligarchy—has struck these United States. An armed Soviet brigade has been discovered in Cuba, two or three thousand armed troops—a gift to the Reaction from Brzezinski, who had ordered intensified surveillance of Cuba in hope of finding *something* the war party could use against Carter,

SALT II and détente. A "combat" brigade, Brzezinski calls it, "deployed in a deliberate attempt to test the limits of Carter's patience and will," so Reaction's spy in the White House insinuates to the press, though not for direct attribution. A "combat" brigade *sans* ships and planes, no more than the half-forgotten remnant of some 20,000 Russian troops stationed on the island in 1962.

Secretary Vance breaks the news first to Senator Church, chairman of the Foreign Relations Committee, requesting discretion, but who would spare Carter in this pitiless season? Not his 1976 rival for the presidency. "The President must make it clear that we draw the line at Russian penetration of the Western Hemisphere," thunders Church at a press conference in Idaho on August 30, before returning to Washington to make matters worse. "There is no likelihood that the Senate will ratify the SALT treaty as long as combat troops remain in Cuba." Thus Church threatens on September 5, a friend of arms control offering a "godsend to treaty foes."

In vain Vance and Carter plead that the brigade has been in Cuba for years—more years than they know, alas—threatens nothing, violates nothing, signifies nothing. No matter, says Oligarchy. They must be removed. The Senate "reverberates" with clamorous cries for withdrawal. Church keeps demanding it. Baker demands it. Jackson as a matter of course demands it: "SALT II is dead unless the Soviet troops are taken out of Cuba." Vance and Carter, hopelessly rattled, promise to do something; accomplish nothing—more charges of "appeasement" rain down on their heads.

The Senate "reverberates," too, with attacks on Soviet "adventurism" and bottomless Soviet perfidy, reverberates with hysterical warnings of "Fortress Cuba" in the making. The *Wall Street Journal* warns of the Soviets landing "troops on Long Beach or Long Island," retaliates by demanding "Reject SALT Now." Carter's "posture of continuous self-abasement" before totalitarian regimes has grown intolerable, cries Mrs. Kirkpatrick, "traditional liberalism" sweeping her into the camp of Reagan and the Right. "Undiminished alarmism" rages day after day, week after week, the fear-mongers of the Reaction battening on this pitiful trifle, escalating "a minor diplomatic squabble," writes

Time, "suddenly and improbably . . . into a major domestic political issue." Turning 3,000 landlocked Soviet troops, even more improbably, into the pretext for a sweeping three-year arms buildup voted by the Senate on September 18. The vote is so sudden that old Senator Stennis protests, "hawk" and "hard-liner" though he is. "What are we voting for? Nobody knows. There has been no listing, no report, no examination, no priorities," complains the seventy-eight-year-old chairman of the Armed Services Committee, left behind by the onrushing Reaction, left bewildered by its headlong contempt for order and propriety and even the thinnest pretense of statesmanship.

No glimpse of the Reaction's bleak, spiteful heart is more telling than this: Former Secretary of State Dean Rusk could have stopped the whole boiling mock-crisis at once by calling Secretary Vance and informing him that the "combat" brigade was known to, and acquiesced in, by President Kennedy as part of the settlement of the Cuban missile crisis back in 1962. Had the State Department called *him,* so Rusk boasts years later, he could have "straightened them out . . . in five minutes—but no one called." Why did the Honorable Mr. Rusk not call the State Department? Why did he choose to smirk spitefully in private? Does this man so signally honored by his country owe nothing to his country in return? Is he not honor-bound to see the U.S. government shielded from needless ignorance and groundless fears? The Honorable Mr. Rusk thinks otherwise. Is he not on the executive committee of the Present Danger? Why should he *not* think otherwise? What are honor, patriotism and probity compared with the grand task of corrupting a free people with hysteric fears, false alarms and dangers "pretended from abroad"—the national security of Oligarchy?

"If appeasement were an art form, the administration would be the Rembrandt of the age," brays John Connally, neoconservative Podhoretz's choice for President until October, when he speaks favorably of Arabs. "We stood toe-to-toe with the Soviet Union," says Minority Leader Baker of the unremoved "combat" brigade, "and, unlike 1962, we blinked instead of the Russians." Reagan detects in the great crisis of the brigade "the sorry tapping of Neville Chamberlain's umbrella on the cobblestones of Munich." Licensed by the Nitzes, the Rusks, the Nunns and the Jacksons, panjandrums of the popular party, the jingoism of the Right grows more frenzied and coarse with each passing week. "Dear Friend," says a New Right agitator mounted on his direct-mail soapbox, "I have enclosed two flags: the red, white and blue of Old Glory—and the white flag of surrender. I want to show you by these two flags what is at stake for America under the SALT II treaty with Russia. If the U.S. Senate ratifies SALT II (the Strategic Arms Limitation Treaty negotiated by Kremlin Boss Leonid Brezhnev with Jimmy Carter) it will mean the permanent surrender of the United States of America to the military superiority of the Soviet Union. You and I must choose—and the Senate must decide—whether we will personally accept the white flag of surrender or America's banner."

SALT II is threatened and Carter must pay: Kennedy threatens and Carter must pay. Patronage, grants, preferments pour into the eager hands of the old party gang in every key state in the Union: The vast resources of the presidency are marshaled to fight off the Kennedy challenge. Local machines are pampered and praised. "We're just startin' to squeeze the guy," says a Cook County alderman after Carter visits Chicago to laud the memory of the late Mayor Daley, who "understood the basis for party strength"—killing off political "outsiders" being basis the first.

One by one the remnants of détente are cast aside, in appeasement of the war party. On July 20, Carter scuttles his battered plan to withdraw U.S. troops from Korea, last vestige of the republican foreign policy of 1976. In mid-August, Carter dispatches Vice President Mondale to China on a pointedly "strategic" mission, deliberately inciting Kremlin fears, bordering on nightmare, of a U.S.-China alliance, flouting Vance's desperate warnings against just such a bellicose "tilt." With SALT II at the mercy of the war party, Carter is putty in the hands of Brzezinski, who urges in a September memorandum "a tough line on Soviet adventurism" and an end to U.S. "acquiescence"—meaning Secretary Vance and what is left of détente, on which memo the President writes "good."

On September 11, half-yielding to Nunn's ultimatum, Carter promises a "further real increase in defense spending," and Jackson that day, contrapuntally, tells CBS that "no divisiveness" would result if Kennedy tried to overthrow the President. The brazen lie is aimed at hollow-hearted Kennedy, who must be assured and reassured and reassured yet again that his candidacy will not wreak havoc with his party, the one thing it is certain to do, the one thing the Reaction wants it to do, for the Republic cannot be well and truly stifled until the Right takes control of the Executive. "You're not talking about taking the nomination away from a sitting President," says a White House aide in mid-September, "you're talking about delivering the White House to Ronald Reagan or John Connally." And where would Kennedy's poor and ailing be then?

A simple man, or an honorable man, would see at once the hideous falsity of his position, but Kennedy is—a Kennedy. Great clouds of windbaggery befog and blind him, are bellowed forth to befog and blind him—the "Camelot legend," the "Kennedy legacy," the presidential "destiny"—a "destiny" he thrice denied already, in 1968, 1972 and 1976, so many an egger-on and hanger-on points out.

An all-but-declared candidate since September 7, when he tells the President he no longer supports him, Kennedy now moves inside a wind tunnel of "drooling adulation." So Jody Powell puts it. A "frenzied atmosphere" surrounds him. The press hangs on his every word. Scarcely a day goes by without an endorsement, a wink or a nod, scarcely a day without some "old pro" expressing delight with his forthcoming candidacy and the easy victory over Carter in store for him. Through August and deep into September the drums of "Teddy-Mania" beat ever more loudly, the whole whirligig spins ever more wildly until, so *Congressional Quarterly* shrewdly observes, Kennedy "can find no persuasive reason not to run."

But why, persuasively, is he running? In order to provide "leadership," says Kennedy. Because "this *outsider* cannot solve our problems," he explains to Teddy White, celebrated chronicler of presidential elections, now beginning his newest one. Does Kennedy mean that a President elected *only* by the people is peculiarly unsuited to govern

them? That the party which did not choose him is loath, to put it
mildly, to help him? If this is a persuasive reason, it is surely not fit for
public consumption. "What would you do different from Carter?" an
NBC reporter, Roger Mudd, asks Kennedy on September 29, for an
interview that will air on November 4. "Well, in which particular
areas?" replies Kennedy. "Well, just take the question of leadership"—
to which, alas for Kennedy, no honest or honorable answer can be
given. "Well, it's a—on—on what—on—you know, you have to come
to grips with the—different issues that we're facing. I mean, we can—
we have to deal with each of the various questions that we're—we're
talking about, whether it's in the question of the economy, whether it's
in—in the areas of energy."

This ditherer promises "leadership"? This dreadful blather—and
this is but a sampling—justifies destroying a President of one's own
party? Watching the devastating interview, Kennedy's well-wishers are
stunned. Kennedy, says Garry Wills, "was being destroyed by TV,
before our eyes." The voters are shocked as well, and worse than
shocked. Dubious ambition so feebly justified revives all the old mistrust of Teddy Kennedy, freshens Chappaquiddick memories of a
drowned girl and a terrified careerist. And the voters judge rightly.
Kennedy is no leader, no rebel, no honest champion of anything he
champions, just Oligarchy's dupe, whom the party leaders abandon
the moment he is safely ensnared in rebellion, whereupon the "old
pros" desert, adulation ceases, the press begins snarling and Kennedy
suddenly suffers, notes Drew of the *New Yorker,* "an extraordinary
reversal in the political standings." The fool of the Reaction's cruel
farce, he will avenge himself, party tool and hollow heart that he is,
not against his party entrappers—that is the path of honor not
taken—but savagely, brutally against the Democratic President, continuing his assault on "this *outsider*" month after month after month,
long after every last hope of victory has fled, a "cardinal sin" in party
politics, but a sin no longer, for Oligarchy, which invents the sins, has
the power of absolution, of binding and loosening. Encouraged by his
very entrappers, Kennedy will carry the destructive fight into and
through and even beyond the 1980 Democratic convention, will read

the Democratic President out of the Democratic Party for his want of sympathy for the poor, the elderly and the ailing until the hopes of the poor, the elderly and the ailing lie buried beneath a landslide for Reagan and the Right. Was this not the object of "Teddy-Mania" in the first place?

Inflation and the "hostage crisis"—that prolonged incitement to national self-pity and the growing mob-spirit—complete what Oligarchy has set out to accomplish since the election of 1976: the disgrace and destruction of the first President since the early days of the Republic elected without the approval of his party. The Teheran hostage-taking, in truth, is more effect than cause. It is a "crisis" because Carter is weak; because all that he does or does not do is seen through the prism of weakness, adjudged the proof of weakness. It is a "crisis," too, because Carter is marked out for destruction; the hostages are a weapon in the long, brutal campaign—"Americans Held Hostage"—Day 49, Day 187, Day 365, Election Day, no less, last nail in the "outsider's" coffin. But the Reaction is already ascendant before the end of 1979, has already smoothed the way for the "Reagan Revolution" of 1981.

The triumph of the war party is completed on December 12, when Carter, caving in to the Nunn ultimatum, announces the commencement of a major military buildup—a 4.5 percent real increase in defense spending for the next five years, beginning at once, necessitated "by the steady military buildup of the Soviets and their growing inclination to rely on military power to exploit turbulent situations." America's military power was "unsurpassed," said Carter as recently as October 1, but it is unsurpassed no longer. America's nuclear deterrent was a mighty shield a few months ago, but it is a mighty shield no longer. A vast, devastating first-strike capacity—U.S. nuclear supremacy, in fact—is needed to avert a surprise Soviet nuclear attack. The President has at last become, albeit grudgingly, the leader of the fearmongers, as the war party had demanded on July 25.

What is more, says Carter, America must develop a large and powerful "rapid deployment force" for swift military intervention in every nook and cranny of the globe. We must cease to fear "potential

Vietnams," says Carter, passing the death sentence on the republican foreign policy of 1976. Brzezinski is exultant: The President has declared "the end of the Vietnam complex," he explains triumphantly to the press. The democratic *distemper* has been cured; danger once again lurks everywhere for America; national security once again stands menaced by trifles. Our "will and resolve" to fear shadows—for the American Empire is but an empire of domestic fears—has been restored to the government, strengthening Oligarchy, devouring liberty. Such is the gift which Jimmy Carter, sad and contemptible, betrayer and betrayed, lays at the feet of the Reaction on December 12, 1979. When the Soviets invade Afghanistan two weeks later, Carter calls it, preposterously, "the greatest threat to peace since the Second World War." How sweet it is to be at one with the war party, which, alas for Carter, refuses to be at one with him. Secretary Vance says little. In April 1980 the vanquished advocate of détente will become the second Secretary of State in American history to find the foreign policy of his President so intolerable he feels compelled to resign.

By the autumn of 1979, too, the Democratic Congress has made itself a mere adjunct of the corporate swarm, an open auction for corporate wealth. "Access was now openly for sale," writes Teddy White, normally a celebrator of American public life, unable to celebrate this new "loose money" which has grown "more important in the purchase of political influence than at any time in living memory." Congress, for sale, is more than ever the mouthpiece for corporate quackery, ever more daring in its quackery. It declares that the poor are not poor enough (having declared in 1978 that the rich are not rich enough), must be made poorer to "combat inflation." The Federal Trade Commission, empowered by the democratic awakening, disagrees; looks to monopoly and oligopoly as a prime cause of inflation. The very thought is now forbidden, taboo. The inflation, by decree, is an instrument of the Reaction, and of no other ideas or thoughts or initiatives. Inflation is caused by government, caused by egalitarianism, caused by republicanism; capitalism is flawless. So Oligarchy decrees, as quackery spreads, thickens, buries public life beneath it. The FTC, persistent, tries to "strengthen the role of competition," gets savaged, humiliated, decimated by Congress this autumn, for so the corporate swarm would have it and so Capitol Hill, for sale, obliges, obliges so eagerly the very bribe-givers are ashamed for the bribe-taking Congress: "I don't like doing this—it's terrible. But it's you guys who've put Congress on the auction block."

Does this money pollution, which can shame a lobbyist, shame the Democratic Congress? No, the Democratic Congress, our Dixie-Daley Congress, finds the money pollution even now insufficient, inadequate, a mere trickle. More, ten times more, corrupt money—and money ten times more corrupting—must be sucked into the vortex of Oligarchy before Oligarchy can begin to feel safe from the democratic menace, which, Antaeus-like, never dies, however crushed to the ground it might be. So, on December 20—the same day, coincidentally, on which the Senate Armed Services Committee *unanimously* condemns the SALT II treaty despite all that Carter has paid and betrayed for it—Congress enacts a campaign-financing measure which destroys what is left of democracy's shield against the corrupting political power of wealth. The measure passes quietly, in "a rare demonstration of harmony," passes by acclamation, votes unrecorded, not without reason. The measure, which is strongly urged by the United Auto Workers—another "liberal" Democratic gift to "labor"—allows the political parties to spend limitless amounts of money for "party-strengthening activities" and "get-out-the-vote" drives in presidential elections. Funds may come from any source whatever, from sources forbidden since 1907—union treasuries, meaning the workers' dues; corporate treasuries, meaning the stockholders' money; as well as the deep pockets of "fat cat" donors—no need even for a PAC. Why put corrupters to trouble? This limitless PAC-less soft money, so-called, goes *unrecorded,* cannot be traced. A corporation could give "twenty million bucks and you don't have to show it," says a Republican Party official.

This limitless, secret, corrupting money goes straight into the hands of the national party leadership, gets redistributed to its favored local candidates, its favored local parties, its favored aspirants for presidential nominations. It makes a mockery of federal funding of presidential elections, tried only once—in 1976—and already turned into a fraud by the all-devouring Reaction. It is meant to make a mockery, too, of popular control of presidential nominations, this being, perhaps, the most important object of all. It favors the powerful few; it weakens, inexorably, silently, in ways hard to measure, the political voice of the many, for it restricts the public realm to Oligarchy's hacks and handmaidens, or will in due course. It is of immense and immediate advantage to the presidential chances of Ronald Reagan, enacted this December 20, 1979, just in the nick of time, by the Democratic Congress, by acclamation—for "labor." The thinnest and flimsiest of pretexts can conceal from honest citizens the brutal fact of collusion and complicity in American party politics, so let this be said as forcibly and as candidly as possible, marking the turning point in this chronicle of the Reaction: Two political parties have united to destroy a feeble democrat. Now they will unite—collude more deeply still—to exalt, protect and sustain a feeble tyrant, will call upon him to bring the *populares* to heel, like a *signor* summoned by frightened magnates to quell some turbulent Italian city-state.

B O O K   T H R E E

THE CRIME OF '81

9.
THE TRUTHLESS MAN

A distraught and befuddled electorate troops glumly to the polls on November 4, 1980—their turnout the lowest since 1948; unhappiness with both candidates greater than any previous Gallup Poll ever showed—and casts 50.7 percent of its ballots for Ronald Reagan, who has promised an immense tax reduction, a giant military buildup and a budget painlessly balanced by 1983 through careful paring of "waste and abuse" and the miracle of revenue "feedback," edible, keepable supply-sided cake.

A tremor of fear ripples through Republican ranks—with reason, reason most compelling. Inside supply-side quackery an immense and dangerous force lies latent, coiled up within it like a boa constrictor. Once the Federal Reserve succeeds in disinflating the economy, the one certain result of Reagan's huge promised tax cut is huge annual budget deficits—more than $100 billion a year; $150 billion, perhaps, counting the military buildup. So calculates Reagan's future budget director, David Stockman, age thirty-four, a former protégé of Senator Moynihan's. No menace in Stockman's eyes are these huge crushing deficits, but an "opportunity," he calls it, a once-in-a-lifetime chance for "a frontal assault on the welfare state." Given the "battering ram" force of those deficits, a titanic reversal of history lies within the power of the Right: "Forty years' worth of promises, subventions, entitlements and safety nets issued by the federal government to every component and stratum of American society would have to be scrapped or drastically modified," so Stockman recalls himself thinking in those heady autumn days of 1980. The "craven politicians" would have no choice: dismantle the enterprises of government, liberate and exalt the power of capital—trampled and brought low for so many years—"or risk national ruin" from the crush of those deficits.

Therein lies the true beauty of the scheme: no choice. No need to persuade a feckless electorate that mitigating gross inequality is an enterprise unworthy of a republican commonwealth. No need to persuade them that a house of one's own, yeomanly independence, security in old age, clear air and clean water, the principles of liberty and equality perpetually upheld (however ill served), a public realm shielded from hungry mobs and criminal despair (for misery is the enemy of liberty) are utterly impermissible public goals—"bloated, wasteful and unjust spending enterprises," so the future budget director calls them. No need to undertake the hopeless task of teaching the national mob the sublime, icy truths of laissez-faire economics; no need to persuade them—for it is equally hopeless—that no purpose beyond "economic efficiency" is fit and proper for a capitalist country, for America as "just one big business," for America the "industrial giant," as the President-elect likes to call this Republic. Are we not something other than that, the feckless rabble would ask? Have Americans not died on a hundred battlefields for something other than that? For something more like government of, by and for the people, which is supposed not to perish from this earth? No need to turn aside such questions. The American people are drowning in inflation, are clinging to the balanced budget idea like a shipwrecked sailor clutching at flotsam. Let Congress enact—but will it?—these huge tax-reduction deficits and then let Reagan demand they be wiped away and there is no need to persuade a free people to abandon their feckless public goals. Under the crushing weight of "fiscal necessity"—a false necessity, necessity brutally, deceitfully contrived—the judgment of the vicious many shall be subjugated to the will of the righteous few, to us, the Right, keepers of the flame, dwellers in the political wilderness for fifty years, in the wilderness no longer.

Such is the latent power coiled up within supply-side quackery—

the power to carry out a brutal plot, a deceitful scheme, a political crime, a crime against government by consent of the governed, a tyrant's crime against a free people's freedom to decide their own fate, a crime by no means deeply concealed. On October 14, poor, unheeded Carter had presciently warned that his rival's program must lead, inevitably, to a $130 billion deficit by 1983, to a bloated military establishment and a federal government stripped, impoverished and paralyzed for years to come. Suppose the supply-side plot were launched and the people rose up against it? What would become of the Reaction then? What possible hope would there be for Oligarchy restored?

Skepticism of the Right is rampant in the country. The huge party of nonvoters would have elected Carter, so the *Times* cautions on November 9. Other cautionary warnings are sounded from within high Republican ranks. Have the American people repudiated Democratic Party goals? "Absolutely not," says Bill Brock, chairman of the Republican National Committee. Is there a "mandate" for a sharp turn to the right? No, but rather an "apparent absence of a mandate," says Richard Wirthlin, the President-elect's own polltaker. George Will, the conservative columnist, is Reagan's informal adviser; he, too, cautions the new President-elect: The election "was not a national conversion to conservative ideology. It was a desire to see Carter gone."

Go slow, be moderate, resist the firebrands of the Right; launch no frontal assault on the popular party: So say the cautious warnings. You are not the man for such courses, Ronald Reagan, have not the strength, skill, knowledge, force of mind, strength of character, depth of understanding for such high and dangerous enterprises.

The President-elect has fine and potent gifts, fully commands the arts of popularity. He is a speaker, a *rhetor*, a master of euphemism and the perfect half-truth, has immense powers of personal attraction, has about him an air of manly resolve, invincible self-assurance, unblemished candor, yet, withal, lightness and charm and ebullience. "There was an ease in his manner." So Copperfield describes J. Steerforth, hero of the school. "A gay and light manner it was, but not swagger-

ing—which I still believe to have borne a kind of enchantment with
it. I still believe him, in virtue of his carriage, his animal spirits, his
delightful voice, his handsome face and figure, and, for aught I know,
of some inborn power of attraction besides (which I think a few people possess), to have carried a spell with him to which it was a natural
weakness to yield and which not many persons could withstand."
Much like Steerforth, hero of the school, does Ronald Reagan appear
in public.

Yet what brutal truncation, what cutting back of the plant, produces that splendid blossom! What lopping away of knowledge, of
curiosity, of truthfulness, to produce that public aura of candor and
confidence. What lopping away of realism, foresight, even the very
capacity to govern. Reagan is ignorant, deliberately, willfully ignorant,
scarcely knows who works for him, rarely asks a penetrating question.
William Casey, his campaign manager, his intelligence director, the
innermost member of his inner circle, describes Reagan as passive,
friendless, "strange." "He gave no orders, no commands, asked for no
information, expressed no urgency." So a startled David Stockman
observes at his first informal meetings with the President-elect, who
will spend two years in the White House without learning that most
Soviet missiles are based on the land. His arms control proposals
sound fairer to him if he does not know and so he never inquires. The
new budget director tells the President-elect that no revenue "feedback" will be forthcoming from the proposed Kemp-Roth tax cut.
Reagan looks puzzled, but says not a word. What happened to the
heart and soul of his promise to the people? Reagan does not care to
know. What good would the knowledge do him? How can he maintain that marvelous air of candor if he knows for certain he is telling a
lie?

For candor's sake and seeming, intellectual honesty must be lopped
away and with it the ability to see the true aspect of things. A
Democratic governor warns Reagan of forthcoming deficits, to which
Reagan angrily replies, "We didn't invent deficit spending"—the *idea*
of it is not his and so how can he be held responsible for his deficits?
"He seemed unable to acknowledge that he might have made a mis-

take," Gerald Ford says of Reagan in his memoirs. Bottomless self-deception protects the public blossom—the self-deception of a man who spent World War II serving in the Air Force at home describing himself as "coming back" from the war, eager "to make love" to his wife. "All his war-making has been in his mind," says Garry Wills, "and he will make it the way he wants." An appalling capacity for repelling truth and believing falsehood is the one truly outstanding gift of the fortieth President. "He believes that he can think a thing true and it will be true," says a Democratic leader. Reagan is "not devious," so a longtime associate says. "He doesn't deliberately alter things. Things go into his mind and whirl around and come out how he likes." Or the unwelcome information is simply spurned, becomes noninformation. "If you bring him facts that don't fit into what he wants to believe he just rejects them," Majority Leader Wright remarks six years hence. Or it leaves Reagan "depressed," for harsh reality, bad news on television, readily dispirits the ebullient popular leader. "He gets that pained look," says an aide, "and you don't want to make him suffer"—and wither the blossom of public ebullience.

What, then, is the source of Reagan's wonderful air of resolve? It, too, is mainly a hothouse bloom, artfully cultivated. "What's so incredible is Reagan's sense of confidence, but it is like death not knowing itself," says an oddly poetical ex-aide of the President's. No real inner strength supports that air of assurance, but rather a desperate clinging to a dogma—the virtues of "the market" and the evils of "government"—and headlong evasion of the terrors of doubt. So Reagan, the most "ideological" of American leaders, often calls upon Edwin Meese III, former county sheriff, now his principal adviser, to pick out from among a series of "options" the "Reaganite" position, lacking the nerve himself to face contradictions and conflicts, lacking the courage, too, to look ahead, or think ahead, to where his dogmas might lead, preferring blind optimism, instead, the faith, says Mrs. Reagan curtly, "that if you let something go, it will eventually work itself out. Well, it isn't always so." Clinging to dogma, Reagan finds unbearable the sight of his advisers disputing; it gives me "knots in my stomach"—knots of terror, for if "Reaganites" disagree is there not a rip, a rent, a tear in the seamless web of "Reaganism"? So Meese, protecting the precious blossom of confidence, constructs "a bubble of obliviousness" around Reagan, as sharp-eyed Stockman observes. "Whenever there was an argument, Meese would step in and tell us to take our arguments to some other ad hoc forum. The President would smile and say, 'Okay, you fellas work it out.'" When the "fellas" do so, endorsement generally follows and thus affairs of state are managed.

Reagan does not govern because he dares not govern, for reality rushes in upon governors—facts and figures, harsh and conflicting, sparing no dogmas, bursting all bubbles—and the Reagan blossom—resolute, candid, ebullient—would wither and die. General Haig, newly named Secretary of State, attends his first Cabinet meeting and discovers to his horror that Meese and James Baker, two of Reagan's triumvirate of senior advisers, have taken seats at the great Cabinet table. "A startling departure from tradition," says outraged Haig; mere presidential aides, flunkies, adjutants, seated in the place reserved for the great sworn officers of state, confirmed by the advice and consent of the august Senate? "Robert Haldeman and John Ehrlichman at the height of their pride would never have dared such an act of lese majesty." But Reagan's advisers are not mere "President's men." They are "managers of the presidency," so Haig belatedly discovers. Every morning at nine they meet the President in the Oval Office and give him the "line," Stockman calls it, on what he is supposed to think about "any significant topic in the morning's newspapers—El Salvador, unemployment, whatever"—whatever being the vast array of public events about which Reagan will not or cannot be bothered to think for himself. The triumvirs care not a fig for "tradition" or rules, or forms, or even, it soon turns out, for the laws of the land themselves.

Such, in brief, is the vulnerable, truthless man who is about to become the fortieth occupant of the most powerful and glorious office in the world. Gimlet eyes, sharp and skeptical, will surely scrutinize with minutest attention the soft stream of lies and half-lies, the euphemisms and evasions, that issue so readily from demagogue lips—and what will the air of candor look like then to the American people? The harsh torrent of events will flood the White House, bursting bubbles, tearing dogma to shreds, bringing news, depressing news—and what will happen then to strengthless self-confidence? How long will the blossom survive unwithered should Reagan compel the popular party, grizzled, guileful veterans of so many political wars, to stand up and defend its people? Not, it would seem, for long.

10.

THERMIDOR

But wait! The democracy has something to announce a fortnight after the election, something to allay groundless fears. The party leaders have gone into "retreat," have pondered party past, present and future on Chesapeake Bay. They emerge and announce to the world that they have been utterly repudiated by the American people. Poll us no polls, says the Democratic leadership. We have been swept away in a "conservative tide." Democratic leaders profess themselves stunned, crushed, "shell-shocked," it is said, by the appalling extent of Carter's defeat, after tearing him to shreds for four years, which shredding has cost them control of the Senate, doubtless a genuine shock. Only one course lies open for the popular party, swept away, as it were, by fiat. We must give the new President-elect a free hand—and more: a helping hand, whatever is needful. "Uni-formly, in one interview after another," so the *Washington Post* reports on the morning of November 17, "Democrats from House Speaker Thomas P. (Tip) O'Neill Jr. (D-Mass.) on down talked about cooperating with the President-elect and giving the GOP a chance." Abject self-abasement is democracy's order of the day. "We're going to cooperate with the President," says Speaker Tip. "It's America first and party second." Senator Byrd, in his Heepish element, will not be outdone by Tip. "We shall be cooperative. We shall offer our assistance. We certainly want to see the new President succeed." At what, pray tell? At the generating of huge strangling deficits, paralyzing the popular party for years to come?

What the Speaker would like to see, reports *Newsweek,* is "a six-month moratorium on criticism." What love of liberty burns in these hearts! Six months with no light save the presidential light! Six months with no voice save the presidential voice! The public realm a darkened theater with one spotlight playing on the President, magnifying his popular gifts, concealing his appalling limitations. What, pray tell us, Mr. Speaker, is this great blessing the President wishes to bestow that cannot stand up to scrutiny? And what is the great good to be enacted that needs to be perpetrated in the dark? We shall see soon enough.

Nor is cooperation, assistance, self-abasement all that our swept-away democracy declares it must practice in order to rise from repudiation and defeat. We must purge the party of the Kennedy "cadres," having used them to purge the party of Carter—so urges Senator Moynihan. We must make the popular party "a centrist" party, by which glib-tongued, mackerel-bright Moynihan means a party syndicate stripped to its true "cadre" of regulars and bosses, hacks and fuglemen, a party freed at long last from independence in word and deed, freed from active citizens—beloved by the civics books, detested and feared by the powerful—freed from all who refuse to be regulated by the aims and interests of Oligarchy, for thus regulated is what "regulars" are. We must also "broaden our financial base," says the swept-away democracy, replacing "left wing" with business wing, with PAC-money machine wing, which will not, most assuredly, disburse funds to Democrats who aid and abet the evils of "activism." For in this season of self-abasement the Democratic Party has not forgotten—how can it possibly forget?—the Great Matter itself, without which all other efforts, purges, shrinkages, collusions, abasements would prove utterly unavailing—namely, the harrowing business of regaining control of the presidential nomination, for which the time is ripe, as ripe as ever it will be.

Carter is an evident disaster; ergo, says Oligarchy, rigorously logical, party democracy is disastrous as well. Is not Carter's failure to get on with us absolute proof, ocular proof, proof incontrovertible, that *we* must alter the system that brought the presidency to *him*? Thus

Oligarchy argues and thus parrot the pundits, being pundits, in the main, by virtue of parroting. Since "the people have acquired the power to nominate Presidents . . . the governments they elect have in the process lost the authority needed to govern." Thus the eminent James Reston of the *Times*. Carter failed because he came to the White House without "the alliances that made it possible for him to organize the coalitions and support necessary to lead a government." Thus David Broder of the *Post,* twelve years in mourning for the "death of the parties." "Jimmy Carter, the outsider, would not have been the nominee in 1976 of an organized political party; he is what can happen when the choice of party leader is taken entirely out of the hands of the party elite and turned over to the people." Thus James Sundquist of the Brookings Institute, bringing Political Science to bear on the Great Matter. All being in complete agreement that the trashing of democracy by Oligarchy demonstrates the preeminent virtues of Oligarchy, a Democratic Party commission will shortly be formed to alter the party rules so that the powerful party few shall once again have the last word—or perhaps even the first word—as to who will and who will not traverse the Democratic road to the White House. Thus Power, as usual, dictates to Thought, or what passes for thought in this corrupted public realm of ours, where knaves hire fools to protect them.

In the meantime the President-elect and his wife have arrived in Washington this November 17, day of Democratic self-abasement, for a "tightly packed five-day tour" which becomes, effortlessly, deedlessly, causelessly, "a five-day triumphal march through the capital," so eager is "official Washington"—dowagers, Democrats, power brokers and all—to hail and proclaim the President-to-be, to let the onlooking, nightly news electorate see how worthy of their deepest trust, faith and adoration is the man they have just elected, not unskeptically. Reagan pays a call on Capitol Hill, meets behind closed doors with congressional leaders and receives "rave notices all around." Laudations pour in upon him; such "a contrast to Carter," so fatally "aloof" from Congress, who failed so disastrously to "consult" it, who "too often seemed to work against it," so the Washington press corps blathers.

The corpse in the White House—is *he* still cluttering the premises?—issues an angry, sad, absurd report showing that he had consulted with congressional leaders eight times before his Inaugural. Who cares? Shut up, be gone.

On the second day of the "triumphal march," official Washington is still more agog with delight: The President-elect and his wife are breaking bread with "the capital's smart set" at a sitdown dinner for fifty at "the toney F Street Club"! It is Reagan's intention to demonstrate "that notwithstanding his anti-Washington rhetoric, he belongs," so *Newsweek* reports, agog with delight. "He will mix with the lords and ladies of Washington society toward whom Carter was standoffish." Two days later there is a dinner for the Reagans at the home of columnist George Will. In attendance is Katherine Graham, owner of the *Post* and *Newsweek* both, "empress of the limousine liberal set," it is said. No "set" is more loathed, loathed to the point of insanity, by the Right, but so delighted is its "empress" with the Reagans that she invites them next month to a party in turn, where they meet the new Democratic Ward Heeler-in-Chief, Lane Kirkland, Meany's heir apparent come into his legacy at last. Some thirty-two of Kirkland's Present Danger colleagues will find a place in the Reagan administration, seven of them founding members of the Coalition for a Democratic Majority. Not even our fiery liberal chieftain Senator Kennedy is missing from the great November Acclamation. He pays a call on the visiting Reagans and emerges "talking of the need for unity." Our prince of divisiveness crying up unity! What firmer proof is needed than this, fellow citizens, that Ronald Reagan, purveyor of supply-side quackery and many another design on your liberties, merits and deserves your deep faith and trust!

No wonder the President-elect so effortlessly "conquered the capital he ran so long and so hard against." The "capital" has surrendered in advance, carrying with it the Washington press corps, which is miraculously restored to "pre-Watergate" deference. "Lions [have] become lambs, typewriters are beaten into plowshares and rear ends at the White House become objects for kissing rather than kicking," says

Jody Powell, embittered by the "double standard." A "suddenly docile press corps," so a press historian puts it, will cushion and protect President Reagan in the weeks and months and years to come—no need to fear gimlet eyes—though the President and his men work ceaselessly to undermine the freeness of the press, which finds it must defer to its very tormentors, for Oligarchy will have it so and the press has no inner life or force of its own.

Bipartisan darkness descends on the public realm, preparation for the rule of the Right. In the House of Representatives on December 8, the Democratic leadership, swept away by fiat, packs every important committee with Reaganite Democrats; makes Jim Jones of the *coup de main* chairman of the Budget Committee, bypassing seniority and a "trusted lieutenant" of the Speaker's to keep it away from a liberal; makes Rostenkowski, of the Chicago machine, chairman of Ways and Means, putting the fate of supply-side quackery into his coarse, shameless hands. Election-day skepticism wanes with each passing week; for the skeptics are no longer heard, have no public voice. We want no "partisan recrimination," warns the Speaker, no "partisan bickering," no Democratic Party *pro tempore*. Let the Right only be heard, and it is. "It was time to be rich again," a gossip writer exclaims, for the rich are no longer "the rich," having become in the gathering darkness "those who save and invest," fructifying the earth. Nor are the poor and needy the poor and needy any longer; they are fast becoming in this gathering gloom a "special interest lobby," a "spending constituency," a "social pork barrel we can no longer afford."

The rich are not rich enough! The poor are not poor enough! Inequality deepened still more supplies the key to prosperity!

And so, says a Washington dowager, in this happy season of political darkness, "You don't have to be ashamed of what you have anymore. At the tea parties the children come in blue velvet and the ladies in $300 suits. You discuss difficulties with maids and you discuss social events." In safety! Without fear of reprisal! As if she had passed through the Reign of Terror, seen Robespierre overthrown, and had finally reached the warm shores of Thermidor—so frightening is revived republicanism to Power in America. For truly there is something Thermidorean in the air this winter as wealth swarms in upon Washington to celebrate Reagan's Inaugural and the restoration of its power and glory. "An armada of 400 corporate jets snarled traffic at National Airport," reports *Fortune*. "A far cry," notes *Newsweek,* "from the populist Peanut Special that chugged up from Georgia for the Inaugural four years ago." No republican simplicity will blight the occasion this time. Instead, "the country's basic values" will be celebrated this Inaugural, says Charles Wick, Reagan's longtime friend and master of the Inaugural revels: four days of dinners, parties and galas, four days of wealth on lavish display, clogging the streets in a new lavish way. "Beautiful Reagan intimate Betsy Bloomingdale leaped into Dupont Circle to help clear a traffic jam of limousines," *Newsweek* notes in the new Thermidorean style. It is "safe again to put on diamonds, designer gowns and—generally speaking—the dog," the *Post* assures its society-page readers. "Laughter is in," says a party reveler, "because Ronald Reagan has a funny bone. His friend Frank Sinatra says that nobody has a funny bone like Ron's." Thermidorean, too, is the twelve-page Inaugural brochure which devotes just one trifling paragraph of its celebration of "the country's basic values" to the swearing-in ceremony, and to the great presidential oath to "preserve, protect and defend the Constitution of the United States," which oath the new President, for the life of him, cannot understand and will not bother to heed, not finding it, perhaps, quite "basic" enough. As he completes his brief Inaugural address, blaming "government" for all our ills, the new President points out the splendid sights on the great Mall before him— ahead the monument to Washington, father of our country, and "off to one side the stately memorial to Thomas Jefferson. The Declaration of Independence flames with his eloquence," says the new President, while at that very moment, give or take a few minutes, Jefferson's portrait is being taken down from a White House wall and Calvin Coolidge's put up in its place.

11.
DARKNESS DEEPENING

It is the evening of February 18, 1981. The new President is about to "unveil" his program for "national economic recovery"—the "Reagan Revolution," the plot, scheme, conspiracy, the crime of '81—before a joint session of Congress and scores of millions of television viewers. There is trepidation at the White House, mounting for weeks. "The image of being . . . narrowly pro-business and uncaring," a team of advisers warns on January 29, "could potentially derail the President's aspirations for a new direction for the country." The President's tax plan looks dangerously like a "rich man's bill," polltaker Wirthlin fears. Deep political pitfalls endanger "the program," a presidential aide named Richard Darman warns Meese, Baker and Michael Deaver, the White House triumvirs, on February 10. The President's budget cuts will affront a large number of "special interests," for one thing; squeezing wealth from the needy will strike many as cruel and unfair; worst of all, warns Darman, the official budget forecast, with its promise of a balanced budget in 1984—the indispensable lie of the hour—is so grossly overoptimistic, so self-contradictory, it cannot pass serious inspection. How much darkness can the popular party provide for the crime of '81? Perhaps not enough, fears Darman, for deep, blinding public darkness is needed, sorely needed indeed.

The President is calling for fiscal restraint. "Can we who man the ship of state deny that it is somewhat out of control? Our national debt is approaching one trillion dollars." Mere paring of waste and abuse, a campaign promise, will not suffice: $48.6 billion must be cut from the fiscal 1982 budget, the largest single reduction in domestic spending ever proposed by a President. Wondrous to behold, however, is "fiscal restraint" in this Thermidorean season! For $49 billion will be added to the Pentagon's spending authority this year—the largest single increase ever proposed by a President in peacetime, proposed atop a $30 billion increase enacted a mere eleven weeks ago by the lame-duck Dixie-Daley Congress. "I am committed to stopping the spending juggernaut," says the President, as he launches a new spending juggernaut on the night of February 18. No fiscal restraint whatever but rather a vast fiscal shift—from domestic commonweal to warfare state; how wanton and wasteful a shift it is Congress will learn in detail two weeks hence.

Deficit spending must end, will end by 1984, the President solemnly promises, his faith in "revenue feedback" undiminished by the budget director telling him that no such revenues exist. The budget will be balanced by a tax reduction for individuals and corporations so huge it will reduce federal revenues, the budget director calculates, by "at least one quarter of a trillion dollars annually after . . . four or five years"—a "staggering" sum even to Stockman, ardent champion of the shrunken fisc. The loss to the fisc from the tax cut plus the cost to the fisc of the arms buildup adds up, Stockman calculates, to a "budget loss" of $1.6 trillion in the space of five years. On terms such as these no balanced budget is possible; only government at every level shrunk, impoverished and paralyzed, and the power of wealth and capital expanded in its stead—a bane to democracy, blessing to Oligarchy, the Reaction truly triumphant.

Privately, many a lawmaker assembled in the House this February evening fears the economic menace of those forthcoming deficits; privately, not one legislator in five, if that, believes in supply-side quackery, but no hint of doubt or skepticism is conveyed to the watching national rabble. Doubt they must not have or all will be lost at the very start. Instead, peals of acclaim thunder through the House and round after round of applause from the lawmakers, "leaving no doubt," recalls Stockman, "that they were predisposed to grant him extraordinary latitude"—for economic quackery, for devouring the fisc, for cruel, dishonest frugality. And when the President finishes his speech, the representatives of the people stand up and give Reagan a final tumultuous ovation—a National Savior has come amongst us! Trust him, follow him, adore him; so Oligarchy adjures scores of millions of television viewers as forcibly as it can this memorable evening of February 18.

On March 4, Congress receives the detailed military budget, a truly astonishing prospectus. The $222.2 billion defense appropriation for fiscal 1982, an immense sudden increase in itself, merely commences a five-year military buildup, growth set at 7 percent a year, discounting inflation; $1.5 trillion to be spent in all. We were the most powerful nation on earth in 1980, with an annual defense budget of $142 billion. We are to spend $367 billion a year by 1986 in this era of "fiscal restraint" and "getting federal spending under control"! Can a republic die of lies? If so, we are dying.

Inside the White House budget office, defense specialists are "shocked and incredulous," Stockman recalls. The huge spending totals and percentages are entirely arbitrary, plucked out of thin air one January day at a meeting between Stockman and Defense Secretary Caspar Weinberger. The whole wanton wasteful enterprise, says Richard Stubbins, Stockman's deputy chief of national security, "had nothing to do with a strategy, nothing to do with a program of what we needed for defense." Four hundred fifty separate military programs are scheduled for a budget increase, not one of them subjected to the customary line-item inspection at the budget office in this new age of false frugality, new age of remorseless, pitiless lies. The budget office—Reagan's own office—compiles a list of wasteful projects: "administrative vehicles" increased from 2,000 to 18,000—pure waste; 75,000 new civilian Pentagon employees—more waste, billions of dollars of waste; the inept new "Sergeant York" gun—$1 billion in waste before its cancellation in 1985; the Bradley Fighting Vehicle— "too expensive to ride in and too vulnerable to fight in," so Stockman describes it succinctly—$3 billion of wasted public wealth; three

143

nuclear aircraft carriers to fight a hypothetical *nonnuclear* global war with the Soviet Union—a neo–World War II—an idea so preposterous the Joint Chiefs refuse to endorse it, but Congress will underwrite it—$54 billion of wasted public wealth; waste of billions in redundant fighter planes, in needless fighting ships, in excessive officer salary increases, in excessive pensions. And waste not included in the budget office list: the B-1 bomber, "a flying Edsel"—$20 billion wasted; preparations for fighting and winning a "protracted" nuclear war—"a bottomless pit" for squandering scores of billions more of the public's wealth, so the chairman of the Joint Chiefs, David C. Jones, says upon retiring in June 1982. What, then, is this Reagan military buildup? It is a titanic engine of wanton waste to enforce a false frugality; a monstrous maw for devouring the domestic fisc, for devouring domestic governance, for devouring public hopes, for devouring the Public Thing, Res Publica, the Republic—a hideous crime within the larger crime of '81.

A reckless, careless, feckless economic menace, too, is this new wanton military spending juggernaut: consumer of savings and capital, supposedly so desperately needed; consumer of skilled labor, engineers, scientists, research facilities, the precious tools of enhanced productivity, supposedly so urgently needed. How little economics there is in all this Thermidorean economic babble! The Reaction, corrupt politics, rules all. "I can think of no priority higher for the nation's economic welfare than close and skeptical scrutiny of all new military expenditures to determine whether they are really needed." So economist Thurow urges, utterly in vain. We dwell in darkness. "Close and skeptical scrutiny" is reserved this Thermidorean season for determining whether a one-legged man can get a job as a night watchman and so be frugally deprived of his disability benefits.

And how is this vast, vile engine of waste received in Congress? A "warm welcome" greets it, so *Congressional Quarterly* reports. The $222.2 billion requested for fiscal 1982 "would appear to be sufficient," writes the chairman of the Armed Services Committee, one Melvin Price, to Budget Committee chairman Jones, but the $367 billion planned for fiscal 1986 may be—too little! The honorable Price fears the administration may be underestimating inflation and endangering the national security. The honorable Price does offer a word of advice. The Pentagon must not "appear" profligate, or the American people might take it amiss. Let Pentagon profligacy nonappear, disappear—by secrecy, concealments, by silencing Pentagon "whistle blowers"—patriots and precisians who cannot bear the ghastly sight of such wanton waste, by plans already afoot within the bowels of the Executive to turn the whole vast engine of waste into a single seamless secret of state beyond the scrutiny of the American people, for the crime of '81, the crime against our sovereignty, generates an endless stream of supporting crimes against our sovereignty.

On March 10, Congress receives Reagan's domestic budget message—an exercise in frugality truly odious in its cruelty, in its rank injustice, in its base and hideous hypocrisy. Student loans to be cut by $1.2 billion—a 9 percent reduction in hopes for a college education; medical care for the poor reduced by $500 million; school lunch and child nutrition programs reduced by $1.8 billion; aid to dependent children reduced by 13 percent; working mothers of three deprived of welfare benefits for earning a few thousand dollars a year; unemployment compensation reduced; home mortgage loans reduced—this by a President who talks so lovingly of the "American dream"; the disabled subjected to harsh new eligibility requirements; the minimum Social Security benefit—$122 a month on the average—eliminated for 3 million people; public housing cut so drastically that existing housing may rot from demoralizing neglect; the food stamp program reduced by $2.3 billion—an 11 percent reduction adversely affecting 22 million Americans; the Legal Services Corporation to be wiped out entirely, a savings of $321.3 million to deprive the poor of fair trials and leave them to the caprice of welfare bureaucrats—this by a President who endlessly inveighs against the evils of bureaucracy.

The poor are financing the Navy's three fisc-squandering nuclear carriers. That is the long and the short of it. The waning hopes of poor working people for a home of their own or college for a child will finance the Bradley Fighting Vehicle. Small farmers will lose their family farms to pay for the B-1 bomber; hunger and homelessness will defray the salaries of the Pentagon's 75,000 needless new civilian employees. The domestic realm will be devoured to finance the warfare state, to fatten the great military-industrial clients of Oligarchy, whose political action committees pour wealth into the hands of party leaders.

The very laws of the land are debauched in this March 10 budget to feed the great engine of waste. "We will use the budget system to be the excuse to make major policy decisions," says James Watt, the new Secretary of the Interior, pure crystalline soul of the spite-ridden Right, subsidizing coal slurries and lumbering in the scenic public wilderness just to despoil what the "market" has not made. There are health laws, safety laws, environmental protection laws which the American people support and cherish, which the Right wants destroyed, is bent upon destroying under the cloak of the new false frugality. "Would you be willing to bring EPA to its knees?" the White House asks a prospective head of the Environmental Protection Agency early this year as Stockman contemplates a crippling 50 percent budget cut for the agency. Let us cut financing for the law enforcement arm of the EPA, of the Consumer Product Safety Commission, of the Occupational Safety and Health Administration, of every agency responsible for upholding laws we abhor and so repeal them *de facto* by nonenforcement. Do we not control the Executive? Let it then be our private legislature. Such is the rule of the Right. "A cruel hoax on the American people," Republican senator Robert Stafford protests; an illegal assault on the rule of law, yet another assault on government by consent of the governed, another crime within the crime of '81.

The die is cast; the plot is launched. All depends now on silencing the popular party, for this Reaganite quackery, cruelty and wanton waste, this debauching of justice and law, could not survive a week if the Democratic Party in the House of Representatives chose to shine the light of public inquiry hard upon it. Mere instruction would be obstruction. The fact of enduring deficits aborts the Reagan tax plan "right then and there," admits Stockman. The wanton profligacy of the arms buildup destroys the Reagan budget, brutally exposes its odious hypocrisy—and much else along with it. So Budget Committee chairman Jones is "desperately" eager, Stockman recalls, to make a deal with the White House: If he gives the President most of what he wants—harsh domestic frugality, profligate military waste, no questions asked—and Republican committee members join forces with him, "the left-wing Democrats would be isolated, hanging out on a limb with no place to go," Jones explains to the budget director.

The real crushing burden of collusion rests on the broad, beefy shoulders of the Democratic Speaker of the House, master of the "moratorium on criticism," and masterly, in truth, he is. What prodigies of care, what ceaseless diligence must our Speaker practice in order to save Reagan—a "ceremonial monarch," so Stockman calls him—from imminent political disaster. What an array of shifting pretexts, strategies and wiles must the Speaker deploy in order to convoy the crime of '81 safely through the Democratic House. Thus O'Neill explains to unhappy liberal Democrats—as one of them recalls years later—why it would be unwise for Democrats to "put forward alternatives" to the Reagan program: "Because then the focus would be on the alternatives, not on what was wrong with Reagan's plan." We can best "focus" on wrongs by endorsing them, says Tip, not really making an argument, but giving an order, a leadership command, tactfully wrapped in an emollient alibi, easing obedience and the pangs of betrayal. When Majority Leader Wright says in early March that even Republicans find the President's tax bill "inequitable," how smoothly does the Speaker quash this untoward breach in the moratorium. The President, he announces at once, will get a tax bill he "will be satisfied with," whereupon Rostenkowski proposes that any tax bill approved by Ways and Means must include a 29 percent reduction in taxes paid on unearned income by the richest people in America! So much for talk of equity, fellow Democrats. *That* well we have poisoned, Tip and I. That gun we have spiked. And through it all, day after day, Tip's lieutenants walk through Capitol Hill reminding Democrats they have been swept away and must, at all times, wear sackcloth and ashes.

How long can the Speaker and his adjutants maintain this delicate, perpetually endangered moratorium? The longer it must last, manifestly, the harder the task will grow. Speed is the ally of silence. On March 10, day of the budget message, "House Democrats convened an unprecedented caucus with Republican leaders," *Congressional Quarterly* reports, "and agreed to complete action on Reagan's entire program by the end of July." Let there be abbreviated hearings, constricted debate, general atmosphere of crisis and emergency, of juggernaut, invincible, presidential force—exactly what the White House wants and needs. The tax bill is secretly loathed by many an old-line Republican. The Speaker wants it "out of the way" by the August recess, out of the way before Wall Street begins to speak out against the huge income tax reduction, which it secretly fears; before Americans, cured of the hostage poisoning, begin asking how a $1.5 trillion arms buildup gets "federal spending under control," and how a trillion-dollar tax reduction balances the budget. Hot headlong haste in the enactment of the most momentous legislation of our time before common sense returns to a distraught and nerve-wracked commonwealth.

"Our enemy is time," says Stockman, and truly it is, for inflation is the grand public pretext for the crime of '81, the disease for which the crime is the proffered cure—"the miracle cure we were peddling," Stockman calls it. Should the Federal Reserve disinflate the economy before the great devouring of the fisc is enacted, enactment will be difficult indeed. So swiftly "out of the way" the Reagan program must be swept. Fixed dates and forced votes are promised by the Speaker, not without cautioning against the dangers of "legislating in haste," lest the press corps suspect, perhaps, that the Speaker is legislating in haste. No loose ends must dangle for objective journalism to tug at in its dim, pertinacious way.

A hitch develops, most infuriating for budgetmaker Jones. White House strategists reject his deal; they have enough southern Democratic votes, they believe, to pass the Reagan budget with every jot and tittle of false frugality intact. And why should they think otherwise? Does not the Speaker go around the Hill saying the President is an "irresistible force," that trying to defeat him in the House would be either impossible or "obstructive"? One or the other, catch-22, for the Speaker swivels about so rapidly these days there is scarce keeping up with him.

In any case, Jones must make up a purely Democratic budget. Shall we propose one that appeals to Reaganite southern lawmakers—"boll weevils," in the current cant? Why do that if the Speaker thinks winning against Reagan is either "obstructive" or impossible? Why not blast the whole Reagan budget fraud to smithereens? Demand an explanation, say, of neo–World War II; ask the Joint Chiefs what they think of it. Expose the whole barrage of Present Danger fear-monger lies adopted by Reagan: the "window of vulnerability," the "dangerous imbalance," the "unilateral disarming" of America during détente— "simplistic deceptions peddled with such zeal from high places," so McGeorge Bundy, former national security adviser, calls them. And smash the monstrous engine of waste. Save what is worth saving in the domestic budget; cut out the real waste and abuse, for waste and abuse there surely is. We could expose the cruel myth that spending on the poor is peculiarly "out of control" when it has not increased as a percentage of our national wealth one iota since 1972; the poor are already getting poorer with no apparent "benefit" to the economy. We could even produce a balanced budget this year, so David Obey of Wisconsin, the liberal passed over for the chairmanship, proposes. What a sharp revealing irony in that! The 1982 budget submitted by our deficit-hating, budget-balancing President has a deficit of $45 billion. Most likely such a Democratic budget would not pass the House this Thermidorean season, but it would be a moral victory, a victory of light over darkness, of truth over quackery, of genuine frugality over false, odious, hypocritical frugality.

Perish the thought! It must not be. We must produce a budget that holds on to our wandering "boll weevils," says Jones, backed by the leadership. A budget that can *win* against the Reagan budget. That is what the party needs! And the Budget Committee produces it on April 9. It provides for the single largest increase in military spending ever proposed in peacetime by the House and a $41.8 billion reduction in our "out of control" domestic spending. Darkness, momentarily threatened, has triumphed.

Now, surely, we will witness on Capitol Hill a mighty struggle for votes between Democrats supporting their winnable "conservative"

Boll Weevil budget and Republican supporters of the Reagan budget. The President, victim of an assassination attempt on March 30, telephones wavering Democratic legislators; Cabinet officials call upon them, and lobbyists and PAC-men and perhaps many a bagman as well. And what does the Democratic leadership do in this titanic budget struggle? "The Democrats, on the other hand, were uncharacteristically silent," the *New York Times* reports. "Instead of orchestrating a counterattack, the Speaker used the Easter recess to make a trip to Australia and New Zealand." He is halfway round the world for two weeks and more while the unilateral battle rages, tarrying a few extra days in Hawaii, just for good measure, before returning to Capitol Hill on April 27. Home at last, our Democratic Speaker of the House calls in the press to announce that the Democrats' *winnable* Boll Weevil budget has no chance of winning whatever and he has no intention of making a try.

"The morale of House Democrats plummeted" at the news that the Speaker "had thrown in the towel on the budget," *Congressional Quarterly* reports. "We have no game plan. We're just going to get killed. It's really pathetic," laments a House leadership whip. Does our good Speaker Tip want to "get killed" by the invincible juggernaut President? Do men desire the obvious consequence of their deeds? They do. So be it. Chairman Jones is furious; claims the Speaker's "perception" is "erroneous." The vote "will be very close," whines poor upstart chairman Jones, used by the Speaker to betray the liberals and now betrayed by the Speaker in turn. "We were behind maybe twenty votes when he started the press conference and then he announced we were behind by fifty votes. At that moment we fell behind by fifty votes," another Democrat laments.

Does the party, belatedly pulling itself together, use its enormous disciplinary powers on straying Boll Weevil lawmakers? "No effort was made to exploit redistricting, for example, through enlisting the aid of twenty-seven Democratic governors and twenty-eight Democratic legislatures," the *Times* reports on May 3. Does the Speaker *now* use the great powers of his office to win back wavering Boll Weevil lawmakers? "He gave them a free ride. He should have called them in and said, 'If you're not with us on this, don't come into my office and ask for anything.'" So yet another Democrat laments.

On May 7, the Reagan budget triumphs grandly in the Democratic House, 253 to 176; a "milestone" victory for Reagan, the press reports; a juggernaut is in the making, the Democrats are in "disarray"—sixty-three of them have deserted to the President's banner. "Tip O'Neill has become Ronald Reagan's secret weapon," William Safire of the *Times* writes a few days later, has become "a boon to Republicans seeking to portray the Democratic Party as a listless hulk," and a demoralizing spectacle to Democrats, who feel "profoundly embarrassed," so Safire reports, "at the amateurish leadership of the man they used to call the Old Pro."

And is he not the Old Pro still? Is he not a Speaker of the House at the very height and crest of his powers, beautifully managing events and appearances? Does the crime of '81 not require political darkness? Then what was more needful than Jones's *winnable* Boll Weevil budget shedding darkness over everything? Does the crime of '81 not require an invincible juggernaut President—associated "with a planned string of successes," as Darman puts it in February? Then what was more needful than wandering aimlessly around the world like a "listless hulk," appearing "amateurish," miscounting floor votes, looking the very picture of an oaf and a blockhead? What does the unflattering picture matter to the Speaker? There is no petty vanity or petty pride in you, sublime Tip, but something of antique virtue in thy selfless devotion to party power and to the loyal doing of whatever is needful, no matter how base, for its prosperity and enhancement!

12.

THE DEED IS DONE

A week has passed since House Democrats achieved, by strenu-
ous feats of clownishness, a resounding legislative defeat.
Now, quite suddenly in mid-May, Democratic leaders declare
themselves "upset," humiliated, hurt by the loss, eager for revenge. "In
the wake of their May 7 defeat," *Congressional Quarterly* notes,
Democratic leaders are determined to "win" a victory over Reagan on
the great question of taxes—a "face-saving tax victory," the leadership
calls it, tossing aside its sackcloth and abruptly donning fighting
armor. We Democrats will do whatever it takes to "pass" a Democratic
tax bill, vows Rostenkowski. "That at least in my training is the final
measure of any proposal." No longer does Speaker Tip fear Reaganite
invincibility, nor Democratic "obstructiveness," nor yet removing the
"focus" from "what was wrong with Reagan's plan." What is wrong
with Reagan's tax plan has grown all too apparent by mid-May, so
apparent it stands on the verge of collapse, requires desperate White
House lying about its own budget forecasts, requires, most of all, the
Speaker's supreme feat of "cooperation" with the rule of the Right.

The chief difficulty, no doubt, is the business community's deep
silent loathing of the President's huge, 30 percent reduction in the
personal income tax—"Kemp-Roth" in congressional parlance; supply-side economics in general, which business leaders regard as a
fraud and a hoax, "an economic theory based on alchemy," says Peter
Solomon of Lehman Brothers, the great New York banking house,

alas, not until this coming October, corporate lips being sealed this spring by a sordid bargain. The "business community" will keep its collective mouth shut about the fantasy of "revenue feedback"; about the near certainty that people will spend, not save, their tax-reduction money; about the near certainty, too, of large and dangerous budget deficits. In return for silent corporate mouths, the administration has agreed to support a massive reduction in the corporate income tax—$500 billion over ten years, 80 percent of which will go to the largest one-tenth of 1 percent of American corporations, "the biggest single tax break in American history"—hush money, more accurately—achieved chiefly by means of a highly accelerated tax write-off of depreciating plants, buildings and equipment. In return for silence over the quackery and menace of Kemp-Roth, the White House champions of the "free market" will avert their eyes from the fact that the corporate tax cut favors investment in shopping centers, commercial buildings and corporate mergers—what the U.S. economy needs least; favors Big Business at its most inept—"social security for the disabled large corporation," economic historian Emma Rothschild calls it; makes good investments bad and bad investments good; comprises, therefore, one of the most massive intrusions into the "free market" ever contemplated by the federal government—about which intrusion the "free market" champions within the White House and their "conservative" allies without will keep *their* collective mouths shut. Thus are we governed in the Age of Reaction—by silence, lies and collusion.

Nevertheless, the "business community," though silent, can still make its qualms heard, and in places not unstrategic. The March 23 issue of *Fortune* tears Kemp-Roth to shreds; notes that "revenue feedback" figures being peddled by Reagan officials look like a fantasy to "most economists"; quotes with deadly effect a budget office economist who says that the White House espouses supply-side economics only because "we had to justify the tax cut" to old-line Republicans frightened of budget deficits. Poor old-line Republican senators—"the College of Cardinals," Stockman calls them. They sit paralyzed between opposing terrors: the terror of defying the President, for there is party power out there—direct-mail agitators, New Right thugs, Reaganite zealots ready, nay eager, to punish Republican oligarchs who undermine the rule of the Right. Terror, contrariwise, of huge budget deficits against which they have been inveighing all their political lives. "They're very cagey about what they say about Kemp-Roth," Stockman confides to a *Washington Post* editor in mid-April. "Privately, they're scathing, some of these guys." For nobody seriously believes—though there is much make-believing—in Reagan's promise of a balanced budget in 1984, for even in Thermidorean darkness common sense, it seems, cannot be utterly mocked. In the year 1984, so *Congressional Quarterly* estimates, the federal government's annual revenue, after the Tax Act, would be poorer by $150 billion. The military would be spending perhaps $100 billion more than it is currently spending—a $250 billion deficit in the year of the balanced budget, to be made up how? And if "revenue feedback" is a confidence trick to "justify the tax cut" and the ensuing deficits, then what are the deficits for? The question hangs in the spring air of the capital like Damocles' sword, while Rostenkowski, of the brass forehead, talks privately with White House officials from April 9 to June 1 about a possible tax compromise, conducting his own little moratorium-on-criticism despite endless White House "rebuffs."

On April 30, however, the *New York Times,* our good gray "newspaper of record," most resoundingly supplies the answer to the hanging question. The Kemp-Roth tax plan is no plan for economic recovery, but a scheme, productive of "horrendous deficits" concocted "for those who want most of all to shrink the federal government." So the truth is out. A light, eminently respectable, shines in the political darkness, a journalistic light owing nothing to the ruling politicians, a journalistic rarity, revealing perhaps more than anything else how terrified of the reckless Right are the great financial interests of New York.

Three days after the resounding editorial, the *New York Times Magazine* carries a deadly critique of the entire Reagan tax plan by economist Thurow. To arguments already made by *Fortune* (and elsewhere in freer, pre-Reagan days) Thurow notes that the proposed reduction from 70 percent to 50 percent in the maximum tax on unearned income—an "incentive" for the rich upon which Reagan and Rostenkowski wholeheartedly agree—will not encourage "productive" investment, but more tax shelters and real estate speculation: gross economic folly pitilessly conjoined to gross economic privilege. For consider this: The Reagan-Rostenkowski bonanza for "those who save and invest" lowers the tax paid by millionaire idlers to a level *below* the maximum rate paid by a laboring hind toiling for $12,000 a year to support a family of four.

Injustice and folly odiously conjoined—the injustice truly brutal and coarse, virtual "class warfare," historian Arthur Schlesinger calls it on the pages of the *Wall Street Journal* in early June. What the President describes as "an equal reduction in everyone's taxes" is sharply unequal in its result. According to the Treasury Department, some 35 percent of the total reduction will go to the wealthiest 5 percent of the country, which already enjoys a 16 percent cut in taxes— with no visible economic benefit to the nation, as if that mattered to anyone—from the "millionaires' relief act" of 1978. A mere 9 percent of the total reduction goes to the lower half of the population, whose tax burden has *increased* 50 percent since the triumph of "trickledown" in 1978. The combination of tax cuts and budget cuts will eventually make the richest one million households richer by more than $8,000 a year and the poorest 19 million households poorer by $390 a year—a willful deepening of inequality in America. Industrial countries with less inequality of income have more productive economies than those with greater inequality of income, so the Joint Economic Committee of Congress reports in 1982 after Reagan and the popular party combine to carry economic babble to victory over the principle of equality and the citizen-idea.

The public is skeptical of the tax cut, so Wirthlin's subtle polls reveal. Wall Street, that great mythic "money power," stands, for the nonce, on the side of justice. Surely, with such an ally justice will triumph! On May 13, the stock market falls into disarray after the Senate votes 78 to 20 in favor of Reagan's budget. Senate Republicans are still paralyzed by opposing fears. In mid-May, Senator Dole's Finance Committee still cannot muster a majority in support of the President's tax plan, which is meeting "increased congressional skepticism," *Congressional Quarterly* reports. One hard shove from House Democrats and the tax plan is finished, the crime of '81 aborted. One long instructive series of public hearings; a lining up of the leading "conservative" economists in the country—Alan Greenspan, Milton Friedman, Arthur Burns, Murray Weidenbaum, the President's chief economic adviser, each one a disbeliever in supply-side quackery—a lining up, too, of brokers, bankers, Business Roundtable, breaking the vow of silence, and supply-side quackery and its White House peddlers will stand exposed to light and truth, would die of the exposure. The fisc would not be gutted; the government would not be paralyzed; the public realm not shrunk, the popular party not liberated from popular demands and expectations. A demagogue would stand exposed as the smiling mask for shark's teeth and shark's motives.

The shark's teeth are showing all too clearly already. On May 12, the administration, clumsily overreaching itself, proposes sharp reductions in Social Security benefits. The average worker who expects to retire at age sixty-two in January 1982 would find his monthly benefit reduced from $373 to $247—the rich shall devour the fisc and enforced frugality shall gnaw away, ratlike, at the laboring hinds. Shark's teeth are already rending the Republic, so eager and vengeful is the Right in power after so many years in the wilderness. Swiftly and steadily, the Reagan Executive cuts itself off from the press and the people. Telephone calls for public information are suddenly given short shrift. Press briefings become so grudging, notes one veteran reporter, that a State Department spokesman says "no comment" and "I can't say" more than thirty times in the course of one forty-five-minute session. Scholars discover that government documents, routinely available in the past, are available no longer. Information coming out of the Executive is being reduced to a "trickle," so the *Post* reports in June. Pentagon officials are warned that the polygraph test—which accuses the guilty and the innocent alike, an instrument of terror, not detection—will be used to identify those who "leak" information to the press. How this President hates "leaks"! They "have the capacity to rouse the President from his customary passivity," says a reporter who has followed Reagan for years. They "make our work more difficult by stimulating inquiries about the subject matters mentioned," says a Reagan official. Inquiry is not to be borne; why should the government tolerate the snooping of the governed?

In late April, the White House declares a moratorium on the preparation and dissemination of government publications in the name of the new frugality. "Elimination of wasteful spending on government periodicals" inaugurates a program of concentrating inside the White House, under cover of executive privilege, unprecedented presidential control—and constriction—of public information, *our* information, without which "popular government," warned James Madison, "is but a prologue to a farce, or a tragedy, or perhaps to both"—regarded by Ed Meese, current triumvir and future Attorney General, as "government property," just as he regards the American Civil Liberties Union as a "criminals' lobby," so he says in a speech delivered this May.

Whatever can be hidden the administration hides. Under the direction of the White House the agencies of the Executive Branch evade public accountability provisions of the Administrative Procedure Act. New regulations are issued as mere "guidelines" so that the public need not be notified. Existing regulations are altered by secret internal memoranda, not without danger of public exposure. The Freedom of Information Act, noble child of the democratic awakening, poses the danger, for it gives a sovereign, self-governing people the power "to force the federal bureaucracy to disgorge rulings made without public scrutiny and documents more politically embarrassing than secret," so conservative Safire points out this May in defense of the act. But how costly it is! The White House is appalled by the expense to the taxpayer: one two-hundredth of the Bradley Fighting Vehicles *per year.* This is intolerable. "Freedom of information is not cost-free," says an Assistant Attorney General in charge of abridging our freedom of information. It interferes with "efficient government," which requires unfreedom of information and much else besides. Accordingly, in late April and early May, William French Smith, an old crony of Reagan's and now Attorney General, issues new guidelines designed to weaken the act and strengthen bureaucracy's power of concealment. The candidate who promised to "get government off the people's back" is determined, as

President, to get the American people off their government's back. And, with utter contempt for his own solemn avowals, to clamp government more tightly on the back of the people. In early April, the White House proposes a "National Recipient Information System" to keep files on 20 million Americans who receive a government benefit of some kind; and, some weeks later, an FBI "Interstate Identification Index" of 40 million Americans with an arrest record—this from a President who two years before had warned against "Big Brother government" keeping "a tab" on the American people. Throughout this busy Thermidorean spring, moreover, the White House is quietly negotiating with the House and the Senate Intelligence Committee over a proposed executive order authorizing the Central Intelligence Agency, for the first time in its history, to spy on the American people—an abuse of presidential power uncovered in the democratic awakening and now to be disabused by making it legal, or, more accurately, by squaring it with the party oligarchs in Congress. "The opening of a Pandora's box with respect to the enhanced opportunities of the intelligence community to intrude into the private lives of American citizens," warns Admiral Stansfield Turner, Carter's Central Intelligence director, and so, in due course, it turns out.

In the midst of these private, undebated negotiations—for what is debated these days?—and casting an ominous light upon them, the President who wants to "get government off the people's back" pardons two high FBI officials convicted last year of violating the "right of the people to be secure in their persons, houses, papers and effects, against unreasonable searches and seizures," having ordered warrantless break-ins of war protesters' homes. The two criminal officials "acted on high principles to bring an end to the terrorism that was threatening our nation," the White House proclaims on April 15. But is the Fourth Amendment not a high principle, a principle of liberty among the highest? So the ACLU asks the White House, which duly supplies an answer published this May 15 in the *Post*. It is a stern reminder to Meese's "criminals' lobby" of the President's "sworn duty to preserve and protect the national security of the United States." Behold! The American Republic has a new presidential oath of office, an oath rewritten for the careless, truthless man in the White House, who not four months ago stood before the grand sweep of the Mall and took his oath to "preserve, protect and defend the Constitution of the United States" and nothing more "basic" than the Constitution, nor "higher" than the Constitution, but it and it alone. The White House has rewritten the oath to make it a shambles, for the difference between the Framers' oath and the Reaganite oath is precisely this: that the former subjects the President to the laws—was this not the "lesson" of Watergate?—and the latter, Watergate-amended, subjects the law to the President. The entire Reagan era of lawlessness and tyranny lies prefigured in that oath so contemptuously redacted. And in Reagan's request that Congress abolish the office of special prosecutor and so put the new criminal regime out of reach of the law.

Thus, at the very moment when the crime of '81 stands on the verge of extinction, a tyranny of shysters and sharks is rapidly taking shape in the Executive Branch, bent upon liberating itself from the people, the press and the laws, bent upon extending its sway *over* the people, the press and the laws, a blessing for the Reaction and the restoration of Oligarchy, though a blessing, be it noted, far from unmixed. Rank and reckless is this rule of the Right, full of factional fury stored up in the wilderness years, requiring restraint and tempering, requiring, above all, the sharpest possible reminder that the interests of Oligarchy are paramount always. On May 20, the Republican Senate fires a shot across the bow of the White House. A "sense of the Senate" vote is taken on the President's Social Security proposal; the tally is 96–0 against Reagan—an extraordinary vote, a "débâcle" the press calls it, a "rebuff," a warning that Oligarchy, without the slightest dissent, in the very midst of a presidential "honeymoon," at the very height of the President's popularity, will not sacrifice its interests one iota to suit the President and the vindictive faction he has brought into power along with him.

The warning shot fired and presumably taken to heart (although the triumvirate's "line" for Reagan the next morning, recorded in a memorandum, is that the Social Security proposal was "only submitted to Hill in response to a request from a congressional committee"), the pressing question of the hour is: How can the President's tax plan be saved? The Speaker, guileful Tip, walkabout Tip, master of his craft, has provided the answer: We Democrats must "win" a "face-saving tax victory." Let us not talk of deficits; let us match the President dollar for dollar in pursuit of a legislative "victory." "We have the votes. Can [Reagan] take them away from us?" says Speaker Tip, "listless" no longer, breathing defiance. Let us not talk of injustice, unfairness, of coarse, brutal "class warfare," of gross privilege dispensed to the privileged. Let us in pursuit of "victory" offer even greater tax favors for corporations, more brazen tax favors for the rich—estate-tax reductions, gift-tax reductions, retirement accounts for the affluent, tax exemptions for oil operators, tax breaks for truckers, scores of tax concessions to scores of narrow special interests— "a battle of the tax cut," *Congressional Quarterly* calls it, a rivalry between White House and Ways and Means Democrats to see who can gut the fisc more deeply, who can offer more favors to the favored. "An amazing spectacle," *Congressional Quarterly* reports on June 27, "Democrats trying to outbid Republicans for the affections of the business community"—a bidding war, so-called, led by Rostenkowski, determined to "win" whatever the price, such is his "training," who "did it with the assent of the entire leadership. I think it's one of the most insidious moves I've seen." So a liberal New York Democrat named Richard Ottinger tells a *New York Times* reporter in January 1984, on the eve of abandoning politics, out of disgust with his party's three-year collusion with Reagan.

Yet strange to relate of this furious fight to win: The Democrats have not the slightest desire actually to win. Why, after all, should they take the blame for the great fisc-devouring deficits to come? So, in the midst of this titanic "bidding war" to gain the votes, ostensibly, of straying southern Democrats, "top Democratic leaders," reports *Congressional Quarterly,* "continue to strongly oppose disciplining party members who might stray from the fold." Is this not an odd way to pursue a face-saving victory? Majority Leader Wright attends a "closed-door forum meeting" of conservative southern Democrats "to tell its members he will protect their right to vote as they choose." Odder yet! Party discipline, says a leadership aide, "is not being applied nor is there even talk of it being applied." In a word, the great "face-saving tax victory" struggle is a complete and utter sham, a sham so gross House leaders feel compelled to supply an alternative explanation to satisfy the more cynical. We are trying to "broaden our financial base," say leadership spokesmen to sundry pundits, party operators and Capitol Hill onlookers. We are "tailoring" our "legislative strategy to woo corporate donors," says a Democratic Party official. House leaders "felt they had to bid for corporate money," a Democratic fugleman later explains.

Yet strange to relate, this furious truckling to "corporate donors," this proffering of tens of billions in tax-break bribes brings next to nothing to the party coffers. For even the sordid commercial excuse for the "bidding war" is just another party lie, as false as the "face-saving tax victory." Two layers of lies, a palimpsest, to obscure the appalling truth: The House Democrats have launched the "bidding war" with Reagan in order to save Reagan's tax bill at the moment of crisis, to save the devouring of the fisc, the shrinking of the public realm, the crime of '81 and the shyster tyranny behind it. This is a motive so base that selling legislative favors at auction sounds innocent beside it, for commercial republics, alas, accept commercial excuses, and economics often becomes, for that reason, the first refuge of scoundrels in America.

On July 29, Reagan's tax reduction plan, now larger and unfairer than it was before, carries the House by a vote of 238 to 196. The *New York Times* editorial this morning speaks the mournful truth: "The Democrats had their chance for glory by exposing the economic fallacies and risks in the President's plan. Instead they pursued him over the same cliff. . . . They spent wildly to pass their bill rather than his. For every tax break the White House offered the rich and powerful, the Democrats offered one of their own, sometimes two. . . . The Great Tax Cut of 1981 assures a yawning federal deficit and another rampage through federal programs to try to offset it." But the price of "glory" would have been steep: the end of the Reaction, quite likely. The prospective profits of baseness seem great: party power fortified and restored under the forthcoming reign of false frugality, political paralysis and popular government relentlessly besieged. Truly, the ambitions of oligarchies are as pitiless as the passions of princes.

13.
SECRET LAW

In the midst of the "bidding war," a House Commerce subcommittee issues a report, momentous in its way, concerning "issues which are of paramount historic importance," issues that "go to the very nature of presidential authority," says the report's introduction, dated July 8, written by Representative John Dingell of Michigan, chairman of the House Commerce and Energy Commission, a man of power and ability, not to be trifled with, nor a trifler himself.

The report is dry and difficult—"an analysis of constitutional issues that may be raised by Executive Order 12291"—prepared for the committee by the American Law Division of the Library of Congress. No member of Congress, however, can mistake or misunderstand the gist of it. On February 17, President Reagan signed an executive order bestowing upon his office control over the implementing of laws, the "rule-making power," which Congress delegates exclusively to the heads of government agencies. Henceforth, under the new order the President's agents in the Office of Management and Budget can veto—in secret—any regulation needed to implement a law if in their private opinion its "potential costs" outweigh its "potential benefits"—the new cost-benefit quackery ensconced in the very heart of the government. No such "centralized mechanism for presidential management of agency rule-making" has ever existed in this country, notes the report, not unsternly. It is a system "without precedent," without constitutional warrant—how lightly does the Constitution sit upon our dozing, glozing, truthless President!—without sanction by any act or intent of Congress, a clear violation of its fundamental intent in the matter: the Administrative Procedure Act of 1946, which "specifically contradicts and precludes the administrative scheme established by the order." The order, in short, is a sweeping act of usurpation, "an unconstitutional act of executive legislation in violation of the separation of powers principle"—a "power grab," so a White House official cheerfully calls it.

And what power does it bestow on the Office of Management and Budget and its new suboffice of "regulatory affairs"? "If you're the toughest kid on the block, most kids won't pick a fight with you. The Executive order establishes things quite clearly," in contrast to timid Carter merely offering White House advice to executive agencies. So James Miller III, first "regulatory affairs" head, brags in the March/April issue of *Regulation.* The February fiat makes "OMB the most powerful agency in the government," says one Jim Tozzi, a Budget Office bureaucrat since Nixon's day, reportedly chief drafter of the order, along with Stockman and Miller—co-conspirators of "economic efficiency," *summum bonum* of the Right, of America as "just one big business." There isn't "anything," says Tozzi, "compared to that power," a power so great that lowly clerks unknown to Congress, desk officers, so-called, can bend Cabinet officers to their will. And General Haig wonders why Ed Meese, the triumvir, dares take a seat at the Cabinet table! His clerks' clerks deal with Cabinet officials, override their experts, rescind their rules, tell them how and when and whether to carry out their rule-making duties, get them rebuked in court for violating the law, as the Secretary of Labor is rebuked this very June 17 for imposing cost-benefit analysis on a law that forbids it. Why is OMB, the operative force, not called into court? Because "I don't leave fingerprints," boasts Tozzi, who wields OMB's power over the telephone, leaving behind only unrecorded threats.

Cost-benefit quackery, now raised to equality with the law, is a hoax as a matter of course, a mere pretext for gutting laws which the Right does not like, for "of course this isn't benefit-cost analysis," says Tozzi. "We're just here to represent the President," whose *will* to "deregulate" sets law aside. When a Reaganite economist at EPA refuses to falsify the "costs" of the Clean Air Act, the agency chief, one Anne Gorsuch, has him fired, because, says a colleague, "Gorsuch thought it should have been obvious to him what the President wanted." Not probity but Cooked Bookkeeping in the service of lawless power. This July, Ralph Nader tries through the Freedom of Information Act to obtain OMB's cost-benefit documents—"if indeed they exist," he adds in an angry letter to Stockman—but Nader tries in vain. "Executive privilege" cloaks the whole operation, conceals it even from Congress. The order, says Dingell, "allows green-eyeshaded OMB officials to manipulate cost-benefit numbers behind closed doors." Allows them in secret to decide that human life is worth as little as $22,500—so Dingell reports in 1985—a "potential benefit" so paltry that lifesaving is far outweighed by the cost of not killing Americans with toxic sludge and cancer-causing chemicals. It allows the OMB, our champions of "economic efficiency," to decide by ignorant fiat this September of 1981 that informing workers about the chemicals they handle will save only 400 lives, not 4,000, as agency experts contend, thereby leaving hundreds of thousands of people in dangerous and deadly ignorance. It allows the OMB this summer—operating through the Department of Transportation—to reinterpret a law so that almost no investigation of defective cars will ever lead to their mandatory recall. It allows the OMB to nullify in secret—public knowledge being deemed "contrary to the public interest"—a law ensuring fair employment for Vietnam War veterans. It allows the freedmen of the imperial palace—operating through the Department of Agriculture—to declare ketchup a vegetable and so curtail "out-of-control spending" on child nutrition; allows them to eliminate preventive medicine for 2 million poor children on the grounds that an ounce of prevention is *not* worth a pound of cure. Common humanity made a different cost-benefit analysis, but common humanity is not a shyster. It is likely that the OMB lies behind the campaign begun in secret this March to throw $2 billion worth of cripples off the disability rolls by declaring that, among other secret redefinitions, psychotics who can boil water are "employable" and so can be thrown to the wolves. The new order allows cruelty, brutality, pettiness and spite to course like an underground sewer through the entire Executive Branch.

In the space of twelve months, the new order saps and weakens civil rights laws, labor laws, mine safety laws, worker safety laws; gives OMB a grip of steel over the Environmental Protection Agency, casts the environmental laws into virtual limbo, prompting a young conservative lawyer at the agency to quit his job in "a matter of weeks," after finding what he called the "conservative approach to the implementation of laws" a chimera. The actual "approach" includes a warning to every regional EPA office that "every case you do refer" for enforcement will "be a black mark against you."

Trafficking in favors at the White House is openly practiced under this new lawless "executive legislation," openly promised, openly proclaimed. If you can't get satisfaction at an agency, says a White House official to a Chamber of Commerce gathering, why, just come to the White House and we will see that thy will is done. See that Dow Chemical this very June is not described in an EPA regional report as "the major, if not the only source" of contaminated water in the Saginaw Bay area, the phrase being deleted by order of—Dow, backed by the White House. See that a coal-mining rule is postponed indefinitely "after a secret meeting between OMB and the American Mining Congress," so a colleague of Dingell's remarks at a hearing this June 19. See that our auto industry does not have to pretreat its vast production of toxic sludge, which ends by poisoning rivers and streams and underground water, the pretreatment rule, four years in the making, being revoked without notice or warning by the White House this April 5, just three days after going into effect. "Access for the auto industry has improved," notes the *Wall Street Journal,* "some would say in an almost revolutionary way."

Revolutionary, indeed, is the power of a President's clerks to dispense multimillion-dollar favors in secret, a tyrant's power, nothing less, grossly abused already, as what tyrant's power is not? "If President Reagan's efforts to reform regulation are seen simply as a set of favors for corporations, a new wave of anti-business populist sentiment may develop in the 1980's," a frightened champion of deregulation warns this summer. The warning is well founded, for despite the tides of inflation, despite the official triumph of corporate quackery, despite the President's urgent appeals for deregulation, the American people's deep conviction that the health, safety and environmental laws are high public goods remains wondrously unshaken. "A large majority of the public believe that government regulations and requirements are worth the extra costs they add to products and services," Gallup reports this June. Only 22 percent of the country, the Chamber of Commerce reports in November, want the laws relaxed to encourage economic growth.

How stupid and incorrigible is this national rabble, as exasperating to the economic Right as once it had been to the economic Left. It refuses to live exclusively in the "economy," cannot see America as "one big business," still lives in the American Republic, still judges of things, however weakly, dimly, sporadically, by the republican standard, so fatal to the ambitions of the Right, so detested, therefore, by the Right. "Government is seen as the defender of the little guy against powerful and uncontrollable forces. Even those who are generally opposed to regulation will support regulations seen as providing protection against powerful forces that an individual could not otherwise control." So reports the judicious *National Journal Opinion Outlook Briefing Paper,* Volume 1, Number 19, this August 24. The American people are almost universally unwilling, says a *Briefing Paper* some months later, "to transfer power to business." Unwilling to do exactly what the Right, above all else, wants done, has waited fifty years in the wilderness for the chance to get done?

The Freedom of Information Act must, perforce, be gutted outright. This summer the administration prepares the "Freedom of Information Improvement Act of 1981," which will "improve" the act by destroying its power to reveal the debauching of laws protecting "the little guy" from those "powerful and uncontrollable forces" the Right wants to make more powerful and uncontrollable than ever. This summer, too, the OMB plans deep, destructive budget cuts—for do we not have deficits to reduce?—in programs that monitor environmental conditions, in programs for gathering social statistics, programs for measuring compliance with the laws. For why should the rabble find out the effects upon *them* of our liberation of capital from

the laws they cherish? There is so much yet to be done! Public dissemination of public information must be brought under "cost-benefit"
veto; the first steps have been taken this June by the tireless, relentless
OMB. The pettifogging federal courts must somehow be kept from
"unconstitutionally dubious and unwise intrusions into the legislative
domain," warns Attorney General Smith, lest they bar *our* unconstitutional invasion of the legislative domain. Dissenting officials must be
silenced somehow; already tens of thousands of officials are secretly
signing agreements subjecting them to lifetime government censorship
of anything they write related in any way to "sensitive compartmentalized information," Carter's bad seed blossoming far beyond the confines of the CIA. A fruitful idea is this of subjugation to censorship by
contract, not lost on the OMB. Thousands of people do social
research in America with government grants; study old-age programs,
computers in school, housing vouchers, pesticides, levels of pollution,
effects of malnourishment; ten thousand and one things that reflect
well or ill upon government policies and the conditions of society.
Why should they be free to publish at will with our money? What
does academic freedom, so-called, mean to us? Let them be compelled, says the budget office, to agree, by contract, not to publish
their findings anywhere, in any way, until a government official
approves it for "accuracy of factual data and interpretation": ignorant
power dictating to impotent knowledge; censorship without precedent
in our history, for the rabble must not be permitted to judge for themselves the costs and the benefits of "economic efficiency"—our Baal,
our Golden Calf, our holy talisman. It is by "economic efficiency,"
standard supreme, that we, the Right, judge the American people—
and find them unfit for self-government.

Thus matters are proceeding at the White House when the powerful head of a powerful committee warns his colleagues that a perilous
usurpation has taken place before their eyes, "of paramount historical
importance," in violation of the Constitution, the laws and the pre-
rogatives of Congress, creating an engine of secret power that can be
used—and is being used—to dispense corrupt privilege to powerful
special interests; which can be used—and is being used—to nullify

laws enacted by overwhelming congressional majorities, laws supported at this very moment by overwhelming popular majorities. Will the
Democratic House, which only last year demanded a *greater* voice for
Congress, the courts and the people in regulatory affairs, rise up
against this brazen act of "executive legislation"? Will it champion the
just sentiments of the people, give voice to their abiding "populist"
fear of private economic power?

The answer is—silence; sovereign silence. The report concerning
issues "of paramount historic importance" falls into the public realm
as noiselessly as a pebble falling into a bottomless well. The Reaction
prevails over all. No mere committee chairman can stand against it.
The smiling mask will not be torn from the White House tyranny.
The budget office will not be checked in its course, will pursue it ever
more avidly year after year. Most of all, worst of all, the republican
sentiments of the country will not be championed—not by Oligarchy
serving itself. Better Reaganite tyranny under our checkrein than
republicanism revived. Thus Power, unslumbering, calculates.

"What we are witnessing," says a spokesman for the ACLU this
autumn, "is a systematic assault on the concept of government
accountability and deterrence of illegal government conduct." True
enough, but "we," the people, alas, are witnessing nothing, for the
powerful keep their own counsel and cloak with their silence the systematic assault.

14.
REAGAN TOTTERING

On December 18, five Senate Republicans, troubled men all, meet with the President at the White House—Baker, Majority Leader; Domenici, Budget Committee chairman; Dole, Finance Committee chairman; Hatfield of Oregon, Appropriations Committee chairman; and Paul Laxalt, presidential crony, the Republican leaders' friend at the imperial court. A feud-ridden court it is, raging beyond Reagan's feeble control, the triumvirs squabbling among themselves, the triumvirate at war with Haig, the feuding fought out in leaks and counterleaks to the press, mocking "the carefully crafted profile of a tough President," says *Newsweek,* just as bumbling Reagan press conferences "shot through with errors of fact" mock the "carefully crafted profile," mock it so thoroughly that by now the National Savior of February last, the juggernaut of August last, has "got to convince people," says a senior aide, "that he has the ability to lead and that he's in charge of his own White House."

Reagan's faltering leadership, his decline in public esteem, his weakening grip on the electorate—the all-important grip, without which disaster looms for the Reaction—lie implicit, unspoken, behind the topic at hand: Reagan's forthcoming budget, second installment of the "Reagan Revolution." An election-year budget it is, fraught with immense political danger; a recession-year budget, too, for 9.4 million Americans are out of work this December 1981, factories are falling idle, the good jobs are vanishing, "traditional family breadwinners" are out on the streets, bewildered and frightened.

The new budget has got to look "compassionate," warns Dole. No defense cuts, no food stamp cuts. The Pentagon cannot simply devour the poor a second time around. The "frontal assault on the welfare state" is utterly out of the question. The others agree, Laxalt included, but they warn and plead in vain. Defense cuts are not to be thought of: Every dollar of the $1.5 trillion figure plucked out of thin air has been forced upon us by our adversaries, says Reagan. Behind the wall of obstinacy is the simple truth: "The President," says Stockman, "didn't have it in him to overrule his Secretary of Defense."

Something must be done about the deficits—another reason to cut defense spending. Mr. President, says Senator Pete Domenici, you are going to pile up in three years a greater addition to the national debt than Johnson, Nixon, Ford and Carter combined: $150 billion is forecast for fiscal 1984, ostensible year of the balanced budget; $170 billion for fiscal 1986, even assuming five years of unexampled prosperity, so Stockman estimates in early November. Deficits huge, unprecedented—and growing, "a massive fiscal disorder," Stockman calls it. A tax increase is imperative, the Republican leaders warn Reagan. Alas, raising taxes fills Reagan with dread. "If our critics heard about it they'd be jumping for joy," he had said at an earlier meeting. The idea of a tax increase—and joyful critics—robs Reagan of his sleep, he complains to Deaver. What, then, is to be done about the deficits? Wait for revenue feedback, says the President. But there is no revenue feedback! How often has Stockman said this? To no avail. Besides, the President doesn't believe in pessimistic forecasts. He believes in "optimism." But the forecast includes the most optimistic assumptions, "supply side" triumphant. How can pessimism include optimism? Reagan cannot understand this.

"Go with your instincts, Mr. President," Treasury Secretary Donald Regan has told him. "These big deficit numbers you are getting are just forecasts anyway." Flight is the President's "instinct." Feckless toadying is Regan's. The "massive fiscal disorder" is bitter to contemplate, dangerous to deal with; sweet and effortless is the fantasy of feedback. The Republican leaders troop out of the White House, danger unaverted, defeated by escapism posing as unshakable faith and by weakness posing as strength.

What a burden upon Oligarchy is this President, a burden almost unbearable when the President's budget reaches Capitol Hill this February 8, 1982.

Stunning, shocking, brutal, a savage affront to justice is this second installment of the "Reagan Revolution." The military buildup, like a ravening beast, eats through the fisc once more: The White House wants a $43.4 billion increase in Pentagon spending authority for fiscal 1983. We are at the $258 billion level now; $116 billion more than the Pentagon commanded a mere two years ago; senseless, wanton engine of waste, grinding away in the midst of unheard-of triple-digit deficits, a proposal so outrageous "it came under heavy fire from prominent conservatives . . . and from liberals," *Congressional Quarterly* reports. Senator Ernest Hollings of South Carolina, ardent arms buildup campaigner of 1979, calls for a one-year freeze in defense spending and a 3 percent increase thereafter. "When hawks like me are talking about cutting military spending you know something is in the wind," says Senator William Armstrong, a Colorado Republican.

And how shall the military Moloch be fed? On last year's cruel diet: the poor, the ill, the handicapped, the schools, local services, student loans, enforcement of laws—$43.4 billion of "deficit-reduction," exact counterbalance to the military's deficit *production*. A lying budget as well, forecasting declining deficits, "out-and-out cooked," says Stockman, believed by nobody in Congress, a political prop for "feedback," for Reagan, for declining public faith in the President's word. A pariah budget is this brutal Reagan budget, has "virtually no support" in the House, is "criticized almost universally" on Capitol Hill—"unusually inequitable," says *Newsweek;* "fundamentally unfair," says the *Wall Street Journal;* "politically stupid," says Minority Leader Robert Michel; for Republicans are anxious, fearful and angry at the thoughtless, truthless President, weakness and obstinacy posing as strength.

So angry that Senator Packwood of Oregon tells the Associated Press how stupidly Reagan replied to a question about the deficits, a gross breach of White House courtesy but a cruel exposure of the glozing President within. Reagan replied with an anecdote—characteristically false—about a man who went to a store and bought vodka with food stamps. "That's what's wrong," Reagan tells Packwood, so Packwood in fury tells the world.

So angry that one Marc Marks, a Pennsylvania Republican, takes the floor of the House on March 9 to vent his rage and despair at the brutal rule of the Right, his rage against the "President and his cronies whose belief in Hooverism has blinded them to the wretchedness and to the suffering they are inflicting . . . on the sick, the poor, the handicapped, the blue-collar, the white-collar workers, the small-business person, the black community, the community of minorities generally, women of all economic and social backgrounds, men and women who desperately need job training, families that deserve and desire to send their children to college." The suffering must be stopped. Let "thinking men and women everywhere raise their voices against this murderous mandate," cries Marks, this mandate which has launched upon recession-stricken America the beast of rankling injustice. Reagan and the Right, in their willfulness, spite and stupidity, are destroying the Reaction, such is the long and the short of it.

The country is stirring; Reagan is tottering. Anger sweeps the country when Americans learn that four huge corporations—Dupont, Texaco, RCA and General Electric, hugely profitable all four—will get a tax refund, a chunk of *our* shrunken fisc to add to *their* profits, thanks to a provision of last year's tax act allowing corporations to buy and sell unused tax credits. Shocking epitome this of a tax code so hideously unjust that a family of four earning $200,000 a year, making average use of tax breaks, loopholes and shelters, pays an average federal income tax of 9 percent, so the *New York Times* reports four years hence, while a family of four earning $12,000 a year pays 16 percent into the Treasury. The affluent feed on the fisc; the deficit gnaws at the rest of us. Such is the beast of injustice now abroad in the land. Even Speaker O'Neill now talks of "fairness," doubtless for want of a weaker word.

Anger, too, unites millions of Americans against James Watt for his spiteful trashing of the wilderness and the national parks; one million people sign a petition demanding his removal from office—environmentalists avowed, and environmentalists unavowed, being sportsmen, rather, and hunters, and members of gun clubs. The environmental movement, torpid for years, springs into life, galvanized by the Right, resolves to take to the hustings this autumn to combat the political ravagers of the land.

Anger breathes life into the civil rights movement when the White House announces on January 8 that racially segregated schools should be given tax-exempt status like any other worthy cause or pious charity, will do it by fiat, in defiance of settled law and policy, stirring a furious storm. "A racial insult," the *Times* calls it, and a "gross abuse of federal power." The White House is stunned, taken aback, ill-judging public opinion, revealing, says *Time* magazine, a "White House Sensitivity Gap," revealing, too, for the first time outside the darkness of collusion, the Right's taste for fiat, contempt for law. "Is it really 'conservative' to play fast and loose with the laws?" asks Anthony Lewis of the *Times,* tearing at one of the Right's many masks.

What transparent masks they are! What prodigies of collusion have kept them in place thus far! Is it "getting government off the back of the people" to call for government censorship of all private research that might help the Soviets improve their economy? A proposal "more compatible with a dictatorship than a democracy," cries one angry scientist when the administration proposes just that on January 7 before the American Association for the Advancement of Science; proposes it and acts upon it, indifferent to any official report, study, analysis, that argues in *favor* of freedom; determined, rather, says a Commerce Department official this March, to combat "the strong belief in the academic community that they have an inherent right . . . to conduct research free of government review and oversight." Is this the object of an administration trying to "get off the people's back"? The answer is obvious. Only let the question be asked, men of power.

Is it "conservative," is it evidence of attachment to "old-fashioned values," is it anything, indeed, but an assault on popular government to issue a presidential directive meant to silence officials who dare tell the people what the ruling Right does not want them to know? Yet the White House issues just such a directive this January 12 to silence officials who tell their countrymen that ketchup is now a poor child's vegetable, that the CIA is now allowed to spy on them; officials, so Reagan explains in private to an interviewer this December, "who are resentful and do not agree with what it is you are trying to do." By what authority is the Executive Branch to be reduced to silence, its old babble and openness, unsung bulwark of freedom, brought to an end? Just ask the question, men of power, and this tyranny of sharks and shysters must topple.

Anger and dismay sweep the country in mid-February when Americans learn for the first time that the CIA is training a paramilitary force in Nicaragua. Is this what the President had in mind when he promised "to make America proud again"? We are not proud of this lawless little enterprise, nor convinced of its necessity, nor frightened by the Soviet threat to Central America cried up "ever louder and louder" by the administration. The "propaganda blitz" is led by Reagan himself—"Taking Aim at Nicaragua" is blazoned across the cover of *Newsweek*—but produces no fear save fear of folly in the White House. By mid-March the administration's campaign is "sputtering," wears, says a Democratic senator, "an air of desperation," which air it is destined never to lose.

The President's budget has begun to hang like an albatross around his neck, filling him with all-too-revealing self-pity. "I'm a Scrooge to a lot of people," Reagan complains in Oklahoma City on March 16, "and if they only knew it, I'm the softest touch they've had in a long time." Rankling injustice is abroad in the land, but the President is a sucker for a hard-luck story; only "paid political complainers" call him unfair, so he complains. By mid-

March Reagan looks inept and inane. His approval rating, slowly falling since August last, now stands at 47 percent, according to Gallup, lower than any other modern President after so short a time in office.

By mid-March even the advancing shyster tyranny loses some of its grotesque impunity. The President's new executive order on "classified information"—documents the Executive is allowed to conceal in the name of national security, 16 million a year on the average—comes under attack in a House subcommittee on March 10. The order expands what Presidents since Eisenhower have tried to reduce, Nixon and Carter most conspicuously—the bureaucracy's propensity to stamp "Confidential" on masses of trivia, on evidence of waste, corruption, fraud and scandal. The Reagan order compels bureaucrats to be more secretive than they already are; creates a vast new category of classifiable information so vague that a U.S. road map, it is said, could be stamped "Confidential"; orders all doubts about concealment resolved in favor of concealment, revealing an appetite for secrecy so gluttonous that Ed Meese blames the order on "zealous bureaucrats" outwitting untried, old-fashioned conservatives, or so he tells the National Newspaper Association four days after the hearings. For the presidential masks are slipping; sharks and shysters are beginning to show.

At this most critical moment, as the winter draws to a close, suddenly, amazingly, the voice of the people pierces through the cant of the Reaction—the voice of a citizenry, of people who talk to one another, who hear one another out, who take counsel with one another in the town meetings of New England, last relic of the old "ward republics" of America, which retain something of their ancient virtue still. What think you, fellow citizens, of this: a resolution calling upon the U.S. and the U.S.S.R. to halt the testing and deployment of all nuclear weapons, the halt to be mutually verified, to commence at once. We are already equals in nuclear strength, let the nuclear arms race be stopped! And in 161 towns in

Vermont, the little ward republics vote aye: The "freeze movement" bursts upon the public stage, surges, too, through California, surges through Massachusetts, beats at the doors of a dozen state legislatures, county councils, city halls, led by the clergy mainly, endorsed by Kennedy, Hatfield and Averell Harriman, old George Kennan, Billy Graham, William Colby, former director of Central Intelligence. It enlists "the unpolitical public," which is worst of all, warns Rostow, late of the Present Danger, now Reagan's arms control chief, in a frantic memorandum to the White House. A vast eruption of public sanity in the midst of the giant arms buildup, "too powerful, too elemental, too deeply embedded in the natural human instinct for self-preservation to be brushed aside" by governments, so Kennan confidently predicts. There are "local initiatives all over the country," reports *Time*. "It is a populist, popular movement that has really sneaked up on us," commanding at once the support of 70 percent of the population.

A vast popular revolt is this nuclear freeze against Present Danger lies and fear-mongering, the Reaction's lies, now Reagan's to defend. He tries, lies, fails, makes matters worse. A nuclear freeze is "dangerous," says the President on March 31, at his first televised evening press conference, after days of anxious preparation. Dangerous because the Soviet Union is the superior nuclear power, dangerous because the United States is afflicted by "what I have called, as you all know, several times, a window of vulnerability," the dreaded window forgotten a few months back when Reagan, obliging supporters in Utah and Nevada, decided to put the MX missile in a vulnerable silo, now hastily pressed into service again, prompting a reporter to ask: "Are you saying that we are vulnerable now, right today, to a nuclear attack?" How can the President say "no" to that, and blather instead about "perceptions" of weakness that nobody except our leaders can believe? A "no" answer vindicates the freeze; undermines the nuclear buildup, undermines the Soviet threat, the Cold War revival, the entire buildup and all that depends upon *that*. So Reagan says yes, why not? "The Soviets' great edge is one in which they could absorb our retaliatory blow and hit us again." Defenseless America, nuclear sword at our throat! America betrayed, too, by Presidents, statesmen and high-ranking generals, criminally negligent almost, until I, Ronald Reagan, arrived on the scene. A storm of protests greets the President's coarse and reckless remarks. The chairman of the Joint Chiefs, General David Jones, feels compelled to repudiate them: The U.S. and the Soviets are nuclear equals; inferiority is a myth, he testifies before Congress. Former Secretaries of Defense curtly repudiate them. "Neither side has superiority," says James Schlesinger, Defense Secretary under Nixon and Ford. Even Senator Jackson demurs. The truthless President is a menace to the arms race, a menace to the entire buildup. Coarse demagoguery works on the inert, unattending mass; on a people awakened it turns on itself, a truth beyond Reagan's comprehension, but how instinctively does truthless Reagan fear and loathe an informed electorate!

What wringing of hands ensues, what sad mournful cries! The whole nuclear buildup "has backfired politically," laments the *New York Times*. "The pro-defense coalition that was emerging in Congress and the country has been ruined," complains Senator Dan Quayle, an Indiana Republican. "I'm getting letters from home now, people are saying 'cut defense.'" Leading Democrats are bitter, too. The "defense consensus of last year has been frittered away," moans Les Aspin of Wisconsin, the House Democrats' newest "spokesman" on defense. The great engine of waste and domestic paralysis, of empty cupboards for the needy and billions for Oligarchy's industrial clients, is suddenly in serious danger. Justice assails the brutal budget; civic sanity threatens the military Moloch. "Large-scale protest now seems certain," two writers predict in the *Nation*.

"The Reagan presidency is at a watershed," White House aides warn the press, is "bogging down." Distress signals issue from the imperial palace. "The question isn't deficits or tax cuts or defense," says a senior White House official in mid-March. "The question is leadership—whether Reagan is going to stay viable as a leader." A cry for help, nothing less, coming at a critical juncture in the

Democratic Party's long, unremitting struggle to regain the keys of its kingdom. On March 26, "with a minimum of debate," the Democratic Party leaders complete their latest revision of the party rules—their post-Carter, anti-Carter, prevent-Carter rules; bestowing upon themselves some 550 "superdelegate" seats at the 1984 convention—we must be able to veto future Carters, must we not? They have altered the rules, in addition, to "make it easier for the party to consolidate around front-running candidates," a party official explains, meaning easier for party leaders, union ward heelers, the party's money men—the newly created Democratic Business Council—to pick one candidate—Walter Mondale is already chosen—fill his coffers, build his organization, bedeck him with endorsements, put the entire AFL-CIO at his disposal and place the party standard in his loyal, trustworthy hands. O, blessed precious nominating power, keys of the kingdom, lost to us for so long, now in our grasp once more. Or almost. There is a hitch, as Mondale's political adviser, one James Johnson, sees clearly. The party establishment can only nominate Mondale in 1984 "if it's a normal year." A normal year? How can such a thing be, with the rule of the Right assailed, Reagan not viable, "activists" swarming, social dregs voting, the banner of justice unfurled? Should President Reagan lose his grip on the country, warns Kevin Phillips, a Republican political analyst, in the *Washington Post,* there will be social upheaval of the most dangerous kind.

The distress call from the fretful palace is not sent in vain. The rescue of Reagan commences this spring, continues for twelve months and more.

15.
RESCUING REAGAN (I)

The "murderous mandate" must, perforce, be lifted from around Reagan's neck, a new budget worked out, the "impasse" ended, or "viable" Reagan will not remain for long. But how shall the popular party do it? Even the most modest alternatives to the brutal budget incite rebellion and undermine "leadership."

Shrunken fisc and tax injustice can be ameliorated together, so many an old-line Republican suggests, by an assault on corporate tax loopholes, privileges and "bidding war" bribes so infuriating to the country at this very moment. The military buildup can be safely brought to a halt, as even conservative Hollings suggests, and billions in hideous waste cut out. The "time to cut is now," says none other than Stockman, speaking unnamed in *Newsweek*, citing the Sergeant York gun, Bradley truck, neo–World War II carriers, the B-1 bomber, F-15 fighter and many another weapon of war chiefly of use in the war on the fisc. Is the cutting not "something in the wind," something now called for in "letters from home"? A mite of tax justice, of honest frugality, of common sense and common decency, of surcease from the grinding of the poor. How easily such demands may be met at the expense of the "murderous mandate"!

And how shall they *not* be met? For not met they must be. A delicate matter, indeed. We are in the season of cheese lines, job lines, hard times deepening, of blue-collar workers streaming southwestward in desperate search for work, with congressional elections forthcoming. Surely the opposition party must do some opposing, for who believes now that the Democrats are swept away in a "conservative tide" and must continue in sackcloth and ashes? So Tip and Jones and "Rosty" fill the air with petulant "partisan" cries. Tax justice is not to be thought of, says the popular party. Why should we help Reagan out of his "budget predicament," the Democratic leadership asks? On tax questions we shall play "a backseat role," *Congressional Quarterly* reports. A Democratic alternative to the brutal budget is not to be thought of either, though for exactly the opposite reason. Democrats "protested that they would not work out a budget compromise unless the President became involved." We will negotiate a deal with Reagan, bring him out of limbo, make him look like a "leader"—how fabricated is this Reaganite "leadership"!—the talks commencing on March 19, not without puzzling punditry somewhat. Thanks to the Democrats' offer, notes William Barrett of *Time*, "Reagan would get credit for leading everyone out of the wilderness" and the Democrats will get—nothing. Where is the partisanship in this? "The very fact of the negotiations has allowed these deficits to be seen as a kind of natural disaster," the *New Republic* rightly observes, instead of the fruit of the President's policies. What prompts this curious altruism on the part of the popular party? Patriotism, of course, says the estimable liberal journal: "They did it for the common good," for surely it is good for the country that the national rabble trust and adore their President and blame triple-digit deficits on Fate!

And what is the "compromise budget" offered by Tip and Jones and Rosty, serving "the common good"? For one thing, the largest *increase* in military spending the Congress can possibly enact. For another, a freeze on cost-of-living allowances for the elderly; lastly, repeal of the third installment of the Kemp-Roth tax cut. Thus the popular party in this year of hard times, elections and blue-collar grief! We shall take money from the taxpayers, money from the pensioners—and stuff the maw of the military Moloch. No demand for tax justice, no call for sanity, decency, honest frugality shall come from the popular party. Republican Marks calls upon Americans to "raise their voices against this murderous mandate." But the popular party, fake opposition, sunk in collusion, raises not its voice. We shall let every fair sentiment that works against Reagan rot unvoiced in the hearts of the people.

"Tip wants talks to succeed." So James Baker at the White House hears from Republican economist Alan Greenspan, who hears it from Democratic polltaker Louis Harris, who is called in by the Speaker himself to deliver the message, a message which says as clearly and emphatically as possible to anxious White House and frightened Republicans—though the talks themselves break down—that not even election-year pressures can weaken the resolve of the Democratic leadership to prop up Reagan and the rule of the Right.

While these budget machinations proceed, so, too, proceeds the freeze movement, catching fire, growing from strength to strength. By mid-April, 150 more New England townships are joined to the cause, 67 county councils, the legislatures of Connecticut, Maine, Massachusetts, Oregon, Vermont, Wisconsin and Iowa. The movement raises questions, demands honest answers. The President promised, as a candidate, to "immediately open negotiations over a Salt III treaty." Why have they never been opened? Why, instead of arms talks, a vast strengthening of our nuclear arsenal—begun by broken-down Carter, set in furious motion by Reagan—the giant MX, the Pershing II missile, the Trident II submarine missile, each of them a first-strike weapon aimed at Soviet silos: arms-race weapons, "will-to-prevail" weapons, weapons in a drive for nuclear supremacy, an ambition so abhorrent to the country that a thick cloak of shabby lies conceals it. We are "catching up," not striving for supremacy; restoring our deterrent, not forging an offensive; desperately undoing the damage inflicted on America by the hideous years of détente, appeasement and "unilateral disarming."

183

Careless contempt is the mark of these lies. The Joint Chiefs will not fully vouch for them, nor the CIA, nor even the Pentagon's annual reports. Careless lies because collusive lies. Why do we need powerful *offensive* weapons to "deter" a surprise Soviet attack? How does a vulnerable MX close the "window of vulnerability"? And if there is no such "window," then why the huge buildup of nuclear weapons aimed at Soviet silos? Why is the MX being built at all? The questions burst in upon the fortress of Oligarchy, a voice from the ward republics, demanding honest answers from ill-prepared liars taken by surprise. "This movement is very dangerous," says a White House aide this April, and so it is, and must somehow be diverted, stalled, nullified, its truths left, too, to rot in our hearts.

Arms talks "as soon as possible" are the way to fend off the movement, so Senator Jackson advises the White House. But what kind of proposal dare we make to the Soviets that will not endanger our perpetual arms buildup—our devourer of the fisc, our chief weapon in the war against the Republic? Needed is a proposal "plausible" enough to satisfy the budgetmakers in Congress, yet one-sided enough to lead nowhere, in short a collusive fraud, proposed by Reagan this May 9 at his old alma mater, Eureka College in Illinois. Fulsomely praised by the *Times:* the start of a "Peace Race"—"a major shift by Reagan"—"the President has moved far from his past confrontational attitude." So Power, unslumbering, would have us believe, though the President's "conciliatory" proposal calls upon the United States to continue developing its huge arsenal of advanced nuclear weapons in return for which the Soviets will reduce theirs by more than one half. A proposal so grotesquely dishonest—old Muskie, retired, suspects it "may be a secret agenda for sidetracking disarmament"—only a President propped up by an entire national leadership could come away praised for so clumsy a hoax.

So cruel and so false that some angry official, it seems, gives the *New York Times* in late May Secretary Weinberger's "Defense Guideline" for 1984–88, an astonishing five-year plan to enable the

U.S. to "prevail" in a limited "protracted nuclear war," a plan "to be ready," says a disgusted member of the Joint Chiefs, "on a moment's notice to destroy all the Soviet Union—everything, everywhere, of any conceivable consequence." A strategic monstrosity—"I don't see much of a chance of nuclear war being limited or protracted," says General Jones on retiring this June. A strategy concocted to justify the endless devouring of the fisc—"a maximalist wish list" of weapons, so one military expert calls it; a "bottomless pit" for the public wealth, says General Jones. A five-year plan for an all-out arms race "difficult for the Soviets to counter." We shall spend them—and the Republic—into submission. "Impose disproportionate costs, open new areas of military competition"— outer space—"and obsolesce previous Soviet investments." A five-year plan for cutting the Cold War loose from even the vague bounds of "national security," for turning it into unrelenting economic warfare, making it a deeper tomb yet for the Republic, already apparent this summer when the Department of Commerce warns universities across the country that anyone teaching advanced technology to a single foreign student may be considered a "U.S. exporter" under the 1979 Export Administration Act and be subjected to a $100,000 fine for exporting technical ideas without a government license. Such is the Defense Secretary's "Defense Guideline" published in the *Times* this May 30, 1982, carrying the official approval of the "conciliatory" President, new leader of the "Peace Race"—truth's perfect, unerring antithesis.

"Runaway government" is the great national evil, says Reagan on May 25, for runaway government is what he is leading—an Executive in headlong flight from the laws, the courts, the people, the light, from accountability in every form. Reagan calls upon Americans to oppose "the great myth that our national nanny always knows best," while the Nuclear Regulatory Agency this May secretly proposes a rule allowing it to meet in secret, then secretly suspends safety regulations without the millions affected knowing anything; while the Department of Health and Human Services proposes in secret this May new procedures for foiling the

185

Freedom of Information Act (which a Senate committee declines to gut), proposes this June that what the department does in the future to the poor, the sick and the crippled be free from review by the courts, which meddle intolerably in the campaign to save the taxpayer $2 billion worth of cripples; while Reagan's appointees to the Legal Services Corporation work to destroy the agency from within and so make it easier for runaway government to trample on the legal rights of the poor, the appointees named "suddenly" last Christmas recess to circumvent the advice and consent of the Senate; while the enemy of "nanny knows best" declines to discuss the resignation of Secretary Haig this June because it concerns nothing that I, President Reagan, think "the American people needed to know for their own welfare." This July the President rails a second time against "runaway government" while his administration proposes laws to weaken the Fourth Amendment, to make it harder to sue government for violating constitutional rights, harder to gain access to federal courts in constitutional cases; while the Justice Department this June issues "guidelines" that override the antitrust laws—and weaken the free market—in the name of "economic efficiency"; while the FBI announces this June new "guidelines" forthcoming to enhance "domestic security." Let the power of capital expand, let the power of the police expand, let the lawless power of the Executive expand—and let the citizenry shrink and skulk in darkness, tend to their "own welfare," leave the public realm to Wealth and Power. Let the American people "get off President Reagan's back so he can get government off our backs," says a White House adviser, one J. Peter Grace, a shipping magnate, to an audience of Dallas merchants this May 27—and much becomes clear in a flash: The *people* are not to be liberated; only business counts as "the people" in the lying, truly Orwellian double-talk of Reagan and the Right.

What say you to that, men of power? Nothing the least audible to your countrymen.

On June 12, the nuclear freeze movement reaches an astonishing, poignant climax before the United Nations in New York City, scene of a special UN session on disarmament. A movement virtually unknown this January has brought together 750,000 people—earnest, respectable, conspicuously clerical, a mighty host calling for an end to the arms race now, before it is too late to turn back. "The largest demonstration in American history"—a mighty plea, a pathetic petition, a cry from the country's heart, nothing less, for sanity and decency and surcease from fear and the rule of the fear-mongers.

And what say you to that, men of power? The answer comes five days later when a House-Senate conference reaches agreement on the budget for fiscal 1983—calls for a $32 billion *increase* in military spending authority, continues grinding the poor and the ailing, delivers "a vicious, venal attack on the working poor," so Congressman David Obey, the passed-over liberal, describes the House version of the budget, a Democratic House budget which is crueler to the needy and kinder to the Pentagon than the Republican Senate version. A budget, too, that forecasts steadily declining deficits—$60 billion by 1985—affirming and confirming Reagan's false, glozing feedback fantasy, knowingly affirming a known lie, for Reagan is tottering still and needs every prop that Oligarchy can muster. "The system is too fragile now to deal with the truth," some economist shrewdly remarks. So fragile that the Democratic House on August 5 votes—albeit narrowly—to confirm its faith in the President's fraudulent arms proposal, its belief in the fictitious "window of vulnerability," for Reagan and truth cannot coexist. We must rally around lies to save him!

Not a single weapon is canceled by Congress; mere "routine cheese-paring" only, says *Congressional Quarterly.* Not a piece of gross squandering is questioned. This year $6.8 billion is to be spent for our neo–World War II carriers and $3.2 billion cut from medical programs; $4.6 billion goes for the "flying Edsel" and the volume of student loans is reduced by 25 percent. "House Democrats," notes the *New Republic,* "again gave Mr. Reagan almost everything he asked for," although election time is nearing, although the recession is deepening, and Reagan himself continues declining in public esteem. Such is the miracle work of collusion. The murderous mandate no longer hangs around Reagan's neck; it now hangs around ours. Nor is there the slightest pause in the arms race. Let the 750,000 people who gathered by the river know this and mark it well. They gather in vain. Let sentiments of justice, common sense, public spirit, decency, sanity and compassion rot and shrivel and die in your breasts. Let every vestige of faith in yourselves—that which Lincoln bid the people never lose—be trampled and ground to dust. We shall make the truthless man your savior yet.

Alas, we have a long way to go, and the congressional elections, cruelly ill-timed, threaten to ruin everything. Unemployment this October stands at 10.1 percent, nearly 16 percent for blue-collar workers, figures not seen since the Great Depression, and though the Federal Reserve has thrown "open the money spigots as never before," as Stockman remarks, is creating money at rates unprecedented in our history, "recovery" must come too late. The Democrats stand to gain thirty to forty House seats, a huge majority in the House of Representatives, sixty or so freshman legislators fresh from the hustings, swept into office by the hard feelings of hard times. How shall Reagan stay "viable" then?

Senate Republican leaders, desperate to weaken the charge of injustice, offer a tax bill that raises $98.5 billion over the next three years, some $50 billion by closing unjust corporate tax privileges. "Something that's better than any bill Russell Long ever put out," says a Nader lieutenant, the handiwork chiefly of Senator Dole. What will the popular party do in the House? For the House of Representatives, under the Constitution, must originate all tax increases. "Make them fairer still," says the *New Republic.* Start a "bidding war in the name of fairness." A battle for tax justice conducted by Democrats? Rankling injustice strengthened. Hopes for justice heightened? Social dregs given heart? Surely, fellow citizens, we know the answer by now.

In a "surprise move," the Democratic House, under the leadership of Tip and Rosty, votes to offer *no* tax bill at all; will merely duck into the darkness of a House-Senate conference to dicker in private with Dole. The popular party wants no part of fairness, no part of tax justice, no part, were it possible, in the public life at all. It attributes this "most unusual" act of inaction to fear of "antagonizing business PACs," to the need for election campaign money, to "reluctance to offend certain interests," Drew of the *New Yorker* reports: the usual commercial excuses for deeper, noncommercial corruption. On the eve of these dangerous elections, let us behold our two-party system: one party's leaders in grave fear of the charge of injustice, the other's in dread of making it.

What the Democrats need, says a campaign manifesto of the vote-repelling sort, is greater cooperation with business. What the Democracy must do with its expanded "financial base" this election year is hoard it. The Democratic Campaign Committee gives scarcely more money to Democratic candidates this year than it did in 1980; gives nothing at all to many a young challenger who stands within an ace of victory. "Ten million Americans out of work—that should be worth 40 million votes," a White House aide remarks to the press. "And the Democrats haven't exploited it." Exploit it so little that *Newsweek* wonders aloud if "they have the will to prevail over the Great Communicator." Well they may wonder.

The election results are nonetheless grim. The Democrats, try as they may, gain 26 seats in the House—the worst reversal for a President at the two-year point in sixty years, giving our poor beleaguered Speaker a 100-seat majority to stifle. Afflicts him with fifty-seven new Democratic lawmakers who, by crying out against the rank injustice afflicting the land, have "resurrected liberal issues from the graveyard to which all but a tiny element of the party consigned them in the course of the 1970s," *Congressional Quarterly* reports. Ten million more people vote this year than voted in 1978, three out of five voting for Democrats—blacks and blue collars, the dangerous dregs, sending an alarm through Republican ranks. Unless we get our supporters registered to vote in 1984, say Republicans, the Democrats, registering the dregs, may yet reverse the "conservative tide"—a registering of the dregs which, however, does not take place, not if the popular party can prevent it. Away with the dregs, for Mondale of "the normal year" is our candidate. Teddy Kennedy, always obliging, bows out of the race on December 1, which "surprise move"—how surprising everything is these days!—leaves Mondale the lone "front runner" as planned, and marks Kennedy for what he so indelibly is—a party hack at the party's beck.

Very tense is the political atmosphere these postelection days, ill-tempered, fretful, more anxious than ever over tottering Reagan's "viable leadership." "The people want action, not partisan bickering," says the Speaker, who must break fifty-seven firebrands to the bit of "get-along, go along," to the vow of *omertà,* and keeping Reagan "viable," like it or not. Democrats, like it or not, "go along" when Speaker Tip and the White House organize a "bipartisan" National Commission on Social Security Reform—ten Republicans, five Democrats, a curious mix—to keep Reagan's "fingerprints" off a $40 billion reduction in Social Security benefits, for we do not want the elderly *blaming* the President for the doing of what the President wants done. Do we not all agree with the *New York Times* that "Mr. Reagan's loss of authority only halfway through his term should alarm all Americans"—of the oligarchical classes?

Alas for Reaganite "leadership"—be-all and end-all of our now degraded public life—Reagan himself is its own worst enemy, the only enemy, politically speaking, his "leadership" has. Reagan's arms proposals, being designed to lead nowhere, are perforce "going nowhere." Where else could they go? Are perforce strengthening the freeze movement, strengthening demands for an end to the arms buildup and, worst of all, most dangerous of all, strengthening demands for canceling the MX, a momentous cancellation, not of a mere missile, but a canceling out, were it to happen, of the whole system of Present Danger lies, a canceling out of the Cold War revival, a canceling out, all too likely, of Reagan's "leadership," but Reagan is hapless to ward off the blow.

In late November, the administration renames the MX the "Peacekeeper," offers a new vulnerable way to deploy it—in a "dense pack" outside Cheyenne, Wyoming, which farcical proposal—"Dunce Pack"—infuriates the champions of MX, arms buildup and Cold War revived. "You just don't seem to understand how much trouble the MX basing mode is in up here," exasperated Nunn complains to Weinberger. Or how strong is "the perception that the Pentagon is out of control," Quayle, too, complains to Weinberger.

What can an ignorant, truthless demagogue do? Poison the public mind, if he can, against those who dare stand in the way. The freeze movement is "inspired by not the sincere honest people who want peace, but by some who want the weakening of America." So Reagan tells a veterans' group in a speech this autumn. Its success is due to "foreign agents that were sent to help instigate and help create and keep such a movement going." So he says on another day this autumn. About this foreign agentry there is "no question," says Reagan. Any evidence? "Plenty"—alas, not forthcoming. The White House refers the inquisitive to the October issue of *Reader's Digest*. Such slander, defaming so many people of honor and esteem, so many tens of thousands of earnest clerics, Oligarchy cannot and will not vouch for.

Oligarchy has its limits. The tyranny of the Right is boundless, stupid, perpetually overreaching itself, never more dangerously so than this November 30—an episode worth relating at some length—when the President invokes "executive privilege," instructs Anne Gorsuch, administrator of the Environmental Protection Agency, to withhold from John Dingell's subcommittee and a second investigating House panel what the White House calls "enforcement-sensitive" documents concerning the cleaning up—and non–cleaning up—of poisonous waste dumps around the country. The "dissemination of such documents outside the Executive Branch would impair my solemn responsibility to enforce the law," would impair the Right's power to nonenforce, trash, suspend and sabotage every law that violates the higher law

of "economic efficiency." Congress shall give way before us, shall
cease snooping into *our* legislative affairs, shall be blinded here and
now, once and for all—in accordance with the "separation of powers." Is it true, as Woodrow Wilson once wrote, that "the only really self-governing people is that people which discusses and
interrogates its administration"? Then let us stifle true self-government here and now. Thus Reagan decrees at the suggestion of the
Department of Justice, which cannot explain how documents han-
dled by EPA clerks, never seen in the White House, can be kept
from the elected representatives of the people.

What a predicament for Oligarchy is this! Reagan's privilege
claim is intolerable to constitutional government, to Congress, to
Oligarchy, to liberty, diverse interests for the moment united. The
claim must be broken and will be broken, one way or another. Not
a Republican on Dingell's subcommittee will support the blinding
of Congress, so their counsel warns Justice. The claim is "unwar-
ranted," "almost shocking," "bizarre at best," warns Marks of the
murderous mandate, senior Republican on Dingell's subcommittee. The "self-evident foundation for executive immunity from
inquiry," a House committee report later puts it, a tyrannical reach
for tyrannical power. Gorsuch telephones the White House,
demands to see the President and warn him of the dangers ahead,
gets cut off with a curt rebuff: "Anne, are you going to be a prima
donna?" says Baker: The President is too busy for this.

Party leaders vainly try to work out a compromise. The shyster
tyranny is adamant, arrogant, determined to "stiff Congress," so
one of the shysters notes in private. Wants a test of wills, imagines
in its thoughtless stupidity that it can possibly win such a test.
Puffed up by collusion, the Right scarcely knows what it is like to
govern without it, will find out soon enough, and all of America
along with it.

Thus the predicament: Oligarchy must break the intolerable
claim without tarnishing Reagan, if possible. Must check tyranny
without reviving democracy. Is this not the perfect prefiguring of
the Iran-contra hearings?

The first step is dramaturgic—to raise the stakes high. At 10:00 P.M. on the night of December 16, after last-minute Republican efforts to work out a compromise with the administration, the House, by a vote of 256 to 105, charges Anne Gorsuch with contempt of Congress, the first Cabinet-level official ever so charged in our history. At once the Justice Department files suit in court against the House subpoena in the name of "The Government of the United States of America"—infuriating Congress. The White House declares in a public statement that "we did everything to reach an accommodation"—an infuriating bald-faced lie, common coin of the Right from Reagan on down. The lawsuit is meritless trash, thoughtless, infuriating bluster, not unlike the 1,200 U.S. Marines now sitting at Beirut airport between murderous Lebanese factions, "keeping the peace."

Breaking the privilege claim is simple in principle, perilous in practice. Cry scandal at the scandal-drenched EPA and make "executive privilege" look like the scandalous concealment of scandal. On January 25, 1983—eight days before the Supreme Court dismisses the meritless suit—John Dingell begins the assault, demands to question one Rita Lavelle, in charge of the corrupted toxic dump cleanup. At once shyster arrogance gives way to panic: "Rita connected to Ed Meese and the President," a Justice Department lawyer notes the next day. We must drop her, scapegoat her, throw her to the wolves. On February 7, Reagan fires Lavelle, but the wolves do not feed—not yet. Oligarchy, instead, unleashes its dogs; three more subcommittees leap into the fray, tear at the throat of the EPA, fill the air with cries of scandal—"sweetheart deals," corrupt special favors, conflicts of interest, shredded documents. Power has spoken; the press plunges in, all "deference" temporarily gone. A journalistic "feeding frenzy" ensues: "Whistle-blowers" are called, Gorsuch mobbed, headlines blare, nightly news, magazine cover stories, "escalating charges," "a political hailstorm"—the first outbreak of opposition since Reagan's election, the last until late 1986. The White House is stunned, confused, cannot understand where its power has fled.

One week without the giant shield of collusion and National Savior, Invincible Juggernaut, Great Communicator is reduced to dithering futility. On February 16, the President calls upon the Justice Department to undertake a "complete investigation" of EPA. Power laughs in his face: Justice investigating EPA? "Tantamount to asking the wolves to go count the chickens." The subcommittees rage on, the press rages on, the hailstorm rages on. The White House "panics," says Gorsuch, fires two more EPA officials, falling deeper into Oligarchy's trap. The investigations continue, "showy and chaotic" but dangerous indeed. Scratch EPA and what stands revealed? The freedman of the imperial palace, budget office power, secret law, and "lightening the regulatory burden" exposed for what it is: dispensing gross favors to corporate polluters, threatening to "reinforce an already widespread public perception," so the *New York Times* warns on February 26, "that Mr. Reagan is too close to business."

The White House, panic deepening daily, blames EPA wrongdoing entirely on Gorsuch, its faithful tool—proto–Oliver North—leaves her "high and dry," she bitterly complains, preparing another scapegoat to be thrown to the wolves.

On March 9, Reagan surrenders to Congress the "enforcement-sensitive" documents and the executive privilege claim is effectively broken, an achievement of Oligarchy, for which all praise is due. It is no small thing. Nor done without damage to Reagan, to "leadership," to the interests of Oligarchy itself. Four weeks of collusion suspended—a grim unavoidable necessity—have "reinforced" all too many unfortunate "perceptions." Two Americans out of every three, so a *Washington Post* poll shows this March 5, think Reagan cares more "about protecting the firms that are violating" the environmental laws than he does about protecting the environment, believe it and resent it. "A bombshell issue," says one liberal Democrat. "The ultimate issue in which the Reagan administration reveals its true self," says another. "A valuable political opening" for the Democratic opposition, a *New York Times* commentator notes on March 10. True enough, heaven knows. On

EPA the eyes of the entire country have been riveted for a month, not happily. Shall we now show the American people "the true self" of the Right? True self of the White House? Shall we delve deep into the corrupted body of the EPA and dredge up Tozzi, usurped power, cost-benefit quackery? Shall we reveal in lurid detail the Chief Executive's appalling contempt for law, appalling appetite for secret power? We shall delve not at all. We shall snap shut the "valuable political opening," shovel out of sight the "bombshell issue." The investigative subcommittees shift their legislative "focus," *Congressional Quarterly* reports, from "specific misdeeds" to general policy, give over all they have discovered about the EPA to the Justice Department, hole of oblivion, seeker after nothing, finder of nothing—as the House Democrats well knew in February and surely have not forgotten in March. Let us return to the great business of the day: exalting a demagogue and degrading a people.

16.
RESCUING REAGAN (II)

F resh from the hustings, the great hundred-seat majority sits idle, does nothing and worse than nothing, betrays every sentiment, virtually, that brought it into being. A majority of Americans want military spending cut, turning a deaf ear to the President's frantic talk of Russia's "evil empire," to his shameless lies about Soviet military spending far exceeding our own. The hundred-seat majority heeds not the electorate, heeds only the President, enacts a $32 billion increase in military spending authority. Does far worse than that: votes without hearings, without debate, without public knowledge, to give the Pentagon authority to conceal from the American people any information it can conceal from a foreigner under the export control laws; turns citizens into foreigners, turns the vast engine of waste and paralysis into a single vast secret of state—or tries to. Henceforth, a patriot in the Defense Department, outraged by the hideous waste and fraud, who dares speak out to his countrymen, risks ten years' imprisonment for violating the export laws, now distorted beyond recognition.

The great hundred-seat majority continues the nuclear arms buildup, although seven Americans out of ten want the freeze movement to triumph, despite all Reagan's slanders against it—how deaf are the people to the Great Communicator! The huge legislative majority continue the great work of subverting the public understanding, help Reagan overcome "the widespread suspicion that he may be unwilling to seek a diplomatically feasible arms control agreement"—as *Congressional Quarterly* tactfully puts it—by hailing his latest proposal for its "flexibility." The hundred-seat majority, most important of all, votes at long last to deploy the MX in a vulnerable silo—"a formidable salvage operation undertaken by a curious coalition featuring President Reagan and Democratic moderates"—after the Speaker and White House organize a "bipartisan" commission to urge deployment. America must aim giant vulnerable missiles at Soviet silos in order to "communicate to the Soviets that we have the will essential to deterrence," says the commission. Meaning what? Meaning nothing. These pretexts are for congressional use only. Nothing to do with thee or me. Public life is not for thee and me. Collusion, like a vampire, drains it of all meaning, relevance, truth; of all that speaks to our condition as citizens.

So the hundred-seat majority takes pains not to harm the President by forcing him to veto popular programs, acts of justice, compassionate deeds. "Constant give-and-take between Congress and the White House produced bills that Reagan could sign." Why not give him bills to not-sign, asks Richard Ottinger, the angry, anguished liberal Democrat. Let us restore student loans; it would "sail through Congress" and let Reagan veto *that*. But the leadership will not allow it. The grinding of the poor is producing real misery and ugly neglect. "Two million kids are not getting measles and polio shots due to the budget cuts. That's something you can dramatize," says the angry, baffled liberal Democrat. "But the leadership is not doing anything." Three of five Americans polled this June think Reagan favors "the upper-income people." Do we of the hundred-seat majority wish to "dramatize" that bitter truth or any bitter truth? When Reagan threatens to veto a $1 billion appropriation for "politically popular programs," reports *Congressional Quarterly*, Democratic leaders, in panic, reduce it to $98 million, vetoing it themselves to spare Reagan the burden. "O'Neill has given the ball game to Reagan," says Ottinger, given the country to Reagan, given the American people to Reagan.

Given tyranny to the American people, for the Right's assault on the Republic grows more intense than ever this year, becomes a kind of mad, jeering defiance that almost unmasks itself.

In January, the White House creates a lawless private government for itself, calls it "Project Democracy," first suggested by Reagan on June 8, 1982, in an address to the British Parliament. Is there not jeering mockery even in that? He calls for a privately funded public enterprise to "foster the infrastructure of democracy" in nondemocratic countries; plans to give this "Project Democracy" a secret non-public side, make it a private arm of the White House, run by the National Security Council staff, funded by secret private donations— billionaire contributors meet this March with the President—to carry out extended "covert operations," to counter "the Soviet Union or Soviet surrogates," to serve, in a word, as a private CIA, unnamed in law, unbound by law, beyond congressional reach, beyond that most fundamental of parliamentary checks, the congressional purse strings, brought into being this January when Reagan signs National Security Directive 77—infrastructure of tyranny planted in the innermost sanctum of the American Republic.

On January 7, the Justice Department, mocking justice, mocking law, issues illegal guidelines that bestow upon the Executive the power to charge prohibitive fees to those who use the Freedom of Information Act to enlighten the people—who are supposed to pay nothing, if possible, under the law as written and now debauched. "Federal agencies are obligated to safeguard the public treasury." Such is the thin piping pretext for this lawless assault on public information, our information, without which popular government is a farce, the frugality "saving" $150,000 a year, not to cut off the "liberal mass media"—the Right's pretended enemy— but rural weeklies, rather, and local radio stations, small-town dailies, free-lance writers; whatever is left of liberty, diversity and independence in our public life. That is what the Right truly fears and strives to stifle further this January 24.

The instrument of stifling is bizarre, jeering, mocking: a budget office change in its Circular A-122—"Cost Principles for Non-profit Organizations." Proposed are new accounting rules for the thousands of private organizations that receive federal grants to carry out government functions. All such organizations—from the Girl Scouts to the Izaak Walton League to the Association for Retarded Citizens—must forfeit federal funds if they speak out on public affairs, will be punished by forfeiture if they bring a fact to a congressional committee, make a comment on a federal regulation. The new rules "would inhibit the free flow of information between these parties and all levels of government," says an angry Chamber of Commerce. "Operated in tandem, the scope and inherent vagueness of the terms 'political advocacy' and 'unallowable costs' can easily become a giant pincers for the stifling of the free and unfettered exercise of First Amendment rights," the National Association of Manufacturers cries out in anger and bafflement, cannot understand this wanton White House assault on civics-book virtue: Is not "citizen involvement in the political process" a good thing, an honored thing, the NAM asks? Once, but no longer. The Reaction rules over all, bewildering even the NAM. Citizenship is a vice, a disease, a crime. What we admire at the White House, says one Michael Horowitz of the budget office, chief designer of this assault on free speech, is "Americans who live in real-world communities, have real-world jobs, real-world concerns, who are not political in character." And how differs this from Democratic Party thugs railing against "activists"? It differs not at all. And what of Reagan's praise for "the spirit of volunteerism"? What of night calling itself day?

Representative Frank Horton, a New York Republican, is outraged, calls the revised circular "a gag rule if ever I've heard of one." Yet "I cannot believe that this could possibly be the intention of the administration." Tyrannical motive for a tyrannical act? Not to be thought of, not in America. "Who in the White House imagined this could be sensible public policy? Why?" asks the *New York Times,* which feared a "Big Brother" in the White House in November 1981 and now, with its worst fears answered, bleats in sheeplike puzzlement. What is the puzzle? What is the mystery? Those who know the real effects of "economic efficiency" on American life, know it firsthand, from hard-won experience, are not to be heard by the representatives of the rabble.

So the administration stops funding the publication of the *Survey of Income and Program Participation,* which measures the effect of its welfare policies; stops publishing the *Annual Survey of Child Nutrition, The Handbook of Labor Statistics* and the *Annual Housing Survey;* stops publishing bulletins on occupational health hazards; stops issuing warnings about newly discovered toxics; withholds health care data from local officials; eliminates or reduces "at least fifty major statistical programs," a House committee reports, on such matters as nursing homes, medical care expenditures, monthly department store sales, labor turnover. Stops publishing "U.S.-Soviet Military Dollar-Cost Comparisons," invaluable CIA reports that refute fear-monger exaggerations of Soviet strength. Let the rabble look to the White House, look to the Great Communicator, look to our Ministry of Truth for the lies, the "leaks," the official propaganda by which they shall live, henceforth.

On February 10, Reagan signs an executive order barring from the federal government's lucrative on-the-job charity drives "any organization that seeks to influence . . . the determination of public policy," yet another assault on public life and activity. Assaults our public life again a month later, by calling for an end to postal subsidies for libraries, schools, other nonprofit organizations, for why should we *waste* public money to support the diffusion of knowledge, to subsidize a free people's *conversation* with itself? That waste goes back to the early days of the Republic. The Ministry of Truth shall stop it here and now in the last days of this loathsome Republic, enemy of all we hold dear.

On February 24, the Justice Department orders three prize-winning Canadian films—two on acid rain, one on nuclear war—labeled "political propaganda" under the 1938 Foreign Agents Registration Act. For we control the borders. Why should we leave them open to ideas we want kept from the people? So on March 3, the State Department denies a visa to Mrs. Salvador Allende, wife of the slain Chilean president. Her scheduled speech to church groups in San Francisco is deemed "prejudicial to

United States interests." We shall use every power of government to suppress what we prefer the rabble not know.

On March 7, the Justice Department issues its new "guidelines" on "domestic security" and puts under police purview a vast range of our public life; allows the FBI to infiltrate any group, however free of criminal intent, on mere unsubstantiated charges that there is something to "inquire" about; allows the infiltration of any group that "supports" the infiltrated group, spreading the surveillance net wider; authorizes the Bureau to file "publicly available information" on *any* American it chooses to monitor, for any reason it wishes. Dare to emerge from "real world" obscurity, dare to enter the public world, and a free people falls under the purview of the federal police power—and into its files if it chooses.

And what say you, thus far, men of power, to this ruthless assault on freedom? Something is said and well said, in this subcommittee or that—honor to them—but nothing the least audible to the country at large. So little audible that three years hence this tyranny is still routinely described as "getting government off the back of the people." Such is the power of the lie in this age of collusion.

On March 11, the White House issues National Security Decision Directive 84, outwardly to stop "leaks"—a "high priority for the administration," says an accompanying statement. Less openly, to assault public life yet again, to gag the well informed by other means. Even outwardly the directive is brutal enough, another step in the Right's unresting campaign to terrify the Executive Branch into silence. The polygraph test, henceforth, will be used throughout the government to trace the source of "leaks"—an instrument of fear and intimidation, of false accusations, pretext for ugly harassment, arbitrary firing, invasions of privacy. Are you a lesbian, asks a polygraph tester of a thirty-seven-year-old spinster? "Have you ever put your mouth to another woman's sexual parts?" The FBI, henceforth, will investigate leaks, even when no crime is suspected, "thereby placing FBI agents at the beck-and-call of bureaucrats wanting to terrorize subordinates." So Safire angrily puts it this April 24.

Attached to these "anti-leak" measures, obscuring its purport momentarily, the President's directive orders all government officials with access to "secret compartmentalized information"—SCI—to submit their writings, books, articles, lectures, letters to the editor, to government officials for "pre-publication review" and approval. They are already doing it in utter secrecy; the new order broadens the government's review powers, Carter's bad seed bearing still more bitter fruit. "How many officials are you talking about here?" a reporter asks an official at a Justice Department briefing. "SCI access is given out only to a handful of employees." "Hundreds, thousands?" "It would probably be classified." The "handful," unclassified, is 128,000 officials across the government and destined to perpetual increase, for "pre-publication review"—prior restraint, official censorship—applies to officials not only employed but "for all times after." Something is wrong, very wrong about this. Leaks are anonymous, not issued in signed books and articles.

At House hearings this April 21, an official is asked: How many times have government officials, employed or retired, disclosed classified information in their writings during the past three years? "A half dozen," he answers. And how many of these damaged our security? None, *not one*. A whole class of well-informed citizens—retired State and Defense Department officials mainly—are to be oppressed by mass censorship in order to prevent *what does not occur*. The falsity of the pretext—"leaks"—cries out to high heaven, creates a "furor," so the *New York Times* reports. Thousands of distinguished Americans, whose patriotism cannot be impugned, whose opinions command respect, who can challenge the word of a President, are to be gagged by a truthless demagogue who cannot bear to be challenged, who this very May fires three sitting Civil Rights Commissioners, an act without precedent, destroying the commission's historic independence, for daring to question the Ministry of Truth. "It is not difficult to lie and deceive," Victor Hugo wrote in exile as he watched an elective despot degrade his beloved France, "when the tongue of contradiction has been torn out." In the degraded Republic right now, tongues of contradiction are being mutilated so that the Right and its allies may more easily deceive us.

Has this tyranny of shysters and sharks not grown intolerable by now? Is its hatred of liberty, hatred of truth, hatred of law, hatred of every republican virtue not brutally clear by now? What will you do, men of power, for the question is not idle, but pressing, rather, for suddenly the lawlessness and duplicity of the White House stands exposed before the entire country. A guerrilla force of 5,000 men, trained and armed by the CIA, has entered Nicaraguan soil, so the *New York Times* and the *Washington Post* inform the nation this April 3, "the first solid evidence that the Reagan administration is aiding groups bent on overturning the Sandinistas." "The Secret War Boils Over," exclaims *Newsweek* the next day—a "full-scale push" far beyond the "purported U.S. objective" of stopping arms shipments from Nicaragua to rebels in El Salvador. The "purported" objective is a lie. The real objective is a crime: violation of a law enacted by Congress December last, forbidding the U.S. to aid any armed force, our Hessians, for the "purpose of overthrowing the government of Nicaragua." Congress stands defied; U.S. law stands defied; international law is mocked; public opinion is trampled upon; White House avowals are shown to be worthless, CIA testimony to Congress—from William Casey, director—is shown to be false. "A crisis of confidence," Senator Moynihan calls it, and so it is. Will the hundred-seat majority meet in caucus and cry out with one voice against this lawless tyranny and its truthless shill, against this White House demagogue who tells schoolchildren that free speech is a "privilege" which carries the "responsibility to be right," who talks of a "government right to confidentiality," who poisons the public mind, poisons the Republic itself, with his private, pseudo-constitution of tyranny? Is there just one senator in a hundred to force that truth upon the sheepish mass media giving it heart? One senator alone suffices, if he is brave enough and eloquent enough and makes the Republic his sword and buckler. The answer is: Not one in that hundred can be found, despite a "firestorm" over the gag rule, despite a "furor" over lifetime censorship, despite anger and dismay over the FBI's new police state powers, despite hostile subcommittee hearings. No matter. The Reaction rules over all, terrifies all, and the Reaction needs Reagan propped up, protected, exalted if possible. Seeks chiefly this of the tyranny of the Right—that it take care not to awaken, out of its own jeering spite and malice, the waning republican spirit of the country. The A-122 gag rule is reduced to vague intimidation through the efforts of Jack Brooks and the House Government Operations Committee. National Security Decision Directive 84 is revoked in part. Let Reagan be lauded and his tyranny tempered. So Oligarchy decrees.

This April 27, the President appears before a "rare" joint session of Congress, appeals for "bipartisan" support for his Central American policies. Half of Congress and more distrusts and detests those policies. Fury over the contra war is "running over" in Congress, deeply dismays the country at large. But the watching rabble get no hint of this. Doubts about the "leader" must not be encouraged, not while the leader performs on this televised stage. When Reagan finishes telling the people's elected betrayers how communist subversion causes all the unrest in Central America, the lawmakers rise from their seats and loudly applaud him: a "standing ovation" for this good and wise man. *We* know what he is, but you must not. Trust him, follow him, adore him; we beseech you, now as before.

Away from the bright lights of television, with the electorate's attention once more diverted, this congressional committee or that threatens contra aid, bans contra aid, denounces contra aid—a congressional guerrilla war against the contra war ensues, lasts for years—legalistic, complicated, tedious, unclear, a useful vent for the hundred-seat majority, and not without its larger political purpose: to remind the White House that Congress will not be publicly mocked with impunity, that it can close down the contra war at will should the lawless White House force our hand. The White House reportedly breathes a huge private sigh of relief, for the legalistic opposition to the contra war is itself a compromise between President and Congress, between coarse bungling tyranny and watchful Oligarchy.

On and on, day after day, the propping up of Reagan continues, for though the economy revives and Reagan's public esteem with it—from 38 percent "approval" in January to 48 percent this June—Power, unslumbering, can take no chances. The lying, lawless, ignorant "leader" must be exalted; the uneasy electorate suppressed and degraded; public life drained of all meaning and relevance. The Reaction is safe no other way.

In June 1983, a bizarre scandal erupts in the White House, threatens "the President's valued nice-guy reputation"—a curious little episode revealing much. It appears that David Stockman, while preparing candidate Reagan for his historic debate with Carter, had a copy of the President's briefing book, knew word for word what the President would say, the book reportedly provided by "a Reagan mole in the Carter camp." James Baker, now Reagan's chief of staff, admits he got the briefing book from Casey, then Reagan's campaign manager, a Wall Street blackguard, habitual liar, a "longtime Reagan favorite," *Newsweek* calls him, one who "inhabits a charmed circle within the Reagan administration," assiduous feeder of falsehoods to the President disguised as CIA reports. Casey has "no recollection" of any such book.

Such are the basic ingredients of "Debategate": a spy in Carter's entourage dedicated to his defeat—epitome of much in that! A momentous personal contest deeply tarnished by Reagan's cheating aides; and two of the President's closest advisers virtually calling each other liar. "Much ado about nothing," says Reagan on June 24, but not so to the American people. The scandal commands "surprising public attention," poses a deadly threat. "For the first time in his presidency," notes *Newsweek*, "Reagan is faced with the erosion of his most priceless political asset—his nice-guy reputation for trustworthiness and fair play." A House subcommittee chairman, one Donald Albosta, vows to "probe this issue fully." But this must not be. This must be stopped. On June 28, day of a presidential press conference, O'Neill sallies forth to help rescue the President. The Speaker wants no investigation. "Briefing book or no briefing book, our candidate was extremely unpopular." The Speaker's remarks are described by *Newsweek* as "O'Neill's instinct"—for surely he has no *intention*—"to downplay the matter."

At the press conference a few sharp questions expose the whining spiteful spirit behind the carefully crafted "nice-guy," actorish figment, artifact of collusion. "I had never heard anything about this until you all started talking about it," Reagan, aggrieved, complains to the press. Reporters keep pressing the President. What of the "ethics" of filching the briefing book? To which Reagan replies: "It probably wasn't too much different from the press rushing into print the Pentagon Papers, which were stolen. And they were classified. And it was against the law." Not much difference between secret sneaking and a bold public deed? Between your private advantage and the enlightenment of a nation? A few days of mild adversity lays Reagan bare, reveals the workings of a twisted, truthless little mind. White House aides "turned unmistakably grim." Public interest is remarkably intense. Eighty-two percent of the country knows of the scandal; three of five Americans think it is a major political issue. And are White House treachery, cheating and lying *not* a major political issue? Do the people not have, as John Adams wrote, "an indisputable, unalienable, indefensible, divine right to that most dreaded and envied kind of knowledge, I mean of the characters and conduct of their rulers"? Dreaded indeed by Oligarchy is the people's knowledge of Reagan's character. In public, the Speaker says nothing, is described as "uncharacteristically quiet." In private, Albosta is rudely checked, his investigation stymied. The House Democratic leadership fears to look excessively partisan, so *Congressional Quarterly* reports; wants to "distance current Democratic officeholders from Carter's unpopular legacy," says *Newsweek,* while collusion, unmentioned and unmentionable, continues to drain public life of all meaning and relevance. The Justice Department takes over the issue and the waters of Lethe close over "Debategate," a sordid scandal turned into nothing, as "Goobergate" was nothing turned into a scandal.

Oligarchy's long struggle to exalt a tyrant and degrade a republic now draws to its sadly successful conclusion, the denouement hastened, strange to say, by disaster and folly, catastrophe and cowardice.

The disaster strikes this August 29 when two U.S. Marines are killed and fourteen wounded at the Beirut airport, felled by a Moslem mortar shell. Felled by folly, more truly, the folly of taking up large gratuitous goals—propping up a weak, murderous regime in Lebanon, driving out a powerful Syrian army—with small inadequate means, 1,200 marines in bunkers; the folly of cowardly meddling, timorous bluster. The country is angry, deeply disturbed, can smell, perhaps, deaths piling up atop these, just as these were prefigured last April 18 when a Moslem car bomb blew up the U.S. Embassy in Beirut, killing forty-seven. "We have no business playing policeman with a handful of Marines," cries an angry Senator Goldwater. The President's approval rating plummets overnight from 53 percent to 44 percent, according to Gallup, a stunning decline.

Not yet is Reagan the "Teflon President," impervious to blame and failure. Reagan is vulnerable still, perhaps feels so himself. "He's out of sync, out of rhythm," says a White House aide a few days later. "The whole administration seems to be flailing." Flailing stubbornly, stupidly in Nicaragua, shedding blood without purpose, to the satisfaction of no one, flailing with its sham arms proposals, breeding distrust. A Republican polltaker says, "I would rather have an arms treaty with the Soviets than a drop of three percentage points in unemployment." Flailing feebly at the huge budget deficits, approaching $200 billion this year with no end in sight, mocking Reagan's feedback fantasies, balanced-budget vows; menacing the economic recovery, itself a mockery of Reagan's claims and promises, driven not by "supply-side" savings and investment but by frenetic consumer spending on houses and cars, by our vast Pentagon profligacy, by unprecedented government borrowing, consumer borrowing, corporate borrowing, overseas borrowing, by a vast profligate imprudence with ultimate consequence still unfathomable. "Uneven and unpredictable," *Newsweek* calls the recovery.

For the plight of the marines, Cold War raving provides tempo-
rary distraction. On August 31, 1983, a Korean airliner with 269
people aboard is shot down by a Soviet pilot hundreds of miles
inside Soviet territory, after passing near sensitive military installa-
tions. Swiftly, Air Force intelligence puts together the story and
passes it on to "the policy-makers." Nervous Soviet defenders had
confused the off-course plane with a U.S. intelligence plane operating nearby, had tried and failed to identify the plane before
destroying it. A confused, frightened Soviet air defense has
hideously blundered, but what use is that truth to our leaders? Let
it rot in limbo, while Secretary of State George Shultz goes before
the American people to denounce the Soviets for coldly, deliberately, knowingly destroying a harmless civilian airliner. "Murder in
the air," cries the press. A "heinous act," cries the President. The
"Korean airline massacre" is denounced at the UN by our representative, Jeane Kirkpatrick, champion of Cold War and party oligarchy. Denunciations resound in the Congress. "An unbelievably
barbaric act," cries Speaker O'Neill. "Horrible, inexcusable, outrageous," cries Minority Leader Byrd. By unanimous vote Congress
declares the shooting "one of the most infamous and reprehensible
acts in history"—nothing less. Mass hatred and bellicosity, twin
banes of liberty, how dearly does Oligarchy love them! Reagan
"couldn't have written a better script," says a Democratic Senate
aide. "He looks like a man of reason, caution and balance—he
looks like the *President*."

But not in Lebanon, where civil war erupts on September 4,
killing two more marines and wounding three on September 6.
"Caution and balance" are badly needed now, but not to be found
in the White House. On September 8, a U.S. warship opens fire
on a Moslem position, angering liberals, angering "pro-military
conservatives" as well. Our marines are "sitting-duck targets in an
undeclared war," cries Representative Clarence Long, a Maryland
Democrat determined to block further folly. Let there be a cutoff
of funds for the marines unless the President invokes the 1973
War Powers Act, reports to Congress that the marines face "immi-

nent involvement in hostilities," setting in motion the congressional role in warmaking.

On the thirteenth, the heedless President authorizes the marines to call for naval bombardments against Moslem positions. Surely we are "in hostilities" now, surely in a quagmire of bloodshed and folly. At the White House, temerity, as usual, gives way to panic. The political position is "frightfully dangerous," says a White House aide; support from Congress is desperately needed, a "bipartisan" prop, sharing of blame. In Congress, opposition to the President's murderous folly is rapidly growing, grows in the country as well. The Democrats stand to "gain politically from a congressional rebuke to the President," so *Congressional Quarterly* reports. Long's resolution conveys the rebuke: no War Powers Act invoked by Reagan, no funds for the "sitting-duck" marines.

The Democratic leadership is terrified. Long must be stopped, the rebuke foiled at all costs. Reagan and his folly must be protected. On the nineteenth, frightened White House and frightened Speaker work out a "War Powers compromise" of uncommon moral shabbiness even in this age of trash. Congress will pass a resolution giving complete unquestioning endorsement of Reagan's murderous, meddlesome folly, will roundly approve the propping up of a feeble sectarian regime in Beirut, will call the ousting of Syrians from Lebanon "an essential United States policy objective," will approve the "peacekeeping mission" (now openly bombarding Moslem villages) for eighteen more months. In return for becoming "a partner in Reagan's policy," as *Newsweek* aptly puts it, Congress—not the President—will invoke the War Powers Act (like a policeman arresting himself for want of a perpetrator), and the President in return will be allowed to "declare in writing that he did not recognize the constitutionality of the War Powers Act." Thus is Reagan saved from "rebuke"—supreme goal of our new degraded politics—at the expense of prudence, at the expense of the law, at the expense of the U.S. Marines in Beirut, neutrals no longer, but marked for certain death, a "tragedy waiting to happen," so many a lawmaker warns in vain.

We stand on the very eve of the tragedy when *Newsweek* editors prepare the issue scheduled to appear this Monday, October 24. Discussed on its pages is the still wobbly state of the President, the discussion noting that "Reagan has the support of less than half the electorate and that his disapproval rating in the polls is nearly as high as his approval ratings. The 'fairness issue,' furthermore, has hardly disappeared." Senator Quayle, quoted, agrees. The economic recovery, he says, is all the President has to his credit. If the economy turns sour "there is no fallback" for Reagan. Oligarchy has striven to weaken every public sentiment opposed to Reagan— only the contra war excepted; has toiled unceasingly to undermine a citizenry's faith in itself, to exalt its faith in a "leader"; has shielded a President to set off a man; has shielded the man to set off the charmer. With what success no one can tell. Not much, it would seem, on the eve of catastrophe.

At 2:27 in the morning, Sunday, October 23, the President, on a golfing weekend in Augusta, Georgia, learns that a suicide attacker carrying a bomb in a truck has blown up the marine barracks in Beirut; 229 marines are reported dead. A demonstration, says the President, his voice "quavering" with emotion, of "the bestial nature" of our Levantine enemies, who, perforce, cannot bombard us in perfect safety from offshore warships, but must actually die in order to retaliate. The attack is "an appalling shock to the American people," so reports the press. But what is the shock? Is it the spectacle of wanton, predictable death that shocks, the folly of blind murderous meddling? In part at least? The United States has got to "retaliate"; the President has got "to do something," *Newsweek* remarks most urgently. "There is a lot of circumstantial evidence," says Defense Secretary Weinberger, "that points to Iran."

On October 25, the United States, in all its might and majesty, invades the tiny Caribbean island of Grenada, site of a communist coup against a communist ruler, site of a medical school attended by a thousand Americans said by the White House to be in danger of their lives. No reporters join the armada. A total press censorship is put into effect. For the first time in our history, all military news will come from official bulletins as several thousand Americans attempt to subdue an airplane-less army of 700. "Members of Congress and ordinary citizens alike," notes *Time,* "wondered what had prompted President Reagan to take such drastic action against a tiny island. Coming only two days after the death of 229 Marines . . ."

Well we might wonder, ponder, ask ourselves hard, cruel questions. Is a demagogue President giving us a shabby bully's triumph to distract from a hideous bully's defeat? Believe this, or something akin, and the public world of America grows grim and cold indeed. Believe this and there is precious little left to believe in; nothing, in truth, to believe in, except in ourselves, politically alone, politically deserted, daily subverted by collusion; and in the Republic, daily corrupted, utterly voiceless. For twenty-four hours the country wavers in an agony of doubt—our moment of truth and dread of the truth. On the twenty-sixth a planeload of medical students from Grenada lands in America, television cameras present, countless millions watching. A few students kiss the ground. One cries out "God bless America, God bless Reagan, God bless our military." Suddenly, relief of the greatest intensity sweeps over the country, and joy unbounded, the "Grenada high," so-called. Away with terrible suspicions and gnawing doubts and the American world grown cold and grim. America is triumphant; Reagan is innocent. Let us hear no critics and no bad news. We will not listen, we will stop up our ears, stop our own hearts if we have to. Has the press been kept from Grenada? Good, cry millions of Americans. For they "only would have turned us against the decision to invade," turned us against our leaders, turned us back on our fears, our qualms, ourselves. We have not the strength left for this. A fabulist and liar is our leader. Let us live by fables and lies, by "Morning in America" and "America Is Back." A charmer inhabits the White House; let us bask in his charm. Not everyone, of course, but millions, enough for a landslide victory in the 1984 elections. Power, unslumbering, set out to exalt a tyrant and degrade a citizenry. October 26 marks the day its sad triumph stands revealed.

212

BOOK FIVE

OLIGARCHY RESTORED

17.

THE TYRANNIZED
REPUBLIC

Ayear and more have passed since the "Grenada high"—sad
moment of truth and fear of the truth, mass exodus of the
American people from public life, mass abdication of public burdens, mass flight from a public world drained by collusion
of all meaning and relevance.

All is well without us: Such is the message from the White
House. There is still an "American sound," so the President assures
us in his second Inaugural address. "It is hopeful, big-hearted, ide-
alistic, daring, decent and fair. That's our heritage, that's our song.
We sing it still." He sings it again in his State of the Union message on February 6, 1985, sings of a "Second American Revolution
of hope and opportunity," is serenaded in turn by the nation's legislators singing "Happy Birthday," is interrupted twenty-eight
times by tumultuous, rapturous lawmaker applause. Never mind
that the annual budget message—mere untelevised words—warns
Congress that this land of "hope and opportunity," this place with
"no barriers to our progress except those we ourselves erect" has
grown too poor to afford fair trials for the needy, too poor to aid
small businesses, too poor to continue mailing books at reduced
rates; too poor to support the independence of local government
with the annual program of "revenue-sharing." But *not* too poor to

213

afford a $29 billion increase in military spending. Eight Americans in ten want the buildup ended now, yet we do not protest against this travesty of "hope and opportunity," this jeering mockery of all that is "decent and fair." Public life in America has grown sense-less, is not meant to make sense; keeps the people out with its deeply calculated affront to sense.

The Democratic Party must not look "weak on defense," Tip O'Neill announces early this February. To whom? To itself. It must "shed its 'soft-on-defense' image." In whose eyes? Its own. Where is the sense in that? None there is nor meant to be. Where is the sense when the entire national leadership cries up "family values," while family life decays; while half the mothers of *infants* are away from home working, more than ever, up 25 percent since the champion of "family values" entered the White House? What sense is there in a "recovery" which leaves America too poor to afford mothers? What sense is there in a public world given over to empty, mendacious cant? "Decentralization" cried up while the local government decays. "Out-of-control spending" decried while the national debt doubles in five years. "Old-fashioned values" praised while the family farm disappears, 180 of them per day dur-ing the winter of 1985–86. "Conservatism" praised while the President this past November decides to "suspend" a law he per-sonally declares unconstitutional, an act of radical, lawless tyranny, brought to a halt in court. "Judicial restraint" praised while the Justice Department this March asks a judge to decree that the 1917 Espionage Act makes it a crime—a new judge-made crime—to give classified information to the American people, as if we were a foreign power and our enlightenment a menace to the country. "The spirit of volunteerism" hailed while the President this May 28, as part of his "tax-reform package," calls—not in vain—for abolishing deductions for charity made by those who use the short tax form.

What sense does our public life make when the President declares in a speech March 7 that his contra hirelings—perpetra-tors of rapine and terror, led by a deposed dictator's henchmen—

are "the moral equal of our Founding Fathers"? What sense is it meant to make when this truly atrocious scurrility passes scarcely noticed by the nation's leaders? "I can't remember a time in the past fifty years when officials dominated the news as much as they do today," old Reston of the *Times* remarks this January 27, 1985, or "a period when so much obvious nonsense, even so many distortions of fact have gone by unchallenged, or been discussed with scarcely more than a whisper by the public," so Reston notes fifteen months hence.

We sleep like patients "etherized upon a table," while Power, which never sleeps, lays siege to the liberties of the people, to the power of the people, to every source of popular strength—before we awaken and return, for return we shall some day, some year, some decade.

The freeness of the press comes under brutal ceaseless assault, starting on high, spreading far and wide. A too-free press endangers the nation: Such is the theme of high officialdom. "Reporters are always against us," cries the Secretary of State. And who does the Secretary mean by "us," Reagan is asked at a press conference? "Our side, militarily—in other words, all of America." A free press is the enemy of "all of America," cries the Republic's chief magistrate, trying to turn the people into the enemy of their own ancient liberties. The press in its temerity, the press, when it dares disobey the Pentagon, "gives aid and comfort to the enemy," cries Secretary Weinberger, invoking the grim, threatening language of the treason statute. "The press," cries a White House adviser this February, "is trying to tear down America." The press, when it traffics in government documents, is dealing in "stolen property, stolen information," Ed Meese, our new Attorney General, proclaims this March. Officialdom everywhere takes its cue, afflicts the press with huge, intimidating libel suits. A brutal Israeli general sues *Time* for $50 million; a fatuous American general sues CBS for $100 million; Senator Laxalt, presidential crony, sues a small newspaper chain for $250 million—not one of them wins, only liberty loses. In Leonardstown, Maryland, a county commissioner sues the *St. Mary's Beacon,* circulation 12,750, for $8 billion, bleeds the *Beacon* of $300,000 in legal fees before the newspaper fends off the assault. The libel weapon wreaks havoc on local liberty. For fear of a suit, "you won't read anything about a local official getting into trouble," says the publisher of a small chain of suburban newspapers. Small dailies and weeklies "just keep quiet because they can't afford not to," says the counsel to the American Society of Newspaper Editors this spring. With the libel weapon in hand, "people with wealth and influence have found a good way to shut up their critics, especially in small towns."

The national Reaction strengthens thousands of local reactions, thousands of local oligarchies, stifles liberty at its local source, whence it derives its strength.

"Throughout the nation," reports the *New York Times* this February 14, "public officials and others involved in public disputes [are] intimidating people from speaking out on public issues." A wave of defamation suits "brought from coast to coast" threatens free speech as libel threatens a free press, strikes at "outspoken people," the *New York Times* reports, stifles civic groups, cripples local political life, or tries to. On New York's Long Island, local civic organizations are sued for $3.5 million for criticizing a real estate developer. In a Pittsburgh suburb, a civil rights activist is sued for $100,000 by five members of the town council for accusing them of a "racially motivated" firing. "These kinds of suits are coming out of the woodwork," says a California lawyer. "If you take on the powers-that-be in this state you can bet on a defamation suit." Power, unslumbering, takes its revenge on liberty "throughout the nation," for "there is no week nor day nor hour when tyranny may not enter upon this country," so Walt Whitman warned us, "if the people lose their supreme confidence in themselves—and lose their roughness and spirit of defiance."

On December 19 of this first year of the "Second American Revolution"—counterrevolt of the powerful—the high court of New York State declares that a free people has no right to hold public discourse in a shopping mall, nor distribute leaflets at a shopping mall's entrance, nor sit quietly in a mall gathering petitions if the mall's owners decide to forbid it. The decision is meanly, narrowly argued, not isolated either, but part of a "trend," part of Power's assault on the roots of liberty. The American Republic desperately needs forums, agoras, spaces of freedom, havens for local political life. We, the people, desperately need the sight and sound of one another as citizens, the common bond of citizenship. And here is the modern marketplace, meeting place, village square, lively Main Street under a roof. Use it not for the democracy of the marketplace without Property's permission, so the New York high court decides, so "recently" decide the high courts of Connecticut, Michigan and North Carolina; so decide, with slight modification, the high courts of Washington and Massachusetts, and lower courts in Florida and Maryland—although the Supreme Court leaves states free to decide otherwise and California had decided otherwise in 1979, before the Reaction swept into power.

What the Republic needs we can no longer afford. What liberty requires we are too poor to pay for. Such are the uses of the deliberate deficit, false necessity, the crime of '81. At Reagan's request Congress puts an end to general revenue-sharing, stringless funds given to local governments, "this modest cushion [that] lets city halls decide what their towns need most," says the *New York Times,* a $4.2 billion annual boon to local independence, local self-government. "Every community had to hold public hearings on how the money would be spent; there could be no discrimination in its use; public audits would show how it had been spent. It was government at its finest. . . . In fourteen years there was no example of fraud." So one James Cannon, former aide to President Ford, laments when the deed is done. Hard-pressed now are America's towns and villages, deep is the "erosion of local authority," the *New York Times* observes. Hats in hands, our towns must go to state legislatures, to county governments, to "the private sector" for badly needed revenues and services. The subjugation of local government to state party oligarchies, to corrupt county rings, to local plutocracies in the false name of frugality is one more crime within the crime of '81, and not the least damaging to liberty in America, nor perhaps the least enduring.

Under the assault of the Reaction the local roots of liberty are withering, the local soil of liberty is sown with poison.

Subtle, indeed, these poisons can be. From Reagan's Department of Education there had issued forth in 1983 a great donkey's braying about America's failed public schools and a "Nation at Risk," desperately in need of "an educated work force." The braying alarm is not sounded in vain. In dozens of states across the country enthusiastic governors, zealous state legislatures—state party gangs—seize control of the public school curriculum, demean what is left of local control of the schools, another constriction of an ancient local liberty, and take up the cause of "educational reform"—more cant for this canting Reaction. What this Republic needs of its schools is clear as day, has been clear as day for two hundred years. We need schools for citizens, schools that teach all our children "how to judge for themselves what secures or endangers their freedom," as Jefferson long ago advised us. What the "Nation at Risk" gets from Oligarchy-turned-pedagogue is standardized statewide tests and the educational dominion of the short, right answer—training for credulity, drilling in orthodoxy, fatal to independence of judgment, poisonous, therefore, to liberty's soil. And school-business partnerships, so-called—the opening of classrooms to big-business publicists, the loan of young minds to corporate propagandists—how few are the stones the Reaction leaves unturned!

For why stop at the public schools? The private universities of America provide havens for sedition, forums for the quarrelsome; were hellholes of protest a few years back. Now they shall pay and pay dearly for past temerity. On October 28, 1985, the Secretary of Education, William Bennett, a true stalwart of the Reaction, tells the American Council on Education that government has the solemn duty to protect the "higher education consumer" from lazy professors, slapdash colleges. Do you think your university is "private"? Count the public money in your budget. Do you think you are autonomous by ancient honored tradition? You shall be made "accountable" to government, declares Bennett. You shall serve at Power's behest, in Power's interest. We want standardized national tests for all your "consumers." You shall prove to the satisfaction of Power, says Bennett, that they are making "educational progress," that you are an efficient factory offering a "sound product." Let the state governments enforce this new policy, says Bennett, and state oligarchies leap at the chance. The nation's governors confer on "higher education," call for standardized university testing, objective proof that "learning is taking place," demand proof of "teaching efficiency," hold up for emulation by Yale, aping by Harvard, a test-ridden little educational plant called Northeast Missouri State University at Kirksville. Is this some kind of low jest? Power never jests. By 1987, universities around the country "are beginning to reform their curriculums and are making plans to measure what their students are learning"—standardized nationwide, Power-pleasing measurements, of course. What is higher education? Oligarchy and its minions will tell us. What is an educated person? Oligarchy and its minions will tell us that, too. The whole prospect is "chilling," protests Ernest Boyer, president of the Carnegie Foundation for the Advancement of Teaching. And so it is, the chill of tyranny, for an ancient haven of freedom and autonomy is falling into political bondage in this age of Reaction, age of revenge, age of less government, so-called.

We are "getting government off the back of the people" while the Reaction habituates the people to polygraph tests, drug tests, blood tests, urine tests, roadside police checks, surveillance, snooping, official harassment, to subservience to fiat and servility in general, stamping out "roughness" and "the spirit of defiance," enemies of tyranny and so tyranny's enemies in turn. The drunk-driving menace, says the President, is a "national priority," and at once state legislatures plunge, knifelike, into action. Some 400 drunk-driving laws are enacted between 1982 and 1987. It is a crime now in forty-three states to drive a car while carrying 0.1 percent alcohol in one's blood, acquired by a 150-pound person drinking three or four beers in two hours. Not a crime to *do* something, but a crime to *be* something—a bearer of criminal blood, a police state crime, justifying police roundups on general suspicion, justifying "sobriety check points." One hundred fifty cars have to be stopped at the barrier to find a single person with criminal blood. And that particular one in 150 is unlikely to be a dangerous drunken driver. For alcoholics kill, not 0.1 percent blood alcohol. "We're wasting our time in America on three-quarters of the hundreds of thousands of people we arrest," complains a Quincy, Massachusetts, judge, an expert on the subject. Not expert, however, in the politics of the Reaction, for it is no "waste of time" to Oligarchy to make 1.5 million harassing arrests a year, many millions of roadside stoppages, to habituate a free people to highway roadblocks, highway police threats, to constant fear of arrest, to the sight and smell of the Police Power cracking its whip at random in search of criminal blood.

Fear of the Police Power and fear of one another. All through 1985 pictures of "missing children" peer out from the sides of milk cartons, are depicted on posters, billboards, junk-mail advertisements. Lurid tales of children abducted, raped and mutilated fill the magazines, titillate the talk shows—"Stranger-Danger." Take heed, Americans, your children are "at risk, vulnerable to exploitation, abuse and murder." Walk down the streets watchfully, warily, suspecting everyone. Have your child videotaped, cries New York's unwed mayor, Edward Koch, to safeguard him or her. Sign up with Child Find, affiliated to a teachers' union run by A. Shanker of the Democratic Majority, the Present Danger and the onrushing Reaction in general. Subscribe to "Kid Watch" for twenty-nine dollars a year: "We take all your children's data and enter and store this information in the 'Kid Watch' national computer," until such time as the kidnapper strikes. Let the sheriff fingerprint your child; step right up to the sheriff's booth at the county fair. Or purchase special ID cards or make a mold of your child's teeth, should the kidnapper decide to cremate his mutilated body, for "there are sick people out there," says a young mother waiting to videotape her seven-year-old boy. "Child abduction is a nationwide epidemic," she says, for the President says so, has invited the father of a decapitated boy "several times" to the White House in order to say so. Congress says so, too, has passed the Missing Children Assistance Act of 1984, to arouse the public to the danger of child abduction, rape and mutilation, has created the National Center for Missing and Exploited Children to disseminate grossly misleading statistics, to disseminate fear and make it official. To propagate a truly cruel lie, for the abducted children "epidemic" is a fabrication of the Reaction's fear-mongers, the Present Danger brought home, exposed as a "national myth" in a prize-winning series of articles in the *Denver Post.* Why sow fear of neighbors, fear of strangers, in the hearts of the people? The question answers itself: *Divide et impera.* Are we not more easily ruled, more readily tyrannized, more powerless to act for ourselves, when we shrink in dread from one another?

Tyranny advances with each passing month in this age of "less government." For the first time in our history a federal judge can put an accused person into prison for the crime of looking "dangerous" to society in the eyes of the judge, at the urging of a prosecutor. Imprisonment on suspicion that you may in the future break a law, truly an instrument of oppression, almost certain to be abused in a time of unrest, is this "pre-trial detention," enacted in 1984, with the overwhelming support of liberals and conservatives, Senator Kennedy leading the way. We must look for freedom's security, says a jurist, to "the oversight that Congress retains over its dangerous legislation." But who will guard these guardians when passions run high and their "oversight" is most urgently needed? For the enactors of "dangerous legislation" are themselves the danger to watch.

Tyranny advances with every tainted breeze of fear that wafts over national television. In 1986 a famous athlete dies of an overdose of cocaine, and our national leaders, with one thunderous voice, bray for a "war on drugs." The White House tyrant, ever on the alert to oppress and stifle the people, calls for a "drug-free workplace," calls upon local governments and private corporations

221

to compel their workers to urinate in jars, under watchful inspection, and so be enabled to detect, by examination of the urine specimen, whether they smoked marijuana last weekend at a private party—for the "workplace" is everywhere—"drastically assaulting the privacy, dignity and civil liberties of innocent workers," the *New York Times* rightly protests. "It reports on a person's off-duty activities as surely as if someone had been present and watching. It is George Orwell's 'Big Brother' society come to life." So a federal judge declares in ruling against a mandatory drug-testing program. It puts lawless police power, unrestricted by constitutional rights, into private corporate hands, creates an instrument of terror and harassment—at the behest of Reagan, our champion of "less government."

In this age of "less government," the Executive compiles vast computerized dossiers on scores of millions of Americans, in violation of the Privacy Act, in the name of "government efficiency"; expands its computerized crime index on the pretext of fighting "white-collar crime." The President's budget office proposes—unopposed—an appalling master list of "seriously improper" persons, a national proscription list, pariah list, leper list, created by the White House budget office. Go on strike as a teacher despite a no-strike contract, lose your job and default on a veterans' loan, lead a maverick community action group, be a rebellious farmer, quarrel with the bureaucracy at any level of government, and you may fall onto the List, become an official leper, national pariah. No federal agency or state agency or local government, or charitable organization, or school or college or community service, or government contractor, subcontractor, subgrantor, may give you any kind of "federally derived" aid, grant, loan, scholarship, fellowship, subsidy, subgrant, subcontract, or conduct any kind of "transaction" with you, or do any kind of "business" with you without themselves becoming "seriously improper" and falling under the national White House proscription list, available by telephone in this age of "less government." By the end of 1985 the Executive has subjected 316,000 government officials, contractors, contract employees, at work or retired—the ever-expanding "handful"—to lifetime government censorship, and censors more than 14,000 books and articles in 1985 alone in this age of "less government" and black Stygian public darkness, born of remorseless and unrelenting collusion.

What an age of "less government" this is when Americans who travel to Nicaragua are visited by FBI agents, intimidated by FBI agents, harassed by landlords, employers and tax auditors duly visited by FBI agents; when a few feeble little pro-Sandinista organizations find their offices burgled, their files rifled, their office equipment smashed, again and again, by perpetrators unknown. There is scarcely enough active left-wing dissent in America to organize a small parade, yet the full force of police state repression—re-created by the Reaction—crashes down on these harmless heads—in this age of "less government" for the powerful and more oppressive government for the weak, the active, the public-spirited, the citizen. In this age of an administration "more committed than any in this century in philosophy and in fact to reducing the intrusion of government into the lives, minds and livelihoods of the individual." Sc Secretary Shultz assures the assembled members of a glittering conference of writers in New York City on January 13, 1986, fully confident that not one in ten of that enlightened throng understands what a grotesque, monstrous, outrageous untruth he is hearing, for it is not the plain people only, or even chiefly, who have fled the Republic and the public realm.

"Merger-mania" sweeps over the tyrannized Republic in the first year of the "Second American Revolution." In 1985 more than eight hundred public merger and tender offers are made; four times last year's total, almost twenty times the total in 1977. The "mania" or "binge" is the Reaction's child, its fond creation, tirelessly promoted by Reagan's officials, its source of strength the suspension and debauching of the antitrust laws—by formal "guidelines" and informal winks, by assurances to corporate attorneys and corporate boardrooms that the Reaction wants competition weakened—in the name of "economic efficiency"; wants the market weakened—in the name of the "free market"; wants concentration and oligopoly expanded—in the name of "free enterprise" and the "opportunity society."

Let steel companies merge with steel companies, paper manufacturers with paper manufacturers, oil companies with oil companies, let companies buy "corporations in their own line of business," let them "unite with a company that specializes in the same industry," so the press coyly puts it, lest plain speech awaken sleeping dogs. Let private economic power flourish—capital neither checked by competition nor regulated by law. That is the heart of the "mergermania" enterprise. For private economic power looks always to corrupt politics for protection, allies itself ever and always to the rule of the few, stands always against the rule of the many. We, the people, set our face against such power a hundred years ago and more; cherished laws have opposed it for ninety years and more—for political reasons, republican reasons. But the people have fled; the Republic stands empty. Merge while the merging is good, cries Oligarchy. Merge before the people return. Such is the "mergermania" of 1985: the political economy of the Reaction, strengthening its rule while the opportunity lasts.

With the watchful connivance of Congress, the White House seizes—usurps—still more power over the implementation of laws, still greater control over public information. Reagan's executive order 12498, issued January 4, 1985, bestows on the White House budget office the unheard-of authority to ensure that any government activity that "may influence, anticipate or could lead to the commencement of rulemaking proceedings" be "consistent with the administration's regulatory principles," consistent with its "policies and priorities." Under this new dispensation the will of the President stands supreme over law, shapes the law, implements the law, makes the rule of law a mockery, makes the legislature a mere check and overseer of the presidential will. Henceforth under the new dispensation, no injustice or abuse may be examined by an Executive agency of government, no condition studied, no problem officially scrutinized if a President prefers the reign and

224

rule of darkness. No official information that might question the wisdom of a President's policies can henceforth be collected without his permission. Or, under various other guidelines, directives and budget office usurpations, disseminated to the public without his permission. The White House as secret Legislature, the White House as National Censor, the White House as Ministry of Truth. Such is the new-modeled presidency of the "Second American Revolution." Representative Dingell protests in anger. The new dispensation is "a fundamental threat to the separation of powers embodied in our Constitution." Ralph Nader protests in anger. The new dispensation gives the White House the "policy power of life or death, health or disease, equity or inequity, repair or deterioration, information or ignorance, open or closed government," overwhelming the people, eroding still further our capacity for self-government; another blow struck by the Reaction against a sleeping people's power and liberty. For "if once they become inattentive to the public affairs," Jefferson warned a colleague, "you and I, and Congress and assemblies, judges and governors shall all become wolves." In the deserted Republic the wolves are prowling.

18.
RULE FROM THE GRAVE

Carefully, warily, like shipwrecked mariners spying the long-sought land, the two national party syndicates wend their way toward the "post-Reagan era"—era of political peace, if nothing goes seriously wrong, of American politics once again monopolized by the "regulars," by all who live under Oligarchy's rule and all who flourish in its service. Popular government stifled; the nerve-wracking Right dispensed with. Beckoning, indeed, are these post-Reagan shores, but the electorate must be kept down, kept out, kept disconnected from "the public affairs." The republican cause must not revive, despite the mad jeering tyranny of the Right; nor constitutionalism either, though we pass through the bicentennial year; nor devotion to the rule of law, though the rule of lawlessness treads perilously close to scandal; nor love of liberty and equality rekindled, nor any champion of liberty and equality allowed to gain public renown, though liberty stands besieged and equality lies ravaged as rarely before in our history.

The great task of keeping the plain people stifled falls, as always, to the popular party, and the popular party has been laying its plans well, elaborating and perfecting them with tireless devotion since the 1984 elections.

We must make of ourselves a "centrist" party, a "moderate" party, a "consensus" party, cry the leaders of the popular party in unison, not a single voice raised in audible dissent. We must "shed our ultra-liberal image," cry the party oligarchs after four years of colluding with the Right. We must set ourselves upon "an irresistible course toward moderation," says a "conservative" southern governor. We "will have to swing sharply toward the center of the political spectrum," cries the president of the ubiquitous, tireless Coalition for a Democratic Majority. "We must move in a more moderate centrist direction," says one Nathan Landow, party banker and broker and "liberal" promoter of the 1984 candidacy of poor Walter Mondale. The new party "centrism" is to be established under the guidance of the newly formed Democratic Leadership Council, headed at first by Richard Gephardt, chairman of the House Democratic caucus, a pet of the House leadership, groomed for higher things. The great goal of "centrism" is pursued, too, by the new chairman of the Democratic National Committee, Paul Kirk, manager of Kennedy's "liberal" revolt against a "conservative" southern Democratic President, now preparing to lead a "conservative southern" revolt against "liberalism," one revolt as fake as the other.

Multitudinous are the objects of "centrism." Centrism means organization, the perpetual strengthening of the party oligarchy, rule of the regulars, monastic order. We must "enhance the role of state and local party leaders," cries centrist Gephardt. We must restore to party power "the true repository of its legacy: public officials and party leaders locally elected," says the head of Democratic Majority, perpetual voice of the party machine. We must make the popular party "a highly efficient, highly effective infrastructure, creating a party throughout the country"—there are gaps of freedom in too many states—"rebuilding it, strengthening it as a delivery system," cries National Ward Heeler Kirkland. Delivering what? Delivering "centrism."

Centrism is a purgative, antidote to "leftism." It calls for the purging of noncentrists, of "leftists," of "factions" of "liberal activists" and "special interests" and all bearers of "the new strain of neo-isolationism" until the popular party is free of every last vestige of freeness.

"Centrism" is a victory strategy. We must win back southern white voters to the party fold, say the centrists. We must say nothing and do nothing and be nothing save what will contribute to the great southern white wooing, to the final production of a "centrist presidential candidate who will not offend the political and cultural sensibilities of southern voters." Centrism is a gauntlet to run, known as "Super Tuesday"—laid down by the party leaders to enforce the rule of centrism. On Tuesday, March 8, 1988, fourteen southern and border states choose one-third of the delegates to the Democratic National Convention, the choosing in the region strongly influenced by Democratic Party officials, by hard-bitten county rings and well-purged election rolls, the choosing meant to winnow out the independent, the noncentrist, the outsider, the would-be tribune of the Republic, with what success the reader of this chronicle knows better than the chronicler. But such is Super Tuesday's object: to force presidential ambition—always dangerous to party power, always prone to awaken the people—through a southern gauntlet of corrupt county rings.

Centrism is a new party platform set forth by the new Democratic Policy Commission, packed, as a matter of course, with "centrists" by Kirk, to supply "a broader agenda of the Democratic Party and the nation." Let us have done with "the singular agenda of elite groups," says Kirk, pressing into service Kirkpatrick's great Political Science discovery of 1972: Oligarchy is democratic and democracy is "elitist," for Oligarchy's lies never die, while political truth is strangled every day.

The "broader agenda" of "centrism" demands a "strong defense," demands (as of September 1986) "increased combat strength," demands greater "combat readiness," demands in the post-Reagan era another kind of arms buildup to overcome the grotesque fraudulence of the first one. "At the grass roots, people see a bloated defense budget as the reason for the $200 billion deficits," says Senator Grassley, an Iowa Republican, in February 1986. What does the "broader agenda" care about the people? What does it care about America's "grass roots"? We must rebuild "the public consensus on defense," for if the people have grown "weak on defense," centrism will try to elect a new people.

"Centrism" demands an active interventionist global foreign policy, condemns with utmost harshness "Chamberlain-style isolationism," so the policy commission puts it; warns of the "strategic threat" posed by "Marxist-Leninist regimes conceived in the image of the Soviet Union"; calls for "military assistance to authentic democratic resistance movements" around the globe. We must overcome "doubts about the Democratic Party's willingness to back diplomacy with power," we must "contain" the Soviet Union, sharply reduce its influence, compel its leaders to "respect the human rights they have agreed to observe as signatories of the Helsinki Accords." Senator Jackson is dead! Senator Jackson lives on as "centrism," as the republic reburied in the imperial tomb.

"Centrism" calls loudly for "fiscal responsibility," meaning "means tests" for social programs, mean vice taxes, mean excises, meanness, as a matter of principle. Centrism calls for "growth"— abject worship of the gross national product just when deep and rankling injustice cries out for amelioration. Calls for loosening the antitrust laws just when the Reagan administration begins to fear a "populist" backlash against "merger-mania." Blames the U.S. trade deficit on the Yellow Peril. Blames the low productivity of the U.S. economy on the poor quality of American workers— "productivity begins at home," brays the "broader agenda" of centrism—just when Richard Darman, Reagan's Under Secretary of the Treasury, assails America's "bloated," inept "corpocracy." In a word, "centrism" blames all that is wrong with the American economy on everything except corporate America, just when corporate quackery is crumbling of its own coarse self-serving inanity.

Thus the new "centrism" of the popular party—a test, a shibboleth, an instrument of discipline and suppression. Defy the canons of "centrism" and you fall outside the party pale, outside the warm world of money and PACs, of "get-along, go-along," and easy reelections. "Sorry, we can't raise money for you because you're Darth Vader." So a Washington cynic describes the money power at work in the popular party. Centrism, too, is a grim warning to any would-be tribune of the people, any would-be champion of liberty besieged and equality ravaged, that the entire power of the popular party stands united, armed and arrayed against him. Most of all, centrism is a headlong flight from the American people; a ship, a vehicle to carry Oligarchy past the snares and pitfalls that bestrew the path to the "post-Reagan era."

Snares and pitfalls there are. In mid-September 1985, an alarm bell goes off, faintly stirring the comatose nation: The United States has become a debtor nation for the first time since World War I. We consume too much, produce too little—behold this "supply-side" era!—borrow to make up the difference: $400 billion borrowed from abroad since Reagan took office and deeper into debt we will sink, $700 billion deep by 1990, such is one official estimate. Something is amiss and badly amiss. Some 1.6 million manufacturing jobs have been lost since 1980, the administration admits this September. We work harder and longer than we did ten years ago, so polltaker Harris reports this September, work harder at poor-paying jobs. Nine of ten new jobs created in the "recovery"—an "economic miracle," Reagan calls it—pay less than $14,000 a year. Six of ten pay less than $7,000 a year: sweated labor, burger-flipping labor. There is "deep discontent among workers," an industrial relations expert warns this September. People are sliding down the social scale. "There are a lot of coiled springs out there," warns a labor negotiator. And how well centrism knows it, how terrified it is of some future uncoiling! For inequality has been deepened in the land, deepened by the Reaction's war on equality, war on the citizen, war on the Republic. The gap between the poorest 40 percent of the people and the richest 40 percent is the widest since the Census Bureau began making the calculation in 1947. Many sides and harsh aspects has this new era of privilege and inequality. A college diploma, more costly than ever, with less government help in the getting, is three times more valuable on receipt, economically measured, than it was in 1980. Three of five families with children have suffered a loss of real income between 1979 and

1984, so the Joint Economic Committee reports this year. Only one-fifth of families with children have gained—the richest one-fifth. Silently, stealthily, carefully unmentioned, wealth passes from the many to the few. The national debt stood at $907 billion when the champion of the balanced budget took office. It stands at $1.82 trillion at the end of 1985. The interest payment stands at $178 billion a year, an absolutely irreducible increase of $100 billion a year since 1980, an annual $100 billion assault on the fisc, $10 billion of which, at the very least, is transferred from the people to the rich every year, while "Medicare," reports a *New York Times* writer, "now pays only for the most minimal care, short of the level that might draw a possible suit for malpractice." Meanwhile, the number of poor people increases as economic insecurity increases, and more and more Americans find themselves without medical insurance of any kind.

Is this deepening injustice, this legislated inequality one reason why Americans have become "superconsumers," spending wildly, borrowing deeply, saving less than we have ever saved before? Are we trying, with other people's money, to conceal from ourselves the gross inequality inflicted upon us by our erstwhile leaders, by our "popular" President? Americans "have been living in a kind of false paradise," warns Paul Volcker of the Federal Reserve. Do we live so because we can no longer bear the sight of misrule, have not sufficient confidence in ourselves, sufficient "roughness and spirit of defiance," sufficient civic courage left in our hearts? Just possibly so.

At the root of much of this vast dislocation lies the crime of '81, the original assault on the fisc, assault on tax justice, the profligate buildup, engine of waste without parallel, and its known and deliberate outcome—the huge annual budget deficits: $213 billion in fiscal year 1985, a record, until 1986's deficit reaches $226 billion. The deficits have "suffocated the legislative process," says Majority Leader Wright in 1985, have suffocated it since 1982 and will suffocate it for years to come. The deficits put the popular party into a "fiscal straitjacket," reduce lawmaking, in the main, to scrimping and saving, slicing and gnawing. They give the popular party a perpetual excuse for doing nothing at all, being nothing at all, promising nothing at all save the living deadness of centrism. The deficits lie upon the hopes of the people like the lid of a coffin, a blessing indeed to Oligarchy, at long last on the high road to unchallenged supremacy.

Political blessing, economic bane; what is to be done with the deficits as the debtor-nation alarm bell goes off this September of 1985? An arresting moment, pregnant with possibilities, for there lies in the hands of Rostenkowski—brazen party oligarch—the chance to ameliorate the crime of '81. It is a proposal for a "sweeping overhaul" of the tax code made this May by the President, as the one "major initiative" of his second term, otherwise aimless, pointless, ad hoc and worse. It calls commendably for drastic curtailment of scores of tax loopholes, breaks for the rich, in return for which the wealthy will have their tax rates drastically reduced—from 50 percent to 28 percent in the final version. It calls for a drastic flattening of the progressive tax, flattened down to three tax brackets—two in the final version, 15 percent and 28 percent—with $29,750 marking the bracket line. It is supposed to be "revenue-neutral," so Reagan decrees. Not a cent will it add in revenues to reduce $200 billion deficits. A "fair share" tax bill, Reagan calls it, and cries it up with utmost fervor, crisscrossing the country this spring and fall with ever-growing urgency, for this is Reagan's "domestic legacy," the completion, it is said, of the "Reagan Revolution." Defeat of this bill "would instantly transform the once-high-flying President into a crippled fowl," says *Newsweek,* would make Reagan "an instant lame-duck President," warns *Congressional Quarterly.* Alas for Reagan, he cries up in vain, campaigns in vain, crisscrosses America in vain. The people are deaf to this "fair share" tax reform, "drones of indifference" greet the Great Communicator, and "wide doubts," and whispered misgivings. Half the corporate world wants no part of it; half the Republican Party and more wants no part of it; the great majority of ordinary people want no part of it. To wipe out tax loopholes does justice. So the American people have thought for two decades and more. To give these ill-gotten gains back to the rich is tax justice mocked, "fair share" as fraud. And who thinks the rich will not puncture new loopholes in the "fair share" tax code and make it unfairer still? And where is the justice in abandoning ability to pay as our fundamental tax principle, in abandoning what the popular party long upheld as "the one great equalizer of the tax burden"? Equalizer, for one, of our brutally regressive federal payroll tax, a 1.6 percent burden on a taxpayer earning a $200,000 salary; a 7.15 percent burden on a worker earning $12,000 a year. Where is the justice in allowing no deductions for interest on educational loans, but deductions on summer house mortgages, Palm Beach mansions, million-dollar sleep-in yachts? Where is the justice in allowing deductions for property taxes, but not for sales taxes? Where is the justice in favoring the propertied over the unpropertied, in letting the fisc pay for business lunches and forcing scholarship students—this for the first time—to pay a partial tax on their scholarships? Where is the fairness in this "fair share" tax? Would it not be more just, would it not be more prudent, to close the unjust loopholes the President wants closed and apply every cent gained to reducing the menacing deficits? Whatever Reagan may say, *that* is what the bulk of the country deems sensible and just.

In the House on September 17, liberal Democrats plead with the Speaker to use the tax bill to enlarge the shrunken fisc. Let the rich reduce the deficit for a change, instead of the poor, the ailing, the crippled; instead of the laws, the roads, the schools, the towns and liberties of America. Let equality and prosperity, republicanism and economic prudence—sundered in the 1978 *coup de main*—be brought together again. Let us dig out at last from under the midden heap of quackery and cant. True enough, the President stands adamantly opposed. What of it, say the liberal Democrats; the people are with us, not him. If he wishes to become an "instant lame duck," so be it. Why should Democrats "bail out the President," angry liberals ask? Why should we save *his* tax bill and see the progressivity of the federal tax system "destroyed," as Nobel-laureate economist James Tobin puts it? Why should we fight for "revenue-neutrality" when the economy cries out for deficit-reduction?

Thus the liberal Democrats plead, but they plead, as usual, in vain. Let Rostenkowski "go ahead" with his work of pushing Reagan's tax bill through his closed-door committee and thence through the House, the House Democratic caucus decrees. Let Reagan's "domestic legacy" become our "priority bill," says the Speaker. Let us gather the 170 or so *Democratic* votes needed to save the President from "instant lame-duck status," from being "Carterized" by his party, so one writer puts it. "Rostenkowski and O'Neill have been the administration's main allies," reports *Congressional Quarterly*, have been so for years, but never quite so blatantly as now. The "unlikely troika of Reagan, Rosty and House Speaker O'Neill," reports *Newsweek*, will save Reagan's "fair share" hoax, for the Speaker and Rostenkowski are powerful and the popular party bends to their will. For while punditry bemoans the "weakness" and "breakdown" of America's political parties—vainly awaiting the return of checked trousers, derby hats and Tammany beer parties—two national party machines, powerful centralized syndicates, have been re-created before their unseeing eyes. Thanks to the popular party machine this autumn, tax injustice is secure for a decade; the deficits are preserved for cutting and gnawing and mean excises—for revenues must be enhanced, say the champions of "revenue-neutrality," once tax injustice is saved. And saved, too, is the truthless tyrant, this above all, as always. And the belief in the harmony of justice and prosperity will be left, like so much else, to rot in our hearts.

One pitfall averted, but by no means the last, for the people seem to be stirring, faintly but perceptibly, as the year 1986 begins. "A sudden surge of support for a wide variety of social programs" registers strongly in opinion polls. The whole fierce boiling Reaction, the huge crushing weight of orthodoxy and cant, seems to have left the people unchanged in their views, however weakly they care, however deeply they despair of seeing them voiced in the public arena. Amazingly unchanged, in fact. Two of three Americans believe "continuing environmental improvements must be made regardless of cost." Three of four Americans want an end to the nuclear arms race. Most astonishing of all, two of three Americans, so the *New York Times* discovers in the mid-January poll, want the government to spend more money on programs for the poor, "Great Society" programs, universally despised by our leaders for years, but not by the people, which "seems to run counter to the view of many Democrats that there is no longer any political mileage in such federal poverty programs."

Punditry and bankers fret this January about a populist "backlash" inspired by Wall Street, by its unmuzzled wolves, its "insider" traders, its conniving, law-breaking, privileged youths; by the spectacle of giant corporations traded like stock shares. "The cancer called greed" is menacing the security of wealth and privilege, an investment banker warns a Senate committee this January. An angry Texas jury fines a grasping oil company several billion dollars and more shivers run through the ranks of privilege. Is *this* the feared firebell in the night, signaling the beginning of the end of the Reaction?

Meanwhile, contrariwise, the legions of the Right are beginning to dwindle and disperse. The Right's feared agitators have become mere bogeys and scarecrows. Jerry Falwell is a hissing and a byword, cheap ward heeler dressed up as a cleric, his Moral Majority has become such a stench in our nostrils, Falwell creates a new organization this January—the Liberty Foundation—in order to make a fresh start. While Richard Viguerie, direct-mail demagogue—"we are ready to lead," cried this tool of Power back in 1980—has sunk into bankruptcy, so the *New York Times* reports this January, this new year's month of faintly discernible stirrings and signs of life renewed.

The stirring spurs the White House to frenzy, tempts it to dangerous courses, to selling arms to Iran in exchange for hostages—these, it is later said, to be triumphantly displayed before a joint session of Congress, or brandished on the eve of the 1986 elections—wild, desperate demagoguery. For power is slipping from the President's grasp just when the Right needs power most desperately, needs it to safeguard a vile tyrant's dream, for the Right does not intend to give up power in the "post-Reagan era." It dreams and schemes and relentlessly plots to rule America from the grave, to crush us from the grave, to keep us impoverished, impotent, enslaved from the grave, enslaved by a fisc perpetually wasted, by an arms race made endless and costly beyond measure—the crime of '81 perpetuated indefinitely, the hideous crime against a free people's freedom to live by our own lights, our loathed and hated lights.

The tyrant's dream comes cloaked in an official "dream," a presidential "dream," glozing and heartwarming, outlined by Reagan on March 23, 1983. Let us, said the President then, call upon the marvels of science to give America and the world a perfect impenetrable shield against nuclear missiles; a defense based in space, covering the cities, protecting the people, rendering offensive nuclear weapons "impotent and obsolete." Perfect security shall one day be ours; science and its wonders shall transport us back to the blessed days when two broad oceans shielded America from the Old World and its evils. Thus speaks the truthless demagogue in the White House. For the President's "dream"—Star Wars, Strategic Defense Initiative, SDI—is a hoax and a fraud, "totally speculative," a "trillion-dollar mirage." It outrages the elders. The speech is "one of the most irresponsible actions by any head of state in modern times," cries George Ball, a former Under Secretary of State. The idea of protecting whole populations with a perfect missile shield "borders on the absurd," cries former Defense Secretary Brown. It is heartless demagoguery that "plays cruelly on the fear and hope of every citizen," cries Averell Harriman, constrained to protest this madness in his ninety-third year. "It is totally out of sync with reality," says even icy, cautious Senator Nunn.

A mere outer husk, however, is this presidential "dream," an alluring package, false advertisement for the real Star Wars project, the official, unmentioned, project. An "enhanced deterrent," the Pentagon calls it, so a presidential directive calls it. It does not, cannot, will not shield populations. At the very most it would shoot down enough Soviet ICBMs to protect our land-based missiles from a theoretical, suicidal Soviet attack. Scandalously wasteful, utterly needless, a menace to the world is this "enhanced deterrent." It would give us a deadly mixture of offense and defense, a generator, inevitably, of an endless arms race, defense spurring offense, offense spurring defense, today and tomorrow, ever and anon, a double arms race "run . . . to infinity unfettered by treaty restrictions," says Townsend Hoopes, former Under Secretary of the air force. The "dream" conjured up for Reagan, not by scientists or defense experts but by two ignorant, willful, right-wing millionaires, one Coors, a beer brewer; one Dart, the drugstore magnate; two chief promoters of Reagan's political career and of this conspiracy to rule from the grave. Their lunatic scheme would bring not peace but a sword, not security but instability, first strike threats, "hair-trigger" readiness, the deepening shadows of nuclear holocaust. And the fisc devoured, the public realm shrunk. For the cost of the "enhanced deterrent" is appalling in itself: $100 billion just to put up some kind of space station defense. Some $100 billion to $200 billion *a year* to keep it there, ever needing improvement to fend off Soviet offensive improvements, so Brown and McNamara testify before Congress on April 10, 1986. A giant maw, a hungry Moloch, a truly hideous engine of wanton waste to be put up in space as soon as possible, for we must "make it impossible to turn off by 1989," say the schemers and plotters of rule from the grave, while the White House demagogue keeps prating of his "vision," his "dream," his perfect shield. Lying through his teeth as usual, but the lie is absolutely essential to the plot, for public awareness of the real SDI, the official SDI, "would knock the bottom out of public support for the project," the *New York Times* rightly observes. The lie is promoted by a legion of hucksters, neoconservatives, Present Dangerists, liars in uniform, liars in laboratory coats, by falsified research results, by pseudoscientific publicity stunts—BEACON: "Bold Experiments to Advance Confidence" and STAR: "Significant Technical

Achievements Research"—conveying a vague aura of impending miracle, of presidential dream materializing. The liars and blatherers are free to speak while skeptics working in scientific laboratories face imprisonment for telling the truth to the American people, for so we are now ruled in the tyrannized Republic, where truth is an "export," truth is "espionage" and the people an enemy country under laws distended and distorted in the service of Oligarchy.

On December 31, 1985, Star Wars becomes the "highest priority" of the Pentagon, to be put up in any junk form when the time is ripe—and then the Right shall rule us from the grave.

Fortune enters the picture, bedeviling the tyrant's scheme. Russia's newest ruler, one Mikhail Gorbachev, is bent upon the domestic reform of his country, bent upon its economic and political revival, wants, therefore, what the overwhelming majority of Americans want, what the Republic desperately needs—an arms control treaty that can end the nuclear arms race. Does the ruling Right in America not demand "deep cuts" in the Soviet arsenal of intercontinental missiles? It does indeed, most ardently, unremittingly, has demanded them for years, has flayed Carter to ribbons for want of "deep cuts" in the SALT II treaty. Has the administration not launched an enormous nuclear buildup, avowedly, for the want of Soviet deep cuts? Is it not planning an "enhanced deterrent" in space in lieu of Soviet deep cuts? Why then, says Gorbachev in 1985, you shall have the deep cuts agreement you so ardently desire, and the price for that grand desideratum, Present Danger goal, Reaganite goal, "Jackson wing" goal is—no price at all: chiefly continued adherence to the 1972 Anti-ballistic Missile Treaty, signed by Richard Nixon, ratified by the U.S. Senate, barring development, testing and deployment of defensive weapons in space, scotching the menace of an endless double arms race, one of the most valuable treaty agreements into which the U.S. ever entered.

The Soviet offer comes down to this: security for U.S. land-based missiles, "enhanced deterrence," thereby, vulnerability's "window" closed, the nuclear arms race effectively restricted at almost no cost whatever. Or consider the alternative: an "enhanced deterrent" in space, an endless arms race, security lost, stability lost, at the cost, perhaps, of *one trillion dollars every five years,* at the price of our sovereignty, of our freedom, of our public life now faintly stirring. The choice must not be seen and known to the people, or the Right cannot rule from the grave. The choice must be shrouded in darkness, grossly distorted, the people left puzzled, bewildered, confused; public life turned into a demagogic riot, irrational frenzy, insofar as the White House can do it. Led by reckless Casey, presidential "favorite," in alliance with feckless Regan, the President's new chief of staff, Reagan launches a campaign of fear and hatred, alarums and excursions in 1986, desperate to stay the slippage of his power, to halt the flight of the people, before the Damoclean sword of "deep cuts" falls once again, piercing the black heart of the Right.

Let there be blood lust and vengeance, first and foremost, the White House decides in early January. We accuse Libya's Qaddafi of two bloody and hideous airport bombings, the President proclaims on January 7. The evidence of his blood guilt is "irrefutable"—a lie, but Qaddafi is hated, Qaddafi is friendless, Qaddafi is safe to attack, as terrorist Syria is not, as terrorist Iran is not. If the economic sanctions ordered this day "do not end Qaddafi's terrorism, I promise you that further steps will be taken"—taunts, provocations, rabble-rousing and worse. Let America wallow in hatred, so the White House decides.

Let America stew in fear as well. A second military buildup is needed, cries the truthless demagogue in the White House, so powerful and threatening is Gorbachev's Russia. The defense budget stands at $287 billion now. Not enough, not nearly enough, cries Reagan. We must give $33 billion more to the Moloch this year; a half trillion increase by 1991, for our "security program is in jeopardy," threatened by those who would bring back the hideous age of détente, appeasement and unilateral disarming, the loathsome "decade before 1981," before I, Ronald Reagan, came to save you, when "the Soviets were the only ones racing." So the fear-monger in the White House cries and lies—the very CIA contradicts him—growing coarse and reckless with lies, as power slips from his grasp. "Almost more than a human being can bear," cries poor forgotten Jimmy Carter a few days after Reagan's speech, constrained at long last to protest against a President who says things "he knows are not true and which he personally promised me not to repeat." Promised but repeats again, and then again, and again, and again, with utter contempt for truth, for vows, for honor or decency; caring only to shill for the Right, advance its cause and perpetuate its power. From this regimen of lies shall we ever recover? After this reign of mendacity will public probity ever return? For "the triumph of demagogies is short-lived," warned the French poet Charles Péguy, "but the ruins are eternal."

Gorbachev's Russia is gaining a "beachhead in North America," cries the White House fear-monger on March 16, in a rabid, hysterical Sunday night speech. Let the "cancer" of Sandinistas survive in Nicaragua, let the "malignancy in Managua" endure—anti-Semites they are and drug traffickers they are, says the false, frothing President—and Gorbachev's Russia "will be in a position to threaten the Panama Canal, interdict our vital Caribbean sea-lanes, and ultimately move against Mexico," sending "desperate Latin peoples by the millions" into the "cities of the southern United States," black nigger-spic infestation, cries and implies the shameless demagogue in the White House as he "spews out rage and hate, fear and falsehood," so Anthony Lewis of the *New York Times* angrily protests. Spews forth, too, vile allegations of communist influence in Congress itself, of communist dupes, communist stooges, victims of a "Sandinista Disinformation and Public Manipulation Plan"—a CIA report concocted by Casey, brandished before Congress, poisoning the atmosphere in Washington, as it has not been poisoned in years.

There has been a Nicaraguan "invasion" of Honduras, cries the White House demagogue a few days later. Skeptical reporters rush to the alleged scene, are barred from the area, for the Ministry of Truth, lying as usual, protects its lies with the new press censorship policy. "For most of the week news organizations were entirely dependent on the Reagan administration for details of the incident." But not a word of "complaint" is heard from the press, so the *New York Times* ruefully reports. For the press, which raged over the Grenada blackout, is now utterly cowed and supine. A few days later, in Mediterranean waters, three U.S. carriers and thirty escort ships taunt and provoke the Libyan dictator, attacking and destroying two Libyan ships, conducting two raids against the Libyan coast—a naval dance of hatred and bullying, of murderous rabble-rousing, preparing the people for the next assault. And the press, barred from the fictive Nicaraguan "invasion," is barred from this combat as well. And again from the press "no complaints" and worse: praise for the military that keeps them in blindfolds, feeds them official bulletins and lies. "They have been as open and as cooperative as we can reasonably expect," says ABC News, groveling. "The military has been extremely cooperative," say CBS News, NBC News and the *Washington Post,* their views "largely echoed," says the *New York Times,* by "several large news agencies," which praise "the unusual harmony between the press and the Pentagon"—the harmony of the bootlick and the boot. For in the tenth year of the Reaction, freeness of the press lies in ruins. Will *this* ruin of demagoguery prove eternal? Will the cowing of the press by one tyrant provide the deadly precedent and easement for the next one? And one question more ominous yet: Will this demagoguery leave behind a permanent faction for tyranny in America?

On April 14, eighteen U.S. war planes bomb the city of Tripoli to "punish" Qaddafi—and kill one of his children—for blowing up a discothèque in West Berlin. The accusation is false, the White House evidence trumped up, carefully kept from all government experts, pronounced "irrefutable" by the Ministry of Truth. The target was chosen long before the Berlin bombing—hated Qaddafi, friendless Qaddafi, safe to attack as Syria is not, as Iran is not. Such is the pride and honor of the new America, such our new standard of conduct, for true honor has fled and much else besides. The ancient idea of a national interest is being effaced, destroyed, consigned to oblivion by these demagogue strikes, alarums and excursions—Grenada one day, Lebanon another, the Libyan shore, the Persian Gulf, a Berlin dance hall, an Angolan village. America is here, there, everywhere. No sparrow falls but we are there, or might be or could be or should be. Let machete-wielding guerrillas chop off the head of a communist official and America is there supporting them; let them kill pregnant women in a communist-held village and there, too, we shall be proffering arms. A Republic no longer, a vast imperium, rather, spread-eagled, global, ever "in search of monsters to destroy"—and monsters to deploy—for the Reaction is triumphant here, too, is triumphant everywhere, so it seems.

While the White House "spews out rage and hate, fear and falsehood"—and Reagan's credibility silently, invisibly oozes away—Oligarchy consolidates its gains. Lifts the 1976 ban on covert aid to Angolan guerrillas, a "major victory" for the revived imperium, so the Cato Institute, being genuinely conservative, rightly laments. Quietly, privately, without a word of debate, Oligarchy affirms in October 1986 the usurped legislative power of the White House budget office, stipulating only that White House legislators be subject to Senate confirmation; Oligarchy again checking tyranny. Quietly, stealthily, it weakens the Freedom of Information Act—also in October 1986—by making it harder to discover government spying, closing a loophole in the restored surveillance system. Weakens it, too, by giving government agencies the authority to charge high fees for requests deemed insufficiently useful to the "public interest"; ensures that false frugality will likely prevail over public enlightenment by putting the law's administration into the hands of the budget office, more strengthening of the Ministry of Truth. One by one the achievements of the republican revival are being dismantled before our unseeing eyes, while "centrism" smothers the people's faint stirring. Do we at the grass roots "see the bloated defense budget as the reason for the $200 billion deficits"? Let the defense budget for 1987 increase by $8 billion, for reduction equals "isolationism," warns mackerel-bright Moynihan, chief among "centrists," anxiously scouring the horizon for every fell sign of republican sentiment.

Most of all, centrism protects the tyrant from the people, vouches for his lies or keeps a discreet silence. In May, David Stockman, the former budget director, publishes a memoir, describes with devastating effect the lies, the frauds, the wanton military waste that made up the crime of '81, but "political Washington" turns from the sight and the press, at the nadir of servility, attacks Stockman for criticizing our leader. "Strangely," notes a press critic a year later, the commentators "focused more on Stockman and his supposedly disrespectful tone toward his former boss than on Reagan's policies." For thus Oligarchy would have it and so punditry, groveling, obeys.

Centrism knows full well, too—has known since August 1985 at the latest—that Reagan's White House aides are raising private war funds, conducting illicit private war, violating the Constitution—and turns a blind eye. Centrism knows full well, too, that the President's "dream" of a perfect space shield is a huckster's hoax, a shill's cruel lie, but the people must suspect nothing. The President's "sincerity," his "faith" in his "vision" must not be doubted by the national rabble. We shall check the conspiracy our own way, for it truly imperils the safety of the world, but inform the common people, speak sooth to the common people, hold up a light for the people to see by? Not if Power, unslumbering, can keep us in darkness.

19.
CENTRISM TRIUMPHANT

S uddenly, on the high road to the "post-Reagan era," an
immense political scandal erupts, as momentous as any in
our history, sheds light at long last on the mad, jeering tyranny of the Right, threatens to awaken a citizenry, threatens to revive
the republican cause. On Election Day, November 4, 1986, centrism stands triumphant, powerful, exultant. On November 25, it
trembles for its safety, ponders how darkness may be restored, a
citizenry smothered, the Republic stifled; how the Constitution
may be openly trashed in the very year of its bicentennial celebration. Fortunately for the powerful few, they are powerful enough
now even for this.

"A new era of American politics" has begun, proclaims
Moynihan on November 5, for the electorate is tepid, tractable,
apathetic. Their turnout is the lowest since the war year of 1942. A
"centrist" electorate truly, which sends several right-wing senators
to defeat, gives "centrism" control of the Senate once more,
demands nothing, it seems, save centrism. Whatever stirred last
January stirs not this November 4. In the House of Representatives
scarcely a seat changes hands, scarcely an incumbent loses, scarcely
more than fifty House seats are closely contested—officious electoral partisanship has been reduced by the rule of Oligarchy to its
lowest level, perhaps, in our modern history. Liberty besieged and
equality ravaged have made no mark on the election. Nor has the

President's cowardly flight from a conference with Gorbachev, flight from a "deep cuts" proposal, clutching his tyrant's "dream." Nor has the sensational downing of an American cargo plane in Nicaragua this October 5, linking the CIA and possibly the White House to a lawless private war against the Nicaraguan regime. A "vast, secret, bewildering" campaign, the *New York Times* calls it this October 22. "A new Watergate-type scandal," says a writer in the *Los Angeles Times* this October 26, about which the electorate seems to care little. "We have exorcised the war, the riots, the rhetoric," cries exultant Moynihan, "and thank God that time is over." Democracy is dead, republicanism is dead, the mad jeering Right, useful but nerve-wracking, is on its way out. Party oligarchy stands supreme, triumphant, unchallenged at last.

Or almost, for the press on this exultant day has extraordinary news to relate: The United States has sold weapons to Iran—hated reviler of America—in exchange for the release of a few hostages in Lebanon, "with the personal approval of President Reagan," notes the *Los Angeles Times* on the sixth, in "marked contrast" to the administration's public policy, in grotesque mockery of "Operation Staunch," the administration's campaign to persuade the world to stop arms shipments to Iran, in violation of the laws requiring the President to notify Congress of such secret deeds; in violation of the Anti-Terrorism Act of 1986, which bars, by explicit order of Reagan himself, any sale of arms to Iran, in "marked contrast" to six years of Reagan's railing against "international terrorism," in marked contrast to his bragging vow to give no quarter, pay no ransom, strike no bargains with terrorist nations, of which Iran is one by presidential decree.

"A dreadful mistake," says Senator Goldwater, "probably one of the major mistakes the United States has ever made in foreign policy." A contemptible mistake, the mistake of a vulgar demagogue who thinks the sight of liberated hostages reunited with their families at the White House wipes out for a degraded television electorate all thought of public vows, policies, national pledges. That degraded we are not. The entire country is appalled, shocked, angry, disheartened at the vile dishonorable arms-for-hostages trade. Nor does it rally to the "popular" President's side when he denies making any such trade, when he cries out against the vicious lying press, assails its "utterly false" charges, its distortion of "the facts," its "false rumors and erroneous reports," its "wildly speculative and false stories about arms for hostages and ransom payments." You lie, Ronald Reagan; you lie in your teeth. The whole country knows it, believes it, will no longer deny it in our hearts. "Now the public is questioning Mr. Reagan's honesty," the *Los Angeles Times* reports on November 18. Four of five Americans polled by the newspaper think Reagan speaks falsely about the arms sale. Four of five Americans believe he has broken the law. Is civic courage returning to America? Are we grown weary at last of our own abject subservience to a demagogue?

For twenty days the arms scandal smolders, sparks and rumbles, and then on November 25, like a volcano long-threatening, it heaves up its boiling innards and spews them forth on the land. This appalling fact the world learns on the twenty-fifth: Money gained in the odious sale of arms to Iran has been diverted by Reagan's National Security Council staff—one Oliver North in particular—to support the private contra war in Nicaragua. Odious traffic for a lawless purpose. So Reagan informs the press in a terse, four-minute announcement, before fleeing the questions of reporters. For there is nothing he can say that will not sink him deeper into lies, crimes and impeachable offenses. The announcement itself creates a sensation "unmatched, perhaps, since the days of the Watergate crisis," the *New York Times* reports, revealing an "astonishing pattern of lawless activity," the *Times* also reports. Lawless and worse.

The diversion itself is a serious crime, subject to criminal penalties: "fraudulent conversion of government funds." The diversion, more scandalous yet, reveals what the White House had been desperately concealing for weeks and months: that the "vast, secret, bewildering" network supplying the contras while the law forbids government aid is not purely private at all. It is a White House enterprise, a secret presidential war fought with a White House privy purse, in "flagrant violation of the Appropriations Clause of the Constitution," a congressional report later declares, organized by a privately funded White House government—behold "Project Democracy" at work!—as if a President of the United States had the right to pursue any private scheme he chooses, as long as he has private means to finance it, as if the elected chief magistrate of the American Republic were a monarch with his own royal treasury, his own private retainers, his own royal sphere above and beyond the meddlesome Commons.

"Dictators, not democrats, create private governments, develop private budgets by dunning the wealthy, traffic with profiteers and lie to legislatures. Tyrants, not elected public servants, decide which laws apply to them." So the *New York Times* rightly, and angrily, puts it. For never in the history of the United States has the constitutional order been so contemptuously ignored, so lightly dismissed, so deeply and dangerously polluted, corrupted, defiled and violated.

What does it mean to "take care that the laws be faithfully executed" when a President claims the right not to know, the right to forget, the crimes his highest aides commit in his service? What does the presidential oath mean if a President can secretly declare a crime "important to national security" and order its commission in secret? What does the rule of law mean when a President obeys and disobeys laws at will? What does law itself mean if it stands inferior to the will of a President and a private purse? What does accountable power mean when a President is free to ignore the laws that hold him accountable? What does the U.S. Constitution mean, on the eve of its two hundredth anniversary, if a tyrant can thrive in its bosom?

On November 25, the mad, jeering tyranny of shysters and sharks, protected by Oligarchy for so many years, stands revealed at last to the American people. We do not flinch from the sight; this moment of truth we can bear. Between November 1 and November 30 Reagan's popular esteem in the polls plummets from 67 percent to 46 percent, the sharpest one-month decline since such polling began a half-century ago. The President cannot save himself; his word is worthless, his "candor" a trick played once too often, far too often. On November 26, Reagan, in desperation, appoints a three-man "special review board" to tell him what his highest aides were doing—ignorance is already his first, corrupt, ignominious line of defense, but it does him no good. Reagan is "covering up," so a majority of Americans believe on November 30. "The public must look to Congress for a solution," warn the editors of the *New York Times:* Capitol Hill alone can restore popular "confidence" in government.

For the nation's leaders, the fork in the road is cruel and dangerous, the choices bleak: If we form a special investigating committee, if we hold conspicuous public hearings in front of network television cameras, before a citizenry awakened, revived and riveted, will it not inspire the people once more with love of truth and justice, with love of the law and the law's supremacy, with love of oaths and fidelity to oaths—all the grave republican evils of Watergate reviving once more? Would not such a committee inspire in the bicentennial year harsh constitutional demands, high constitutional resolves, severe constitutional reckonings? The danger of such a committee is enormous; failure would be catastrophic; the undoing, the ruination, of all we have fought for, struggled for, all we have lied and betrayed for, lo these ten years and more.

Yet the alternative to a special committee would very likely be worse, warns Senator Moynihan on a television program this Sunday, November 30. "Protracted paralysis, rancor, poison in the air" would be the inevitable result. And something far worse than these: the exposure of the whole mad jeering shyster tyranny, for the Iran-contra scandal is a golden opportunity come at last for many a friend of democracy in Congress, a chance to throw off the thrall of Oligarchy and reveal to a people grown suddenly attentive the true extent and depth of the tyranny of the Right, six years at work besieging liberty and law and the power of the people. If Oligarchy leaves a vacuum, the friends of liberty will rush in to fill it.

249

On the morning of November 30, Senator Dole, Republican Majority Leader, casts the fateful die. Let there be a Watergate-type investigation of the Iran-contra scandal, he announces on a Sunday news program. There is no safe alternative. "This is critical. It is not going to go away." What will the committee investigate? Will it pry pitilessly into tyranny, lawlessness and crime, private White House government, secret government, impeachable offenses, guilty knowledge? Let no fatuous friend of liberty mistake the aims of Oligarchy on this historic Sunday, November 30, 1986.

What say you, Senator Byrd, to Dole's proposal, the *New York Times* inquires by telephone? The past and future Senate Majority Leader approves. "This is my President. He's in trouble and I don't want to see the presidency damaged." By what, pray tell us? A light shining on tyranny and crime? A light shining *from* law and the Constitution? What says icy, cautious Nunn? "We must, all of us, help the President restore his credibility in foreign affairs. We can't have a crippled President for two years." A crippled Carter for four years mattered not, but the "credibility" of a liar and a tyrant must be "restored," for the people and the Republic must be kept down.

What says lawmaker Les Aspin, perpetual restorer of the "defense consensus"? "Keep it narrow," advises Aspin, a future member of the special committee. Let us not talk largely of large things but triflingly about trifles. "Let's find out, for example, how weapons assigned to the armed forces can be shipped halfway around the world without the Joint Chiefs knowing." Thus speaks Oligarchy on this busy, historic November 30: "Congressional leaders backing the idea of a special committee said they were primarily concerned with resolving the issue and protecting the President's credibility." From what? From truth? From justice? And secondly to "head off a confusing and time-consuming situation in which several panels start separate investigations." And liberty breaks out!

Let Oligarchy and its minions control everything, dominate everything. Be advised, say Democratic leaders on this busy, message-sending Sunday, that the popular party will not tolerate Democrats holding forth in public "like so many apprentice Torquemadas." Let them not cry out in anger during the six months, ten months, however long it takes us to dim the lights, blur the issues and salvage the tyrant.

Mere Walter Mondale sounds like an ancient republican hero in the midst of this villainous chatter. "We are faced here with the profoundest issue that ever occurs in America: the accountability of elected leaders before the law. Without that we have nothing." And we shall be made nothing, if possible, so Oligarchy decrees. And we shall hear no noble republican utterance. Oligarchy decrees that, too. Petty prudence only, if possible. Private government, secret government, privy purse government deprives a President of "the benefit of those with the expertise in the field." Thus Senator David Boren, an Oklahoma Democrat, on the "profoundest issue that ever occurs in America"—and Boren is perhaps the most powerful senator on the Iran-contra committee. The great task facing the committee is "the larger process of reconciliation" between "the intelligence community and Congress," says Moynihan, for the small shall be made "larger" and the large and noble made small.

"I think the center—troubled and disappointed, but not infuriated—will let Reagan be President," William Safire of the *New York Times* predicts the day after the historic Sunday. While Donald Regan's White House staff sets to work on his latest internal memorandum: "Blame must be put at NSC's door—rogue operation going on without President's knowledge or sanction." While *Time* magazine this Monday carries the words of the President, wallowing in habitual self-pity, talking of "the bitter bile in my throat these days," and of "the sharks circling" around. While Oligarchy puts all its immense skill and guile and power to work to save him and keep the Republic degraded, a citizenry suppressed.

Quickly the President's "defense" takes shape in accordance with Regan's memorandum: The President, for one thing, cannot "recollect" many things. It is a violation of the Arms Export Control

Act to permit a buyer of U.S. weapons—Israel—to sell them to countries to which the U.S., by law, is forbidden to sell arms— Iran, for one. Reagan cannot recall approving an arms sale to Iran via Israel on August 8, 1985. "It's possible to forget" what he did on August 8, 1985. "Everybody who can remember what they were doing on August 8, 1985, raise your hands," the President asks a group of visiting businessmen, "as if sending arms to revolutionary Iran is as consequential as whether or not you sent the brown suit to the cleaners," the *New York Times* scathingly observes. Nor can he and Regan "remember any meeting or conversation in general about a Hawk shipment" via Israel to Iran in November 1985. A triple violation of the law, the Hawk sale, worth more than $14 million, should have been reported to Congress; the CIA helped with the shipment in violation of a 1974 law—a democratic awakening law—which forbids any covert CIA activity without formal presidential approval. In short, what the President cannot "recollect" is White House violations of the laws of the land.

Moreover, Reagan knows nothing about the Nicaraguan activities of his closest national security aides, nothing of what they did to raise a privy purse, provide arms, ship arms, carry out a private war, in violation of the laws of the land, although the funding of the contras, arming of the contras, war of the contras has been Reagan's "obsession" for years. He has "no knowledge whatsoever" of the diversion of funds from Iran to the contras. How can he? "North and Poindexter were running wild, and we did not have control over our policy." So the White House contends day after day, week after week, blaming, lying, scapegoating with shameless abandon. In short, whatever crime the President cannot "recollect" he is innocent of by virtue of ignorance, by virtue of his closest advisers "running wild" in perfect conformity to his avowed aims and wishes.

And at least one claim of innocence more. His power to authorize a "covert action" allows him, he says, to break any law that stands in the way of the action, including the law that requires a

President to inform Congress of the covert action—a lawless claim, a tyrant's claim, outrageous and dangerous both. Meanwhile the Pentagon announces this January 1987 that a crude space defense should be put up "as quickly as possible," so that, explains Meese, "it will be in place and not tampered with by future administrations." As Reagan's power bleeds away, the struggle to rule from the grave grows more desperate, stands on the verge of defeat as this chronicle ends—the "dream" crushed beneath the combined weight of scandal, of centrism, of Gorbachev's drive for an arms control treaty.

On February 26, 1987, the President's "special review board"— John Tower, chairman, former Republican senator from Texas; Edmund Muskie, former Democratic senator from Maine; Brent Scowcroft, former national security adviser to Ford: three spavined old geldings of Oligarchy—issues its long-awaited report. The commissioners declare to the press (for the report, a masterpiece of obfuscation, indicates otherwise) that there is nothing wrong with Reagan's lawless tyranny except that "the President's personal management style places an especially heavy burden on his key advisers," who, alas, have kept him in the dark, usurped his power, run wild. The President stands accused of his own defense! "A crass copout," the judicious historian Theodore Draper later calls it, "so farfetched it makes one wonder about the Tower Commission." But Oligarchy and its trumpeters wonder not. Instead, they rise up as one to echo and re-echo the "accusation." The report paints "an almost pathetic picture of a man wholly out of touch with a central episode in his presidency," writes R. W. Apple of the *New York Times.* It "provides the most definitive evidence yet of his disengaged and remarkably incurious style of management," notes *U.S. News and World Report* (although the report shows Reagan asking about the hostages at almost every morning briefing). It shows that "the President failed to supervise national security policy," note the editors of the *New York Times.*

"Failed to supervise"? What kind of pseudoconstitutional cant is this? The language of the Constitution is plain, clear and inescapably applicable to Reagan's paltry, lying "defense." The President is bound by solemn oath "to take care that the laws be faithfully executed." Ignorance is no excuse, poor memory is no excuse. Tyranny lurks in those excuses. Liberty is menaced by those excuses. "Take care," wrote the Framers, knowing tyranny well, knowing Reagan well. Nothing less will do. Anything less gives tyranny a dangerous precedent, a permanent foothold in the American Republic. But who cares about the Framers? Who cares about "take care"? Who cares about the Constitution in this hideous, hypocritical bicentennial year? Not the great liberal champion, Teddy Kennedy: "The challenge now is for the President to reassert control of his presidency." Not Heepish, mealymouthed Byrd: The President has to "improve his work habits. . . . There needs to be more substance." Not Senator Muskie, speaking for the commission: "We regard him as a person who didn't do his job." A half-dozen crimes are committed by the White House and the President "didn't do his job"! A half-dozen crimes in behalf of a President's policies and he has to "improve his work habits"! Let there be darkness and glozing and infantile tri-fling and the degrading of everything noble. To these base ends does Oligarchy labor.

On May 5, the Iran-contra committee, part Senate, part House, a two-headed body, at long last begins public hearings over network television. General Richard Secord, retired, lays bare at once the scope, the power, the astonishing resources of the secret White House CIA—"Project Democracy," the enterprise, so-called—with its private exchequer, private transport, private arms suppliers and its lawless private war. "A private clandestine intelligence service that didn't report to Congress," notes the *New York Times*, that evaded the laws of oversight and accountability, that illicitly employed "key officials from various agencies" of government, that was known to countless numbers of officials—except, we are still to believe, the President of the United States. Only two men can give the lie to that lie with conviction; can reveal to the watching millions what Reagan knew about the most grievous assault on the rule of law ever discovered in our history. One of them is Robert McFarlane, the President's national security adviser until December 1985. The other is his successor, Admiral John Poindexter, already known to the committee in private as a witness ready and willing to tell any lies—"fall on his spear"—to protect the President. It is McFarlane who begins testifying on May 11, but the committee— Oligarchy's well-chosen minions, in the main—do not want the watching rabble to hear from a high official's lips directly, dramatically, powerfully, what the President really knows about his private tyrant's government.

The baseness and corruption of the committee stuns even the *New York Times*. "In four days of questioning, the congressional committee investigating the Iran-contra affair never pinned down Robert C. McFarlane on what he told President Reagan about the White House staff's activities in behalf of the Nicaraguan rebels." Senator Daniel Inouye, chairman of the Senate half of the committee, a Hawaiian Democrat, asks McFarlane whether he had "advised the President on whatever you were doing" for the contras. "Yes, sir," replies McFarlane and Inouye drops the subject—the subject of subjects dropped. McFarlane mentions discussing Colonel North with the President, alleged "loose cannon," supposedly scarcely known to the President. "Once again," notes the *New York Times,* "Senator Inouye dropped the subject." Questioned by Senator Warren Rudman, a New Hampshire Republican, McFarlane says the President had "a far more liberal interpretation" of his freedom from the laws "than I did." And "Senator Rudman dropped the matter." For the people believe in the supremacy of law. Do we want them to hear over television that the President does not? Questioned by Representative Edward Boland, a Massachusetts Democrat, McFarlane says he himself was well aware of Colonel North's activities, aware of their illegality under the "Boland Amendment" and, in addition, had discussed the contras "frequently" with the President. "But Mr. Boland"—grand foeman of the contra war—"never asked the clinching question, whether Mr. McFarlane had told the President precisely what Colonel North was doing."

255

Why this turning away, the honorable Boland is asked? "It just didn't come to mind," answers the honorable Boland. The question on everyone's mind escapes the committee member's! Why these turnings away, the honorable Inouye is asked? "We are not targeting the President," explains the honorable Inouye. Scandal pervades the White House, crime pervades the White House; tyranny looms over the Constitution, but the President is not to be scrutinized, his lying words are not to be weighed, not before the watching rabble. Let their suspicions rot in their hearts; let their faith in the law rot in their hearts, let every vestige of republicanism wither and die in their hearts. Reagan is too "popular" to be scrutinized, claim the leaders of the popular party. If they gave us a signal we just might reach for his throat.

So the corrupting charade continues. Oligarchy's objectives, outlined on November thirtieth last, slowly but surely come to pass. No powerful voice invokes against Reagan the great principles of the Constitution; no public figure of consequence speaks for the supremacy of law over presidential tyranny, of the sanctity of the presidential oath, of the "take care" clause that binds all Presidents to law, which had bound Richard Nixon a mere thirteen years ago. Oligarchy silences our elected representatives this bicentennial year, a year in which the Framers are lauded in "seminars" for the hundreds and betrayed at the Capitol before millions. Instead of the great maxims of liberty and law, pettifogging and petty prudence, relentless drenching pettiness, rains down upon us. What is wrong with the "privatization of foreign policy"—with the tyrant's private privy-purse government? It leads to "confusion and failure," says one Lee Hamilton, an Indiana Democrat, on June 9, summing up for the House committee the "meaning" of the first part of the hearings. What does the Constitution require? "Trust" between Congress and the President, as if we are not dying of that "trust" already. What does "accountability" mean, without which mere Mondale knows we have nothing? It means that someone should have "supervised Colonel North," says driveling Hamilton, numbing the souls of the people with this soul-numbing, pettifogging inconsequence.

In July, Colonel North and his superior Admiral Poindexter are scheduled to appear in turn. These are the National Security Council staff "rogues," the "junta," the "loose cannons," the advisers "running wild," usurpers of poor "detached-management" Reagan's power, the once-powerful "leader" now required to pose as an utter pea-brained dupe, uninterested even in his own obsessions, although he talks of them constantly to his "running wild" aides. It is agreed between the White House and the committee that the President's avowed ignorance of the "diversion" of funds from Iran to the contras constitutes his complete vindication, absolution, exoneration, salvation, "restored credibility." Secret government, lawless government, private war, "Project Democracy," constitutional oath, "take care" clause shall be as nothing once presidential ignorance is proven before the national television rabble. Such is the little arrangement between shyster White House and shyster committee as they labor to stifle the republican cause.

It is known to the White House, surely, and long known to the committee (having questioned the admiral in private since early May), that Poindexter is going to make the preposterous, incredible assertion that he, a notably drab little order-taker, ordered the momentous criminal diversion on his own and said not a word to Reagan; that he will support this "exoneration" by a welter of lies, self-contradictions and memory lapses of such bald-faced fraudulence that Reagan stands in serious danger of being seen by the American people as a truly dishonorable cheat who rests his entire claim to "innocence" on preconcerted collusion with his former adviser.

Yet another hazard imperils the little arrangement. Reagan's avowed ignorance rests, all too evidently, on four days of frantic document shredding carried out in the White House while Ed Meese, Attorney General and White House henchman, was conducting an "investigation" so gratuitously inept it borders on, or possibly passes into, obstruction of justice—leaving Reagan's "ignorance" looking like what? The elaborate preparation of a massive criminal cover-up. How tiresome and laborious are fraud and corruption!

But "Ollie" North of the NSC staff inadvertently saves the day for Oligarchy. "Ollie" is no fall guy, he boldly, forthrightly testifies, no scapegoat, no "loose cannon," no "cowboy" running wild. Ollie did only what he was authorized to do—directly by Poindexter, indirectly, he believes, by the President himself. Plucky Ollie is popular with television viewers; little-guy candor shining brightly against the murky evasions of the high and the mighty who have made him their scapegoat. Telegrams pour in upon Congress, in part spontaneous, "in part orchestrated," says Drew of the *New Yorker,* noting that Western Union offers North telegrams at a discount price. What does the popularity mean? That the Iran-contra hearings have been too "prosecutorial," cries Senator Boren, publicly humiliating the committee's own legal counsel. The American people want no probing and prying, want no truth, want no light, and we shall probe not and bring no light—a "perhaps mistaken interpretation of the public's reaction to North," notes Drew with biting irony.

Poindexter comes next, to tell his transparent lies. He alone decided to divert the funds because "the buck stops here with me," a mere adviser; because profiteering in arms to terrorist Iran is "a mere detail of implementation." A lawyer whispers in the admiral's ear; the answers sound like evasions, stink of evasion. "Did you brief the President on the fact that the NSC staff was helping the contras?" "I don't recall a specific conversation that would allow me to answer your question in an affirmative way." What did he and Casey talk about at a critical luncheon when the scandal was erupting November last? The admiral can remember nothing, save that the two ate sandwiches. His entire testimony is "literally incredible," cries Drew. "Admiral Incredible," the *New York Times* editors call him.

Most of the country suspects that the admiral is a thorough-paced liar, but not one committee member confirms that dark and dangerous suspicion; let it rot unvoiced in our unhappy hearts. No committee member makes a serious effort to tear Poindexter to shreds, to sum up his lies and falsities. "Though most of the members," notes Drew, "did not believe Poindexter's story, none were willing to explicitly say for the record"—not one: think of Oligarchy's powerful thrall!—"that they didn't, while the President's champions—in Congress and the press—were quick to claim that Poindexter's testimony proved that Reagan didn't know about the diversion." Hear this, fellow citizens: The President has been "exonerated" by his own adviser; the President is truthful, the President is candid, the President is absolved; judge him not by the maxims of liberty; we pronounce him innocent of all charges outstanding. The lie is brayed; the truth is voiceless. So we are ruled. The Attorney General testifies next, fake "investigator," presidential henchman, nothing more. "Tough Questioning Is Awaiting Meese," the *New York Times* predicts, for it cannot yet grasp—as indeed who can?—just how base and corrupt is this Iran-contra "hearing"—a blinding, rather, and a deafening, rather. During his November investigation Meese never asks Casey, who stands at the center of every high intrigue, what he knows of the diversion of funds; never asks Poindexter if he told the President about the diversion; takes no notes, brings with him no aides, for he is not "investigating," but impudently plotting, scheming, obstructing truth and justice. What of the NSC "rogues" destroying documents under your nose, Mr. Attorney General, after you warned them of your coming? The documents may well have been "irrelevant to my investigation," says Meese, and this whole impudent testimony goes virtually unchallenged. Meese passes through the committee unscathed so that a tyrant and a tyranny may pass through unscathed in this bicentennial year.

The deep, calculated corruption does more than deceive and mislead a people; does more than blur all issues; does more than "almost ignore the President's failure to see that the law forbidding aid to the contras, which he signed, was not faithfully executed," so Reston ruefully notes; does more than gloss over the appalling iniquity of a privately funded White House warmaking machine, which "wasn't much focused on," notes Drew; does more than pretend that a lawless, truthless tyrant is the honorable victim of a "secret White House junta," so honorable Inouye calls it. "Ollie North put the United States Constitution through a shredder," say Democratic aspirants for the presidency, obligingly scapegoating the tyrant's own scapegoat.

Oligarchy does more than use its power to avert the menace of a popular republican revival on the road to the "post-Reagan era." Day after day in the closing weeks of these appalling hearings, Oligarchy, in its power and temerity, dins a message of deep corruption into our ears. We live in a "dangerous world." Such is the heart of the message. We cannot afford any longer a stringently constitutional President, a finicking oath and "take care" trammels. We are a government of leaders, not of laws, for this is a dangerous world and demands of us—do we not have a "living Constitution"?—a measure of tyranny, a measure of lawlessness, a measure, and more, of private, secret executive power. We cannot afford any longer the strict accountability of Presidents, for were the Iran-contra troubles not born of lack of "trust" between Congress and President, born of "pervasive suspicion" between Congress and President, so the *New York Times* puts it, born, in a word, of too many checks and balances? Away with these copybook maxims; they are baneful and dangerous in this dangerous world. So Oligarchy preaches, brazenly advancing its cause in the very midst of a menacing scandal. Long live the Empire and the "imperial" presidency. Long live, too, this "dangerous world"—so indispensable to the power of the few, so destructive to the power of the people.

Do we, the people, heed these siren songs of self-serving Power? In our stifled hearts do we believe in the dangerous world, in the lawless presidency, in an end to the republic of laws, an end to the old maxims of liberty? Oligarchy is powerful now, but perhaps not powerful enough for that. An ancient republic cannot be snuffed out quite this readily; a people born to freedom cannot be corrupted this deeply. Sometimes we sleep, said Robert LaFollette, last great republican champion to grace the U.S. Senate, and "sometimes it seems the sleep of death." But we, the people, always awaken, none the better for sleeping, but we awaken, nonetheless, and we "will be heard." Perhaps a citizenry is awakening now beneath the crust of the Reaction. Perhaps the deep, evident unhappiness with the Iran-contra hearings, the deep, evident bewilderment over so many lies and so little truth; perhaps our reported wish to be governed by those who "play by the rules," are signs of a deeper awakening, little sprouts of life in the barren ruins of civic life left by the dying demagogy of Ronald Reagan. There are other signs. When Judge Robert Bork, Reagan's choice for the Supreme Court, declares himself unwilling to admit a fundamental constitutional "right to privacy," the whole country stirs uneasily, sensing that a truly dangerous boundary is about to be breached. We have just let a tyrant escape the rule of law. We cannot—and the popular party dares not—allow tyranny to plant one of its favorites on the High Court itself. That corrupted we are not; that republican we remain. Perhaps some presidential aspirant, sensing undercurrents of thought and feeling and public spirit, will dare break with the rule of Oligarchy and speak to our neglected condition, our stifled hearts. The reader of this chronicle may know; the chronicler is merely guessing and must cease. The chronicle has completed its appointed round and told its tale: One notable day in the life of this Republic a happy people celebrated a joyous bicentennial while Oligarchy watched from the sidelines, sullen, anxious, fearful of the future. Eleven years later a confident Oligarchy celebrates a hollow, hypocritical bicentennial, while the people watch from the sidelines, unhappy, anxious, sensing that something—but what?—is very, very wrong. A bleak round and a grim tale, but, said Jefferson, "we are never permitted to despair of the commonwealth," for power supreme remains with the people and Oligarchy is never secure.

WALTER KARP
1934-1989

Walter Karp was the author of eight books, including *Indispensable Enemies: the Politics of Misrule in America* (1973) and *The Politics of War* (1979). He published more than two hundred articles and essays in *Harper's Magazine, Pageant, Horizon, American Heritage*, and many other magazines. In 1969, in collaboration with H. R. Shapiro, he wrote and published a journal about American politics called *The Public Life.* He was active on the Freedom to Write Committee of the PEN American Center, and wrote the foreword to a 1988 book sponsored by PEN, *Liberty Denied: the Current Rise of Censorship in America.* A collection of his essays on American politics, *Buried Alive: Essays on Our Endangered Republic,* was published last year by Franklin Square Press. Born and reared in Brooklyn, New York, Karp graduated from Columbia College, where he was class valedictorian and elected to Phi Beta Kappa. He died at the age of 55, after complications arising from surgery, leaving his wife, Regina, and two children, Roy and Jane.